HARLEY-DAVIDSON®

1930-1941

Revolutionary Motorcycles & Those Who Rode Them

Herbert Wagner

77 Lower Valley Road, Atglen, PA 19310

To my mother and father, who hated
the motorcycles but loved me anyway.

Published by Schiffer Publishing Ltd.
77 Lower Valley Road
Atglen, PA 19310
Please write for a free catalog.
This book may be purchased from the publisher.
Please include $2.95 postage.
Try your bookstore first.

Printed in The United States.
ISBN: 0-88740-894-X

We are interested in hearing from authors
with book ideas on related topics.

Library of Congress Cataloging-in-Publication Data

Wagner, Herbert, 1952-
        Harley-Davidson, 1930-1941: revolutionary motorcycles &
    those who rode them/Herbert Wagner.
                p.   cm.
        Includes bibliographical references (p.) and index.
        ISBN 0-88740-894-X (paper)
        1. Harley-Davidson motorcycle~History. 2. Harley-Davidson,
    Inc.~History. I. Title.
    TL448.H3W34   1990
    338.7'6292275'0973~dc20   95-37082
                                                CIP

CONTENTS

The Holy Ranger met up with that lost rider often heard on
Wisconsin back routes rumbling gravel shoulders on an Iron
Milwaukee Vision at the edge of summer just before the heat
rises from the day clear into evening's ground gully fog.

©1989 *Martin Jack Rosenblum*

Acknowledgments

The author gratefully acknowledges the following persons for information, photos, and other assistance in the creation of this work.

Stan Ambrose; Roger Ames; Royal Beguhl; Ralph and Evelyn Behrs; John Benner; Adam Beyer; John Birch; Aileen Bonneau; Joseph Borgen; Carman Brown; John Buchta; James Bukovic; Andrew Bushman; Ken Bryne; Joseph "Indian Joe" Campbell; Joseph A. Campbell; Eugene Carver; Bob and Sid Chantland; Bruce Chubbuck; Walter "Junior" Cowen; Arthur Davidson, Jr.; Laura Decheck; Harold "Hal" Deckert; Gerald Effenheim; Larry Engesether family; Tom Engesether family; Bernard Ernst; Mrs. Mike Farrell; Howard Fischer; Russell "Kid" Fischer; Ray and Ellen Frederick; Henry Fuldner; Dr. Paul H. Gaboriault, Director Superior Public Library; Mary Ganzel, Jean Fisher, and Andrew Kirov; the late Morrie Gauger; Virginia Gessler; Alice Gormley; John Gadwood; Mr. and Mrs. Kenneth Gredler; Ray Griesemer; Albert Hech; Elmer Helms; Mrs. Harold Helms; Ralph "Ralphie" Heger; Albert "Squibb" Henrich; Willy Herbold; John Horstmeier; John Howard; Herbst Jahn and Elisabeth Hohlingen; Robert Jameson; Clifford Jensen; Mrs. Harley Johnson; Mary Kakuk; Steve Kakuk; Arthur J. Kauper; Walter Kobs; Joe Koller; Dan Klemencic; Max and Edna Kroiss; Herman Kubowski; Mel and Emma Krueger; Ed Kubicki; Roger Laabs; Ted Mastos; Frank "Stinky Davis" Matheus; Stanley McClintock; Paul Maronde; Erwin Martin; Milwaukee Public Library; Rolland Mouser; Dr. H. Nicholas Muller III, Jonathan Cooper, Harold Miller, Joshua P. Ranger, and Victoria Allred of the State Historical Society of Wisconsin; Bill and Beatrice Nadler; James Nortman; John "Mr. Motorcycle" and Marie Nowak; Dan Olsen; Florence Ortscheid; Roland "Bud" Pater; Karen Pecher, South Wood County Historical Corporation; the late Wilbur Petri; Margaret "Mugs" Pritchard; the late Fred Process; Orville Process; Lavern Radke; Fred Reimesch; Gayle Spiegelhoff Renz; Otto Resech; Adolph Roemer; Connie Schlemmer; Peter Schumacher; Harry and Audrey Sebreny; Henry Seebooth; Joseph Seidl; the late Joseph Simadl; Judith Simonsen, Milwaukee County Historical Society; Joseph Somogyi family; the late Christy Spexarth; Louis Thiede; Matt Thome; Euella Trapp; Frank "Uke" Ulicki; Keith Ulicki; Peter Ulicki; Grace Kobs Valsano; Ray Wheir; Arthur Wilke; and Joseph Zedoff.

Special thanks to Dr. Martin Jack Rosenblum who instigated this book and Peter Schiffer who made it possible. Tom Wagner (31VL1403 and 39EL2007), who originally suggested "The Motor That Saved Harley-Davidson" as a story line which appeared in abbreviated form in the spring 1993 issue of *The Enthusiast* under the title, "The Founders' Legacy." Fred Pettis, who sold the author his first Harley-Davidson. And the late William H. Davidson, who encouraged the author's research and who appeared in a dream shortly after his death where he handed over his winter riding gear with the words, "I want you to have this." An omen surely that wherever he is now the riding is good!

>>>>

Author's Preface

All research for this work was done on two wheels. Research extended to the doorstep of—but not inside—the Harley-Davidson factory archives. Conclusions and opinions expressed in this work are not the opinions or policies of Harley-Davidson, Inc. All interpretation of events are the responsibility of the author alone and not the expressed or implied views of Harley-Davidson, Inc.

Research was conducted under all road and weather conditions: from a cold October day when the author interviewed Joe Seidl—ace frame builder—and got caught in Milwaukee freeway rush hour traffic in a blinding icy rain to a black night outside Madison pitching his "traveling hotel" in a muddy field while lightning flickered and the skies opened and mosquitoes sank their needles into flesh. Or that heartbreaking day when he knocked on Joe Geiger's door and was told by the new tenant that Joe had died a few months earlier.

But there were also good moments like meeting "Indian Joe" Campbell a few days before he passed away; knowing and talking with living legends like John "Mr. Motorcycle" Nowak, "Squibby" Henrich, Art Kauper, Uke, Stan McClintock, "Hal" Deckert, Frank "Stinky Davis" Matheus, John Horstmeier, and the many other old timers whose stories and knowledge made it a pleasure; that fine camp on a bluff overlooking the Mississippi River; that incredible ride home one November after a Halloween blizzard dumped four feet of snow on northwest Wisconsin, with the last five miles ridden over snow, slush, and icy ruts. That smug satisfaction of having made it home alive one more time.

That memorable day looking for "Bill" Davidson himself and seeing an immaculately dressed elderly gentleman walking up a driveway, who turned abruptly and gestured when he saw a motorcyclist go by obviously looking for someone.

He knew.

*   *   *

The author's involvement with motorcycles began in 1970. On the day high school diplomas were handed out he was speeding across South Dakota on a Honda CL160. In the vicinity of the Black Hills a Sportster pulled up alongside and it was the coolest thing he had ever seen. That summer he visited both coasts—put on eight thousand miles—then promptly blew the engine.

Then fate took a hand. That fall on a hunting trip to northern Wisconsin he and some pals stumbled upon a Harley-Davidson graveyard from the 1930s and 1940s. He brought home an assortment of junked bikes: 45s and Big Twins. That was the start of many years of rebuilding old Harleys and using them for four-season daily transportation. For ten years the author's sole means of travel was by motorcycle. Snowy Wisconsin winters were handled with a 1950FL sidecar rig, homebuilt third wheel Big Twin and 45 jobs, and currently a Servi-Car. Summers were spent on a cantankerous 31VL, a 41EL, 49FL, 50FL, several 45s, and other motorcycles. In spite of the foregoing the author considers himself a rider and not a collector.

After a stint working as a high school teacher the author built a log cabin in northern Wisconsin and removed to the woods. He tried trapping and living off the land but went back to an earlier love: writing. He cut his historian's teeth on Indian (Native American) lore, copper mining, and the Lake Superior country. In the mid-1980s he toyed with an idea that had appealed to him many years earlier: writing a history of Harley-Davidson. After testing the water for a season the author decided to jump in with both feet and hasn't looked back since. His research extends to the previously untold origin of the American motorcycle. The present work is a portion of that research.

If there are any errors or ommissions in this book they are the responsibility of the author alone. They are bound to occur when information depends on human memory going back fifty years or more and when most of the principals involved are long dead. The spelling of names was a special problem. In cases where the correct spelling was unknown, the author has followed what can only be called the preferred "Mi-waukee" style.

The author would appreciate any factual corrections and additions for future editions of this work. He would also appreciate hearing from anyone with knowledge or photographs to share of American motorcycles of all brands made before 1954 and especially before 1915. Inquiries to the author can be directed to the publisher. Much work remains to be done. The present volume is just the start.

>>>>

WISCONSIN

· Tomahawk

Wausau ·

· Shawano

Sturgeon Bay ·

· Marshfield

Green Bay ·

·Wisconsin Rapids

· Appleton

· Manitowac

· Fond du Lac

· La Crosse

· Sheboygan

· Lake Delton

· Beaver Dam

· Madison

· Milwaukee

· Janesville

· Racine

· Beloit

· Kenosha

CHAPTER ONE:
VL: A Study in Flawed Elegance

Oh, it's nice to straddle a two-wheeled job
That's flashy, peppy and fast.
And it sure is a thrill, to race up a hill,
And laugh at the cars as you pass.
You know what you have—and they know it too,
They have speed, but you've speed a-la-mode.
So they curse you and swear as you give them the air,
'Cause they know you're the King of the Road.
Francis Schiller
The Derby, 1931.

The Harley-Davidson Motor Company looking east from the Highland Avenue viaduct. Pile of scrapped motorcycle parts was behind trees in foreground. *Photo by author.*

In 1930 a world famous factory stood on Milwaukee's western outskirts. To the east lay city. Westwards lay vacant land until one reached the Washington Highlands subdivision. Beyond that was Wauwatosa. South of the Grand Avenue viaduct was Piggsville. This early farming settlement on the Menomonee River gave the area its descriptive name. In time Piggsville vanished, but the city prospered and the factory grew rich and strong.

Railroad tracks ran along one side of the factory and a fence stood there. But if you knew the right spot you could sneak through a hole that never got fixed. The only hitch was a watchman who made the rounds even after the bell rang and the men went home.

Quick. Duck through. Nobody's in sight. The big red brick six-story factory looms up a few hundred feet away. Countless windows stare down. Is anyone watching? No time to worry. A quick dash brings you to the spot: a large pile of reject parts from the factory. But this isn't ordinary industrial scrap—this is treasure, for the objects the young trespassers frantically dig through are cycle parts from the Harley-Davidson Motor Company.

The scrap pile is no fable. It was there from the teens until the Second World War. Occasionally the junk man would come round and haul off what today are priceless antique motorcycle parts. Some were dented. Others had holes drilled oversize. Maybe there was a stripped thread or a bad casting. For some reason they hadn't passed Harley-Davidson's rigorous inspection and lay rusting on the scrap heap.

But to young fellows with no money in their pockets, that didn't matter. One guy nearly built a complete motorcycle from stuff pirated off that scrap pile—so the story goes. Some took the parts (but keep this quiet!) and peddled them for cash to one of the independent cycle shops

around Milwaukee. As one old timer recalled it, "The scrap pile was about twice the size of a big room. It was back towards the bridge. Almost like a junkyard but where nobody charged for parts. We'd sneak in through the fence, get what we wanted, and put the parts on our motorcycles. Just kid stuff. I got fenders for my Forty-five. A headlight. New wheels. The guard would come out swinging his club. We'd run like hell."

Watch it! Here he comes now. With your treasure you race for the railroad tracks. The guard—huffing and puffing—isn't fast enough. He slams his club along the fence and yells:

"Verdammte kids! Heraus!"

But you're already running down the tracks towards home on Vliet or over on Highland. Maybe this time you copped a nice fender or gas tank. You don't wonder why the hole in the fence never gets fixed. After all, this is 1930 Milwaukee. Nobody cares if kids pilfer a few worthless motorcycle parts. Very probably the founders and chief officers of the company: Walter Davidson, William S. Harley, Arthur Davidson, and William A. Davidson, didn't know the hole in the fence even existed. Or if they did perhaps they recalled their own humble origins and the fact that material for their first motorcycles had been "borrowed" from the railroad shops where some of them had once worked.

But that was ancient if not forgotten history in 1930. The founders of Harley-Davidson had weightier matters on their minds. The stock market had crashed the previous autumn. Business was off. The outlook was uncertain although no one guessed the depth of misery to come. Besides, most people didn't enter Harley-Davidson through a gap in the back fence. Office employees, salesmen, and visitors came through the front door at 3700 West Juneau Avenue. Although many still knew it by its older name: Chestnut Street.

A short flight of outside steps brought visitors to the main entrance and into the lobby where they'd see a phone booth and a potted plant. To the right was pretty Stella Forge the switchboard operator, depending upon their mission, she directed visitors down a long hallway to the various offices. The hall going west took one past the offices of the founders. Let's stroll down that way.

Front entrance to Harley-Davidson in early 1930s with West Coast competition stars Joe Herb (left), "Windy" Lindstrom, and wives. *Courtesy of Stanley McClintock.*

Arthur Davidson (on cycle) created Harley-Davidson's excellent dealer network at an early date. Photo taken in 1916 probably at Lake Ripley near Cambridge, Wisconsin. It shows how founders thought motorcycles should be used. A new generation of riders in the 1930s had other ideas. *Author's Collection.*

First came the office of company secretary, sales and advertising manager, Arthur Davidson. This he shared with his secretary, Francis Miller. This office connected to the sales department where T.A. Miller, Herman Schulke, export manager Eric Von Gumpert, and others were busily at work.

Art Davidson was a compact sandy haired fellow. He was an out front brassy little guy. A handshaker. He loved people. He could sit down next to a stranger on the train and know his life story in five minutes. He liked a good joke and he loved telling stories, and he was good at it too. He had a dozen ethnic accents to tell them in. He used to quip that when he left Milwaukee he went to Cambridge—but that was Cambridge, Wisconsin—not England. Out on the farm they called him "Bunce." At Cambridge he first met another gasoline-sniffing pioneer: Ole Evinrude. It was Art Davidson and Bill Harley who had gotten the motor-bicycle idea off the ground in the first place. By trade, Art was an "apprentice" pattern maker. It was Art Davidson who in the early years of the century rode the Silent Gray Fellow far and wide convincing bicycle men to take on their new powered two-wheeler. If you were a visiting dealer it was Art's office you'd duck into for a hearty welcome, a slap on the back, and the latest gossip.

Back in the hall again and a few steps further brought you to the office of company president and general manager Walter Davidson. Of the three Davidson brothers, Walter was the most reserved—he could be brusque, quick, taciturn, even stern. Perhaps this was due to his great responsibility as company president. He had learned the machinist trade in the railroad shops in Milwaukee and other places. Although possessing little formal education, Walter was a highly intelligent man. In his younger days he had put Harley-Davidson on the map with his 1908 1000+5 win in a prestigious New York endurance run. Before that time

Walter Davidson (right) outside factory in early 1930s as dealer James Trapp (left) and customer take delivery of new Servi-Car 36R2902. Such inventions tried—and failed—to compete with the cheap automobile. *Courtesy of Euella Trapp.*

few outside Wisconsin had known of the Harley-Davidson motorcycle, but Walter's win helped change that forever.

Walter shared his office with Miss Crystal Haydel. Miss Haydel was officially Walter's secretary, but she was no ordinary secretary. She was Walter's right hand. Her position was in fact office manager. From

an old fashioned rolltop desk Miss Haydel handled the payroll, did the books, and kept track of stock transfers. She was involved with hiring and firing. She had been a shareholder from an early date and that explained why she sat on the company's board of directors. One old timer who was office boy back then recalled that Miss Haydel was kind, motherly, and had a gait like a man. Maybe she got that in the early days when she lived a block from the factory and rode her own motorcycle, in fact Crystal Haydel holds the distinction of being the first woman in the state of Wisconsin to register a motorcycle for road use, back in 1911. Like so many others working at Juneau Avenue in 1930, Crystal had grown up with Harley-Davidson.

Down the hall again brought one to another corridor going north. Here was a stairway leading into the shop. Beyond that were the finance and accounting departments where Joe Kilbert and Jack Balsom were in charge. Parts and accessories was there too with Harry Devine running things. Also down that way was the office of the service department. Here a big gruff Irishman with a flair for "colorful" language managed things. That was Joe Ryan, a man who had a memory like a computer. As one old timer recalled, "All correspondence went into the filing department. Joe Ryan would say, 'I think I remember this guy writing to us fifteen or twenty years ago.' He'd go back and look and sure enough he'd find the letter."

One might catch Orin Lamb, who taught the mechanics in the factory service school, up there too. Lamb knew his work but was somewhat of a worry-wart. He chain-smoked incessantly. Nearby was the desk of racing boss Hank Syvertsen. Also down this way was the "fountain pen" department—also known as advertising. Among other tasks the company publication *The Enthusiast* was put together every month. There you'd find Walter Kleimenhagen and Howard E. Jameson—although nobody knew the latter man as Howard. To everyone around Harley-Davidson this was "Hap" Jameson or "Jamie." Readers of *The Enthusiast* knew him by the pen names, "Uncle Frank" or "Hap Hayes." Their secretary—the famous "Steno"—was Nellie Newkirk.

Going back and continuing down the first hallway brought one to the office of company vice-president and works manager, William A. Davidson. This was "Big Bill" or "Old Bill." The latter nickname differentiated him from his son, William H. Davidson, who later became company president.

Bill Davidson had been foreman in the railshop toolroom of the Milwaukee Road and was the oldest of the three Davidson brothers. Outside the business he loved to hunt and fish. He was a big man and a kind man. Likely as not, you'd find him out in the shop somewhere mingling with the men. If you caught him in the office, chances were one or more of his cronies would be there—machinery salesmen—guys who wanted to talk about everything but business. By the door was a large container of peanuts. Old Bill was known to say, "Grab a handful—on your way out." The emphasis being: "on the way out." As his nephew Arthur put it, "He couldn't get rid of them. Rather than being rude he'd dismiss them by that method."

Bill Davidson shared his office with plant superintendent George Nortman. If there was a "fifth" Davidson (the "fourth" of course being Bill Harley) it was George Nortman. He had followed Bill Davidson from the railroad shops in 1907 when the company incorporated. If you got a job at Harley-Davidson chances were you talked to George Nortman first. He was a tall man, reserved, and was seen around the shop even more than Bill Davidson. Nortman was a kindly man. One guy said that if Nortman liked you, you had it made. It was in their office on a separate table where the first sign of motorcycle parts were encountered in various stages of manufacture.

In spite of belonging to the founders and top officers of a world famous company these offices were not pretentious. They were simple, plainly furnished, almost spartan and they were not large. The only decorations were a few photographs of early runs or races. In Walter's office there was a trophy or two, although most were kept down in advertising. The only taste of luxury was the rich dark oak woodwork which in Walter's office had been blonded light. But nothing elaborate. That you felt an officious state of affairs within was only because you

William S. Harley on cycle and William A. Davidson in sidecar show off a fine 1920s walleye catch from Pine Lake, Wisconsin. "Old Bill" had a cottage there for many years. Bill Harley was located on nearby Beaver Lake. This often published photo shows the founders' concept of the motorcycle as recreational vehicle. Bike is typical "JD" with sidecar, 1924 model. *Author's Collection.*

knew who each office belonged to, and not by superficial trappings or fake symbols of authority. These were practical men who were not impressed by big talk or phony displays, only by results.

If a visitor went any farther—most did not—a short walk down the same hall brought one to the office of company treasurer and chief engineer William S. Harley. Unlike the other founders there was a wall between Bill Harley and the outside world: this took the form of his personal secretary, Joe Geiger. Joe was so important he had his own office. He kept track of all engineering drawings and factory records going back to the earliest years. There were thousands of documents and Joe knew them all. He screened visitors and took care of Bill Harley's correspondence. He was a quiet man—he had to be, there was so much to do. So much to remember. He was a life-long bachelor. He devoted everything to Harley-Davidson. He lived across the railroad tracks and took the footbridge home. He was the last man in the place to relinquish his brass spittoon. When he finally retired in 1982 Joe Geiger had worked at Harley-Davidson for sixty-three years and eleven months, more than anyone else in that company's history including anybody named Harley or Davidson. But loyal Joe Geiger didn't live quite long enough because when I went looking for him in 1991 he was six months dead and the vast knowledge that was Joe Geiger's was gone.

A doorway under Joe's watchful eye took you into William S.

Harley's office. Here, too, you'd see motorcycle parts. Some of these were for experimental machines the public might never see. On the walls were photos of racing events. There was a desk and drawing board. A window looked out over the engineering and drafting department. The only other entrance into that secretive area was kept locked and bore a "No Admittance" sign.

If you were lucky enough to get inside—and certain favorite dealers and privileged characters did—chances are you'd find Mr. Harley bending over a drawing table in deep consultation with his assistants L.A. Doerner and Alfred Kuehn. Bill Harley had a fertile mind and was intimately involved with every aspect of motorcycle design. While in later years much of the design work was done by others, he was always extremely active and in full charge of the department, and he called the shots until the day he died.

Bill Harley had been involved with two-wheelers for a long time. At the age of fourteen he worked as a cycle fitter at the big Meiselbach bicycle factory in North Milwaukee. Now he was chief engineer of the world's greatest motorcycle company and he was also the only founder with a university education. Outside the factory his interests were hunting and fishing and he later enjoyed photography and copper etching. In early years he participated in motorcycle events and rode the machines the company built.

Double-wide sidecar was almost suitable for the whole family. Lack of weather protection and cramped quarters did little to make the motorcycle competitive with the family auto. After the First World War only the export market kept Harley-Davidson prosperous. *Author's Collection.*

Another gentleman in engineering was William Ottaway who for years had been in charge of H-D's racing department and was the man most responsible for their early racing supremacy. Originally from New York, Ottaway had been visiting the World's Fair in Chicago in 1893 when he decided to settle in the Midwest. Later he worked for the Thor motorcycle factory in Aurora, Illinois. In 1913 Harley-Davidson enticed him to Milwaukee. William H. Davidson, who knew Bill Ottaway, described him as "A very excellent person. Perfect character. Divine principles. And a fine mechanical wizard."

Along with Ottaway, Rudy Moberg and some other men who became valued foremen at H-D had come from Thor. Moberg was the shop liaison man. All the foremen answered directly to him.

These were the founders and some of the top people at Harley-Davidson in 1930. Most had been involved with the company for many years and the same was true of the men in the shop: sons worked alongside their fathers, brothers, and uncles. German names predominated, a language that was heard around the factory on a daily basis. No surprise that—in those days Milwaukee's North Side was German to the core.

The founders had divided their responsibilities early and stuck with them. They demanded top quality work and usually got it. They desired to build things correctly—they only accepted what they knew was right. For that reason there weren't many unpleasant surprises around Harley-Davidson. The atmosphere was predictable, calm, and relaxed. So many guys had worked there all of their lives that some referred to the company as the "Old Soldiers' Home." It was the last place you'd expect a crisis.

Yet if visitors had dropped in during early 1930 they would have found a much different atmosphere. Bill Davidson's cronies weren't welcome. Down the hall in Bill Harley's office there was a huddle with company engineers and many a glum face. Bill Davidson and George Nortman were there. In the service department the girls covered their ears when they saw Ernie Goldman roll up outside with his sidecar package truck and come in to dump the morning mail on Joe Ryan's desk, whose face turned red and his language promptly turned the air blue.

Walter was more stern than usual. In his office he studied letters from unhappy dealers and a telegram sent from Denver by his nephew William H. Davidson. Crystal Haydel waited patiently with pen in hand. After gazing for a few moments out his office window overlooking Juneau Avenue and south towards Thirty-eighth Street and Highland Boulevard, Walter began dictating a letter to Crystal. The letter promised every H-D dealer that a solution to their trouble was being worked on day and night. That the factory stood behind its product and was determined to make things right.

What was the cause of this crisis at the normally placid and quiet offices of the Harley-Davidson Motor Company?

Motorcycles.

What else?

The trouble centered on the new VL model launched a few months earlier. This 74 cubic inch (ci) side-valve machine was intended to replace the now obsolete and discontinued JD model. In general design the VL closely followed the 45 ci side-valve DL model introduced in 1929. But while the Forty-five had suffered only minor birthing pains—largely confined to its unorthodox vertical generator—the VL had plunged the company into a major crisis.

Just how the problem got as far as it did without being discovered is a mystery to this day. It probably stemmed from Harley-Davidson's intention to make the VL a fast, high-speed solo motorcycle with invigorating acceleration. This desirable characteristic was in response to a basic shift in the motorcycle scene and fundamental to Harley-Davidson's new thinking for the 1930s.

Previous generations of riders had relied heavily on the JD model as a sidecar machine, reflecting the philosophy of the founders as much as market demand. Their conception of the motorcycle favored it as a practical means of transportation that could compete with the automobile which is why in the late teens and throughout the 1920s photos of

sidecars with the girlfriend, mom and kids, or guys on hunting or fishing expeditions are so common. That's how the founders used the motorcycle so that's what they built and emphasized. Anyone who's ridden one knows what a practical and fun vehicle a sidecar machine can be.

But by 1930 the founders were entering late middle-age. They had given up riding motorcycles. A new generation of riders—including several second generation Davidson and Harley boys—were showing less interest in the sidecar. The founders were finally getting the message and coming to accept the motorcycle as a pure sporting proposition in its own right and not in competition with the automobile. The new side-valve models reflected this change in attitude.

The last incarnation of H-D's F-head engine—the hot "Two-Cam" JH (61 ci) and JDH (74 ci)—had been a nod in the direction of a high speed solo mount. As its successor, the new side-valve VL model incorporated certain features intended to carry out the motorcycle's new mission as a fast "hot rod" and not the sidecar plugger of former years. These same features were giving H-D a serious headache in 1930. And this from an engine that was supposed to cure all the ills of the F-head.

*   *   *

Valve layout of "inlet over exhaust" engine is clearly evident in this illustration from a 1920s ad. The F-head engine type was in use from 1911 to 1929 in all H-D Big Twins. There were a number of letter designations for this engine type, but most modern riders refer to them collectively as "JD" engines. *Author's Collection.*

Motorcycle engine technology has always been a compromise between cost of manufacture, performance, reliability, ease of maintenance, emotion, and looking over the other guy's shoulder. Early on, most American motorcycle manufacturers adopted the V-twin as standard. But even V-twins varied considerably: one difference was the angle between the cylinders, another was the positioning of the intake and exhaust valves. Being piston driven engines operating on the four-stroke principle, motorcycle engines use camshaft actuated poppet valves that open and close at the proper time to admit fuel into the combustion chamber and exhaust the spent gases. Probably no other feature of engine design is more critical than valve placement. It has a profound effect upon performance, reliability, styling, and ease of manufacture.

There are three main types of valve layout: inlet-over-exhaust (also known as IOE, F-head, or pocket-valve), side-valve (or flathead), and overhead-valve (OHV). The evolution of the motorcycle engine is largely a reflection of these various design types and the philosophies, science, and crossed fingers behind them.

All motorcycle engines (excepting a few "freaks" built before 1900 like Pennington's "Motor Cycle" with its open-crank, locomotive-style engine) descend from the genius of two Frenchmen: Georges Bouton and the Comte Albert de Dion. In the mid-1890s, Bouton, working for de Dion, invented a small high-speed, light-weight gasoline engine with spark ignition. This novel design was based on heavier and slower speed German engines. This improved French engine was reasonably powerful, reliable, and light enough to mount on a bicycle frame. Being the first engine practical for motorcycle building it was natural that everybody and his brother would copy it. That's just what happened. It was the perfect means to an end and nobody since that time has come up with anything better. Set one of Bouton's original engines beside any early motorcycle—including the Harley-Davidson—and the paternity is obvious. There was no other choice. Bouton's work was that good.

The De Dion-Bouton and countless copies utilized an inlet-over-exhaust valve layout popularized by Daimler in Germany. In America this type of engine was known as the "pocket valve" due to the valves being off to one side of the cylinder in a chamber or pocket of their own. Today this engine type is generally known as the "F-head."

In essence the F-head was half side-valve and half overhead-valve. It placed one valve (normally intake) on top of the cylinder with the valve head directed down towards the combustion chamber. The other valve (exhaust) was placed beside the cylinder in an upwards facing direction. The tops of both valves faced each other. This was how De Dion-Bouton did it and that's what others copied. Writing in 1916 in *The Handbook of Motorcycles* Victor Page said, "[This] form of combustion chamber...has considerable merit...as the fresh, cool gases from the carburetor strike the exhaust valve head, and have a very beneficial effect as they assist in reducing the temperature and by preventing the valve head from overheating, the valve or its seating is not so apt to warp and pit as would be the case if it were not adequately cooled."

Nearly all early motorcycles used the F-head engine and the Harley-Davidson was no exception. However, one complicating factor appeared around 1910. On all early F-heads—including the De Dion-Bouton and early Harley-Davidsons—the overhead intake valve was of "automatic" type. On the intake stroke of the piston a partial vacuum was created in the cylinder. Atmospheric pressure (suction) automatically opened the intake valve and brought in the fresh fuel charge. As engine speeds and the number of cylinders multiplied, the automatic intake valve was superseded by the more accurate mechanically operated type. This was accomplished through a second cam, a pushrod, and a rocker arm.

This complicated matters. While the side exhaust valve had always been mechanically actuated, the method of doing so was simplicity itself: located beside the cylinder with the stem in close proximity to the crankcase, a simple camshaft and tappet arrangement operated it. The overhead intake valve, however, perched on top of the cylinder with the stem pointing upwards needed additional parts to make it work. These parts—the pushrod and rocker arm—were out in the open and were lubricated by hand, acting as a magnet for dirt and dust. This caused rapid wear and the need for frequent adjustments and once wear occurred, the overhead-valve mechanism tended to get noisy. Thus in spite of its long service many weren't sad to see the F-head go. One old timer who ran a Harley-only used motorcycle shop on Milwaukee's north side said, "I didn't want nothing to do with JDs. To me that was an antique motor. I didn't like the way they looked and the motor made noise: 'clack, clack, clack!' You could hear one coming a block away."

Yet the pocket-valve's achievements were many. It served H-D and others for many years. It was an Excelsior (Schwinn) F-head that first officially cracked the 100 mph barrier in 1912. Harley-Davidson's success with the F-head on and off the racetrack is legendary. It had done its job well.

Some abandoned the F-head long before H-D. Back in 1907 Reading-Standard dropped the overhead intake valve and placed both valves on the side. Another early side-valve machine was the Iver-Johnson, the same company once famous for firearms. In 1916 Indian followed suit. From then on all Indian production big twins were side-valves.

In 1919 Harley-Davidson came out with a side-valve flat-twin engine in their Sport model. This smooth, sweet-running machine had several advanced features including a wet clutch, unit construction, and gear primary drive. But according to a man who learned to ride on one it couldn't beat its way out of a wet paper sack. With so little pep the

Sport model wasn't very sporty and only lasted four years. In H-D's V-twin line it was F-head all the way except for special racing engines.

Indian had better luck with the side-valve. This was especially true after 1920 with the introduction of the 37 ci side-valve Scout model and in 1923 and 1924 the redesigned V-twin side-valve 61 ci Chief and 74 ci Big Chief models. In 1927 the Scout was increased in size to 45 ci. The Scout 45 may have been the best loved Indian ever built.

During this same period Harley-Davidson stuck with the F-head 61 ci V-twin. In 1921 a similar appearing but bored and stroked twin of 74 ci displacement made its debut. The Seventy-four was intended for sidecar and high speed solo work. In 1925 the JD received a styling facelift by Arthur Constantine under the direction of William S. Harley. A lower frame and streamline gas tanks replaced the former "square" tanks.

Incidently the unusual four-pipe muffler that appeared on 1929 models was also the brainchild of Constantine. As William H. Davidson remarked, "Constantine wanted a quiet motorcycle and he got it with that little four-tube, V-shaped 'auspuff.' But after a while they'd clog with soot and raise hell with performance. We dropped those early."

The hot JDH was Harley-Davidson's last fling with the F-head. Formerly a competition only engine, the "Two-cam" was put in a road bike chassis for 1928 and 1929. "Two-camming" became slang for burning up the highway in the late 1920s but it was also the pocket-valve's last hurrah. After serving faithfully for twenty-seven years the F-head engine was phased out in favor of new side-valve models. First with the 21 ci single in 1926, then with the 45 ci twin in 1929 and the 74 ci twin in 1930.

The introduction of the Indian Scout in 1920 spelled trouble for Harley-Davidson. Middleweight machine was popular and side-valve engine seemed more modern than the H-D's F-head engine. Fine print in "Jim" Clark's 1920 ad explains the Scout's virtues. Riders took heed. *Author's Collection.*

By adopting the side-valve Harley-Davidson had seemingly thrown in the towel. Indian riders could smirk at H-D's adoption of their engine type. At the time, however, it was perceived as the most logical choice available. The only other alternative was a full overhead-valve engine. But this would have compounded the JD's nagging complaints of noise and dirt by placing all the valves on top. By comparison the side-valve engine was elegantly simple. When it came to designing a

Harley-Davidson production test room around 1926. New 21 cubic inch single-cylinder model on right. Man making final adjustments on single is "Squibb" Henrich. Original photo had a portion cut out to remove evidence of a secret experimental model. *Courtesy of Albert Henrich.*

new generation of twin-cylinder road bikes the founders and their crew opted for the simplicity of the side-valve.

The side-valve had significant advantages. It made a compact powerplant that could be build at lower cost. With detachable heads the necessary chore of decarbonization was an easy job. Its valve stems and springs could easily be enclosed (like Indian had done) with lubrication carried out by crankcase vapor. Because valve tappets operated directly off the camshafts there was no need for noisy pushrods and rocker arms. Having the valves and springs enclosed kept oil in and dirt out. Fewer parts meant a quieter engine. And if the side-valve produced less power than the overhead this was more true in theory than practice as shown by Indian's many racing successes over the years. Just as important was the lack of demand for overheads. The overhead-valve engine had no significant following in this country. The few American motorcycles with overhead engines had gone out in the teens. English overheads were almost unknown here. A side-valve with 45 or 74 cubic inches was deemed more than enough powerplant for anyone riding on two wheels.

The side-valve had a special mystique of its own. It gave Indian a distinctive look that many favored over Harley-Davidson's F-head. While the side-valve has few admirers today it was considered hot stuff back then. As one early owner of a 1929 Forty-five side-valve model told me, "Those flatheads seemed modern to us. They were quieter and smoother than the JD engine. That thing always had the problem of lubrication to the rocker arm. The flathead was all enclosed."

Or as another guy put it, "Those flatheads looked so mighty."

And yet another, "There was something about them. They looked strong. Like a locomotive."

To insure their new line of side-valves would be as advanced as anything Indian had, H-D purchased manufacturing rights to patents belonging to Harry Ricardo. This Englishman had given new life to the side-valve engine through careful analysis and design of combustion chambers. His detachable cylinder head designs produced greater efficiency, increased output, and a cooler running engine. H-D would boast when advertising the DL and VL models of "genuine Ricardo detachable heads."

So side-valve it was. But this change, while a fresh turn for H-D, made the difference between Milwaukee and Springfield's motorcycles even less than before. This isn't hard to understand. Both shared the same history and were competing for the same market: speed-oriented young men (and a few young women) looking for adventure on two wheels. No matter what brand they rode, a motorcycle was the easiest means of finding what H-D characterized as, "The Greatest Sport on Earth."

*　　　*　　　*

In the summer of 1929 Harley-Davidson embarked upon one of the great factory tours carried out at intervals during their long corporate history. This one differed in one important respect. It was being undertaken by second generation Davidson boys mounted on the year old Forty-five DL model and the brand new Seventy-four VL. The trip was intended to kick off a big advertising campaign but unfortunately things didn't go as planned.

The presence of Davidson boys mounted on the new models was more than symbolic. It was a perfect means of getting the message across that these frisky new side-valves were intended for a younger generation. It was sort of a "This isn't your father's Harley-Davidson anymore" campaign. It was a break with the past and the stodgy old JD. When Walter C. Davidson, Gordon Davidson, and Allan Davidson saddled up their Forty-fives in the summer of 1929 and slapped leather opti-

Harley-Davidson dealership in the late F-head era. Signs referring to "80 miles per gallon" bike are for the 21 ci single-cylinder side-valve model. It was intended to put the ordinary man on a motorcycle. It didn't. But the side-valve soon knocked the older F-heads in the photo out of the picture. *Courtesy of John Howard.*

13

Two early side-valve Forty-fives. On the left is a 1930 model and the other is a 1929 model. These machines are similar to those Gordon, Walter, and Allan Davidson took on a 8,000 mile cross country tour in 1929. *Courtesy of Frank Matheus.*

William H. Davidson at time of his Jack Pine Enduro victory in 1930. He was the first non-Michigan rider to win that event. Photo was taken in Wauwatosa woods near Milwaukee. Motorcycle and clothing are same as Davidson used during Jack Pine Run thus photo is authentic in that respect. *Author's Collection.*

14

Having fun in the late 1920s. Frank "Uke" Ulicki pulling his brother "C.D." (Walter) on skis. Bike is 21 ci side-valve single. *Courtesy of Peter Ulicki.*

mism was running high at Juneau Avenue. Shortly afterwards William H. Davidson took the first VL model off the assembly line and with sidecar attached followed in their tracks.

If ever there was a place where Horace Greeley's dictum, "Go West Young Man" holds true it's Milwaukee, Wisconsin. The reason is simple geography. Milwaukee lies butt flush against Lake Michigan. The only way eastwards across this freshwater sea is by boat. To the south are the cities of Racine and Kenosha, then comes Illinois and the outskirts of Chicago. To the north lie the lake cities of Sheboygan, Manitowac, and Green Bay. So west it must be—either straight west over rolling hills and dairy farms to the great "father of waters" the Mississippi River, southwest towards the heartland prairie, or northwest to the piney woods and lakes and finally the wild shores of Lake Superior. From Milwaukee it was—and remains—ever west. The eternal ride towards the setting sun and the evening land.

Think of it. Being the offspring of the founders of the world's greatest motorcycle company. Given new motorcycles and instructions to blaze a trail across the continent. Nor were they pampered or given special favors. The youngest was just sixteen. No support vehicles or repair van followed these guys. That wasn't the founders' way of doing business. No sir! Everything they took along was carried in sidecar and saddlebags.

The three boys on Forty-fives were William A. Davidson's younger son Allan and Walter Davidson's two sons Gordon and Walter C. Allan is something of a mystery. He worked at Harley-Davidson for a time and died young. Gordon officially joined the company in 1930 after graduating from the University of Pennsylvania. He started in sales and became a company director in 1937. In 1942 he became vice-president of manufacturing. Like his uncle William A. Davidson, Gordon felt more comfortable in shirtsleeves than in a business suit and was friendly with the men in the shop. Sometimes too friendly. One foreman recalled him gambling with men on the assembly line to the point where the foreman had to shout, "Gordon we got motorcycles to build!" Gordon Davidson died in 1967.

Young Walter C. Davidson was a cheerful fellow and a good sport who also liked a good drink. One H-D employee who accompanied him on a business trip was sent out twice in one evening for a bottle of bourbon. When asked how he liked the trip, the man quipped, "If it

For Cold Weather Riding Comfort

Handlebar Muffs

These warm and roomy handlebar muffs are lined throughout with thick sheep's wool. They fasten securely to the handlebars with metal clamps. There is ample room inside these muffs for the horn and headlight dimmer switches as well as the front brake lever. With leather outside and wool inside, they keep your hands and wrists fully protected without the use of gauntlets. Price per pair $5.00

Gauntlet Mitts

Sheepskin lined! You bet, they're lined with soft, thick sheep's wool way out into the wrists of the cuffs. The stiff cuffs are large and roomy and the hand stock is tough black horsehide which always stays soft and pliable, and wears like iron. Available in full-mitt or one-finger style. Sizes, small, medium and large.

These gauntlets are unlike anything else on the market. They are designed especially for motorcycle riders and will keep your hands warm in the coldest weather. Prices $5.00 and $5.50

Sheepskin Saddle Cover

The mounted officer who spends hours each day in the saddle will appreciate the added comfort afforded by this extra soft, evenly clipped sheepskin saddle cover. Made of one piece, with long, fur-like wool. Easy to attach or remove. Price $4.00

Leather Police Coat

This highest quality, full 36-inch length, double-breasted, black horsehide coat has been adopted as standard by many City, County and State Police Departments. It is fully lined with wool cloth and has sheep-lined wristlets and adjustable cuffs. Two shoulder straps, a badge strap and all-around belt. Special police buttons. $23.00

Horsehide Leather Breeches

Just what every mounted officer needs for cold weather. The fine quality black horsehide leather used in Harley - Davidson breeches will not scuff, peel or harden. Khaki cloth lining. Strongly reinforced seat. Smart cut and splendid fit. $14.50

Genuine Cowhide Puttees

Well formed, built to keep their shape, these puttees are very smart and durable. Made of full grain black cowhide, or split leather, in the loop front or spring front style. $4.00 to $6.50

HARLEY-DAVIDSON ACCESSORIES

Back when motorcycles were used year round Harley-Davidson offered a full line of cold weather riding gear. This assortment was targeted especially for law enforcement use. Motorcycle pictured behind cop is 1930 Big Twin VL model. *Courtesy of Harold Deckert.*

Two Forty-fives on right, a Big Twin sidecar rig, and a 21 inch single on left. Scene is Pike River outside Kenosha in 1930. *Courtesy of Peter Ulicki.*

taught me anything it's how to spend company money." Walter shot back, "Listen punk, I'm the boss." Walter started working in the shop at H-D in 1935 after graduating from the University of Oklahoma. At college he traded his motorcycle for a polo horse. Later he went into sales and ended up as vice-president and sales manager. Walter C. Davidson died in 1974.

The trip west was great adventure for the three Davidson lads. Goggled, grinning, and leather-jacketed they served as traveling good-will ambassadors for the company. They drank in the freedom and exhilaration of the open road. One of the machines was fitted with extra spotlights, saddlebags slung over the front fender, and a lightweight sidecar in which they carried spare gear. Along the way they visited dealers, chased jackrabbits, shot rattlesnakes, and slept in haystacks. They covered about four hundred miles a day. If that wasn't enough they visited carnivals and rode roller coasters at night when the opportunity presented itself. While the early Forty-five didn't possess great speed, it handled like a dream. Arthur's son (who went into business for himself) remembers riding one the seventy miles between Cambridge and Milwaukee most of the way with no hands.

Finally the three Davidson boys reached San Francisco sunburned and road worn. After cleaning up and donning snappy fresh riding outfits consisting of high boots, breeches, and sweaters—with Allan sporting a bow tie—they were photographed outside the shop of veteran H-D dealer Dudley Perkins. After resting up and having their machines serviced they zoomed off for Denver. Arriving there they were greeted by H-D dealer Floyd Clymer who took them for a ride over the city in his Hisso-Swallow airplane.

While this trio was somewhere between San Francisco and Denver, Bill Davidson's older son, William H. Davidson, was speeding towards Denver from the opposite direction on a VL with sidecar. "That was the first production model off the assembly line," Davidson said before his death in 1992. "Mr. Harley told me, 'Just go!'"

Young Bill Davidson had formally joined the company in 1928. He was born in 1905 and learned to ride on a Sport model owned by the Nortman boys. He got his first motorcycle on his 15th birthday: a pocket-valve twin with sidecar. As a student at Milwaukee's Washington High he rode it to school and the kids naturally piled in. "Fortunately," he said. "By the grace of God nobody ever got hurt."

He attended the University of Wisconsin at Madison. He started out in engineering, but later switched to business. The engineering background did no harm. Davidson said, "I could talk to engineers and know what the hell they were talking about. I could stay with them when things got technical. They couldn't con me."

During his college years William H. Davidson rode one of the new 21 ci singles. During classes he'd lean it up against a tree. Summers were spent in coveralls in the factory. This too speaks worlds about the founders. A college degree was fine, but shop experience was fundamental. All the founders' sons who entered the company started from the ground up. During this training period young Bill Davidson worked in every department in the factory doing two week stints under the guidance of assistant plant superintendent Fred Bahr. He did everything from pound rivets to editing *The Enthusiast*. "Doing everything," as he put it, "from A to Izzard."

His work was careful if not fast. The last thing he wanted to hear was: "That scrap came from young Davidson." So none did. But it wasn't always easy being the boss's son. One guy remembered a fellow worker coming over red-faced with the warning, "Whatever you do don't call him junior!" In 1931 he became a company director, and in 1937, after the death of his father, vice-president. And in 1942 upon the death of his uncle Walter, William H. Davidson became president of the Harley-Davidson Motor Company. This last position he held until the AMF years. Young Bill Davidson was also a crack rider. In 1930 he won the rugged Jack Pine Enduro. He was the first non-Michigan rider

Dealers like Hank Swaske of Wisconsin Rapids covered labor costs for up-grading early flawed VL model. Factory supplied parts, instructions, and expertise of Orin Lamb. Photo taken in early thirties. First year VL model on far left. *Courtesy of Mrs. Mike Farrell.*

to win. Davidson rode motorcycles year round and had a special sidecar garage built at his home. He rode daily until well into his fifties.

At the time of the 1929 trip William H. Davidson was 24 years old. He was working in the factory service department under Joe Ryan and Orin Lamb. He personally set up the three Forty-fives his kid brother and cousins had ridden west on. He had gone over each machine like a detective making sure everything was right. Shortly afterward with a new VL under him, he left Milwaukee for Denver where he planned to meet his brother and two cousins. The first night out was spent in Springfield, Illinois. Next day he traveled on to Kansas City. There he met an unexpected surprise. Waiting for him was none other than Bill Harley, Jr.

William J. Harley was yet another of the founders' sons to join H-D. He too started at the bottom, in the boiler room to be exact. In 1935 he earned a degree in mechanical engineering from the University of Wisconsin. His summers had also been spent working in the factory. Later he would assume his father's position as chief engineer. He died in 1971. But in 1929 when he showed up unexpectedly in Kansas City he was a seventeen year old kid. Photos of the trip show young Bill Harley as a participant, but it hadn't been planned that way. His presence in Kansas City was a total surprise to young Bill Davidson.

"I suspect," Davidson recalled, "and this is purely my assumption, that the senior Mr. Harley realized that the Davidsons had their sons represented on these two trips and he didn't. So he put young Bill Harley on a passenger train for Kansas City. When I pulled into town he was there waiting for me. He piled into the sidecar and we were off to Denver."

Under the hot summer sun the two Bills and their sidecar rig sped across the prairie. In their excitement they neglected to watch the gas and on an isolated stretch their engine began to sputter. There was no town or filling station in sight but there was a farmhouse. They pulled up there and stopped. Nobody was home. Desperate for fuel they made a furtive search of the premises. On the back porch they discovered something that *smelled* like it might work. They left some coins in payment and poured the liquid into the gas tanks. The engine was still hot and started easily. They roared off—but not in the normal manner; the machine began to buck and snort. By luck the distance to the next town wasn't far, for the stuff they had poured into their motorcycle was low octane stove gas or kerosene!

The Seventy-four model they were riding was new from one end to the other. As previously stated the engine was of side-valve construction and similar in design to the 45 ci DL model. The new style forks were of drop forged I-beam construction. Gone was the single row primary chain (between engine and transmission) of the JD. The new side-valve models ran multiple row roller chain which has been subsequent H-D practice. There was an improved front chain oiler. Brakes were modernized. A bigger clutch was fitted. The seating position was lower. Wheels were interchangeable and quickly detachable through the use of splined hubs and brake drums.

The VL was lower slung, heftier, and sleeker when compared to the higher and more spindly JD model. It was designed to match and exceed the performance of the hot JDH. The fly in the ointment was that the VL weighed a hundred pounds more than its predecessor. In order to match the acceleration of the JDH, light flywheels were incorporated in the new VL. While this might have pepped up the new machine some, it led to a nasty surprise which young Bill Davidson and Bill Harley discovered on their way west.

"Long before we got to Denver I knew something was wrong," Davidson recalled. "I wired the factory that I was very unhappy with the bike. I think I told them I wanted to tear it down. I was qualified to do so at the time."

Somehow—and the mystery of how it got by exists to this day—a combination of faulty engineering and a lapse in the testing department allowed an incorrect design to get into production. While giving the bike brisk acceleration, the lighter flywheels did not provide adequate engine momentum. The new motor lacked the smoothness at idle and low speeds that heavier flywheels would have given it.

William H. Davidson wasn't one to pull punches, not even with the company he loved and was his life for decades. Describing his own views on the VL's initial faults Davidson said, "It's always been a mystery to me how that slipped by after months of laboratory and road testing. Being all-new and exciting it wasn't quite clear at first what the problem was or exactly what I was looking for. But something inherently wasn't right. It was a combination of bad engineering and faulty developmental testing. The engineering department was wrong in the first place coming out with flywheels too small. The fact that our experimental department didn't find it was inexcusable."

In fact the problem was a sneaky one. It sort of crept up on the rider. At first Joe Ryan, Orin Lamb, and Fred Nagley in the service department tried tuning the problem away. When that didn't work engineering went inside the engine. To their horror they discovered the fault lay in the basic engine design and flywheels. The only solution was to redesign and install larger flywheels which would necessitate fitting a new larger crankcase and mean more headaches. Complicating the problem was the fact that a considerable quantity of VLs had been shipped out before the cause of the problem had been tracked down, including some to Europe. When the faulty engine design was discovered production was stopped at once. Engineers and production men went on a crash program to develop and build suitable replacement parts and all the while complaints were streaming into the service department. Already a master of coarse language, this disaster propelled Joe Ryan to new heights of creativity.

To Harley-Davidson's enduring credit the VL debacle was not ignored or pawned off on dealers and owners. The factory tracked down every machine shipped and provided replacement parts. One old factory employee recalled, "Orin Lamb went from shop to shop changing the crankcase and flywheel. That's how we got the unequal size flywheels. It started with that first VL. Lamb's wife was pregnant when he left. When he came back home he found he had a daughter."

Other VLs had been shipped overseas. It was young Bill Davidson's job to track down the European dealers and make arrangements for repair parts to be shipped that would bring these machines up-to-date.

"Once we changed the faulty parts the bike didn't look a lot different than it did originally did," Davidson said. "You had to look close to see any change."

Once the necessary alterations had been made, riders and dealers quickly accepted the new VL. Performance and owner satisfaction were quite acceptable. Young riders naturally took to the side-valve engine and the sleek looks of the VL and its smaller 45 ci brother. The collective sigh of relief at Juneau Avenue as the crisis passed must have been audible all over Milwaukee. Not only had fixing the problem been expensive, but the affair was an embarrassment to a conservative and well-established company.

This episode, however, pointed out an important feature about the Harley-Davidson Motor Company. During most of the 1920s the company had coasted along comfortably on adequate domestic sales and a booming export market. The VL crisis had come out of the blue like a thunderbolt. Yet it showed how quickly the founders handled difficulties even when forced to admit they were wrong and mistakes had been made. Years of success and smooth sailing hadn't dulled their basic business instincts. H-D accepted the responsibility and provided replacement parts at their own expense. Dealers were expected to pitch in and help with labor costs.

This aggressive put-it-right attitude showed the level-headed management team that ran Harley-Davidson. As a result the problem was solved before any lasting damage had been done. There was no lingering dissatisfaction or resentment. The crisis was over before many riders knew what was happening. The factory stood behind its product and backed its dealers with the correct parts, tools, and information to bring the VL up to its true potential. Purchasers of early flawed VLs probably felt reassured to be singled out by the factory for special treatment. Luckily Harley-Davidson had sufficient cash reserves to fix the problem but earlier in their history such a mistake would have been fatal. Lesser errors had ruined many an American motorcycle company in the early days.

With the VL debacle behind them the founders looked forward to good sales with their new line of modern side-valves. In normal times it probably would have worked that way. Once again peace reigned at Juneau Avenue. New machines were crated up by Joe Traut and his men and shipped out. Engineering turned its attention towards new projects. Joe Ryan settled down enough so the office girls could uncover their ears. Bill Davidson's cronies were again welcome to hang around and chew the fat. But other clouds were gathering on the horizon. Problems that couldn't be fixed by recourse to the drawing board or the machine shop. But that was yet to come. At the moment at least the future looked bright.

Steve Kakuk on a 1930 Seventy-four sidecar rig. Twin headlights were actually dangerous. They were sometimes mistaken for automobile headlights in the distance. *Courtesy of Mary Kakuk.*

By 1932 the side-valve models were firmly established. Notice of "New Low Price" was reflection of hard times during the Great Depression. *Courtesy of Frank Ulicki.*

BLACK AND
MANDARIN RED

THE 1933 HARLEY·DAVIDSON 74 BIG TWIN MODEL

Fancy paint was hallmark of the mid-1930s. Perfected VL was an elegant machine but serious flaws lurked in air-cooled side-valve engine. *Courtesy of Frank Ulicki.*

19

Three generations of Harley-Davidson motorcycles. On left is a 1924 JD, center an early thirties Seventy-four, and on right a 1930 30.50. Heavier construction is evident over a span of a few model years. *Courtesy of Mary Kakuk.*

The VL in updated form was a good reliable motorcycle by the standards of the time. But how did it meet expectations with regard to performance? Consider this.

After the flywheel problem was solved Joe Ryan sent William H. Davidson to various police departments to replace some faulty valve springs and to install larger covers. At Buffalo, New York, he completed the job on one VL then turned it over to a skeptical police mechanic. He recalled the occasion, "In those days the police speedometer had what we called a 'maximum hand.' It recorded your top speed. I told him to take that thing out and see how it behaved. When he came back the speedometer showed ninety-two miles-per-hour. He said simply, 'That's good enough.'"

Milwaukee motorcycle police in the spring of 1930. Motorcycles are first year VLs. After flywheels were brought up to date the Big Twin side-valve soon found acceptance by riders and police forces around the country. *Courtesy of John Howard.*

CHAPTER TWO:
Frustration and Fun in the Great Depression

*If you like motorcycles you can't get enough;
but if you don't you just cuss them out.*
William H. Davidson

The Great Depression was the most troubled peace time event in the twentieth century. It began in October 1929 with the collapse of the New York stock exchange. At the time few realized the agony yet to come—there had been numerous financial panics in U.S. history, but none as deep and bitter as this would be. When the economy hit bottom in 1933 over sixteen million would be out of work: one-third of the total labor force. Not until the election of Roosevelt and his New Deal economic policies did the country begin its slow climb out of darkness.

Milwaukee did not escape the disaster, nor did the Harley-Davidson Motor Company. Already suffering the effects of Prohibition that had shackled Milwaukee's important brewing industry, that place now saw her vital industrial base grind to a near halt. There would come a day

during the Great Depression when the founders pondered whether Harley-Davidson could stay in business at all. In late 1930 at a convention of Harley-Davidson dealers Arthur Davidson warned of difficult times ahead and that factory and dealers alike should prepare for a long period of low sales and diminished production.

The Depression was worse for motorcycle companies than many other businesses because the mass produced automobile had long since driven the motorcycle to the wall; a trend that had begun in the teens and never let go. The sidecar and package truck had done very little to slow that decline, not when one could buy a used Ford as cheap or cheaper than a motorcycle. Most people saw no reason to put up with the limited load capacity, discomfort, and downright danger of motorcycling. As a result the public abandoned the motorcycle as practical

Harley-Davidson motorcycles were strong competition for English bikes in British home markets during the late teens and through most of the 1920s. Light construction is evident on this BSA overhead-valve single studied by H-D engineers in 1927. Rider is "Squibb" Henrich. After being test-ridden, dismantled, and inspected, foreign bikes were scrapped. *Courtesy of Albert Henrich.*

transportation. Joe Kilbert—an H-D employee since 1912 and number two man in the sales department—once said, "(A dealer) doesn't sell (motorcycles) because he has them in stock or there is an accumulated demand like there is for automobiles. Everybody wants an automobile, but few people want a motorcycle...there is no natural demand for motorcycles."

It was an honest statement. People need food to survive and they need some means of basic transportation, but as things evolved in this country that wasn't going to be the motorcycle. Domestic sales had been declining since 1913. The only thing that kept Harley-Davidson prosperous during the 1920s had been the export market. Late in the decade, however, that door suddenly slammed shut too. Behind it lies an interesting tale.

Foreign sales of U.S. motorcycles had grown from 5.8 percent of total production in the teens to 55.5 percent by the mid-1920s. Up to forty percent of Harley-Davidson's annual production went overseas. Imports into this country were a joke. In 1920, thirty-seven thousand American motorcycles were exported while forty-one foreign bikes were imported. Eleven years later in 1931 an identical number of imports were recorded—twenty-three from England and twelve from Germany. There was simply no demand. In fact at one point in the early twenties Harley-Davidson requested that import duties on foreign motorcycles actually be lowered. They had no fear of foreign competition and thought they could use the lower tariff to pressure other countries into reducing their rates.

The biggest overseas markets were countries in the British Empire, especially Australia and New Zealand. This worked out well for Harley-Davidson. Being south of the equator the seasons in those countries were opposite those of North America. When combined with domestic sales the export market gave H-D a fairly balanced twelve month production and sales schedule.

But this was a precarious situation. Foreign markets have unforeseen risks. H-D found this out when our best allies the "Brits" pulled a fast one in their quasi-colony Australia.

For many years British bikes going to Australia had enjoyed a twenty percent import duty preference over American motorcycles. This didn't concern H-D unduly. Long distances and poor roads in Australia resembled U.S. conditions so closely that only the most ruggedly built motorcycles could stand the strain. Harley-Davidson motorcycles held up where other brands were quickly reduced to junk. In spite of the higher tariff American bikes were preferred and sold well. Then the monkey business began. Under pressure from British interests, Australia reduced tariffs on Brit bikes to zero and to twenty percent on U.S. machines. That was okay too, H-D continued to enjoy good sales. Then the Australian government pulled a fast one by raising the duty on all imports by fifty percent. This—in the words of export manager Eric Von Gumpert—was, "a case of high mathematics." Since the tariff on English bikes was zero—nothing—raising it fifty percent didn't amount to a damned thing. Fifty percent of zero is still zero. American bikes, already at the twenty percent rate, increased to a prohibitive thirty percent and the result was an immediate collapse of exports to Australia.

The same story was repeated throughout the "sterling bloc," including England, the sole exception being Canada. As a result the important export market of the twenties dried up to almost nothing. Thus H-D was hit with a double whammy after 1929. Not only would the Great Depression cut deep into domestic sales, but exports were strangled off as well. The only bright spot was that the twenties had been profitable, this in spite of an expensive lawsuit with the Eclipse company where H-D had to shell out a million dollars to settle. Old timers still recall that Walter Davidson took that especially hard. In spite of that loss Harley-Davidson had some two million dollars in working capital to fall back upon, still, the outlook at Juneau Avenue was gloomy. After decades of profit the company faced losses and layoffs as the economy grew ever worse.

Statistics reveal H-D's decline after 1929. According to *Moody's Investment Manual* for 1935 and other sources, H-D motorcycle production was as follows: 1929, 23,925; 1930, 18,000; 1931, 10,502; 1932,

6,000; 1933, 4,520. Industry wide the Depression's effect on the motorcycle industry was staggering. Between 1929 and 1931 sales dropped fifty percent. Between 1931 and 1933 sales were down another fifty percent. Between 1929 and 1933 employment in the U.S. motorcycle industry declined by sixty-eight percent. Factory hourly wages were down by twenty-three percent. Total payrolls declined by seventy-six percent. Sales for the Indian Motocycle Co.—H-D's main competitor—were even more dismal than Milwaukee's. As listed in *Moody's* Indian production was: 1929, 8,463; 1930, 6,068; 1931,4,360. Indian failed to provide figures for later years and secondary sources vary widely. Indian production for the worst year of the Great Depression: 1933, has been given at a low of 1,657 machines to a high of 3,703. Take your pick. Neither was adequate for a motorcycle company capable of turning out 30,000 bikes a year!

The only other American motorcycle builder of any consequence was the Schwinn-owned, Chicago-based Excelsior company that built the Super X and Henderson Four. When the Depression hit Schwinn threw in the towel and went back to building bicycles. Production of motorcycles stopped at Cortland Avenue in early 1931.

As the Depression deepened the country was gripped by a terrifying paralysis. Fear and dread of the future overwhelmed people, even ordinarily decent folks became suspicious and ready to strike out.

*   *   *

Albert "Squibb" Henrich was born in 1899 in Milwaukee. As a kid he met Annie Oakley and "Buffalo Bill" Cody. He had sixty-four jobs before ending up at Harley-Davidson in 1923. He lost a year's seniority when he quit and was rehired overnight. He hillclimbed with Herb Reiber and Joe Petrali. He made the cover of *The Enthusiast* at least twice. As an experimental test rider he rode the redesigned 1925 JD in the Arizona desert for three months where he hit and killed a longhorn steer—and still has the scar to prove it. It was "Squibb" Henrich to whom Edwin "Sherbie" Becker revealed the secret of the Hidden Room. Henrich was a daredevil who didn't look for trouble but sometimes found it anyway, but even he wasn't ready for what he and his boss encountered that November day in 1931 with their VL sidecar rig.

At the time Squibb worked for Leo Connors in the production test department. These were the guys who made final adjustments, stand tested, and road tested bikes coming off the assembly line. They also tested police motorcycles for speed. Henrich and Connors shared a common interest: they both liked to hunt. So one fine autumn day they headed for Soldiers Grove out near the Mississippi River on a hunting trip. A murder of a young boy had occurred shortly before and the killer was still at large. When the two rabbit hunters started asking directions and the locals saw guns sticking out of the sidecar they drew their own conclusions. Soon the hunters became the hunted. But let "Squibb" Henrich—now in his nineties—tell the story.

"We went out there looking for rabbits never thinking the people were hot and heavy over the murder of that Corrigan boy," Henrich recalled. "We went through Soldiers Grove and I said to Leo, 'Did you see those guys? They must be nuts. They got pitchforks and clubs.' We got out a ways and saw a bunch of guys talking. We stopped and asked for a road to Richland Center. They said just go down there and hit the highway. We said we didn't want the highway. We wanted backroads. That's how I figure we got into trouble. I glanced back and there was a car speeding after us. Rather than eat dust I stepped on the gas. But after a while they were there again. We shot through Richland Center and lost them. A few miles beyond we took a sideroad to look for rabbits. We went up into the hills hunting. Down below we could see the roads. Cars were going past like crazy. Then one turned up the road we were on. I'd just come out of the woods with my gun and was eating a piece of bread. A car came by and stopped. The guy was in uniform. He said, 'Come over here.' So I did. He stuck a Luger in my ribs. His hand was none too steady. Another car stopped and those guys had shotguns. Believe it or not the hammers were back. It was a posse after us. With orders to get two fellows with a sidecar."

22

A love of hunting got Al "Squibb" Henrich (pictured) and his boss Leo Connors in serious trouble in 1931. They may have been on the 1930 Seventy-four VL model pictured here. Swamp buck shot near Rhinelander. Photo taken on grounds of present Milwaukee Zoo. *Courtesy of Albert Henrich.*

When Leo Connors came out of the woods they grabbed him too. Their guns were taken and they were hauled off to the local jail. At first nobody would tell them what the charge was.

"Leo was scared," Henrich continued. "He sat in the middle of the jail cell reading a paper upside down. Later we laughed about that. But not then. I went and lay down on a bunk. We didn't know what we were in for. Finally the courtyard got full. People were hanging on trees. Our sidecar was out there with the guns. They thought they had the guys. Then the witnesses came. Leo was first. Then I came in. The guy said, 'No, the other fellow looked like him but not this one.' So they had to release us. But instead of letting people know they gave us a release paper. We took off. We got a mile out of town and stopped for gas. There was a little country store with some guys sitting around. It was Leo's turn to drive. Suddenly I see these guys jump off the porch and into a car, hanging on the running boards and all that. I said, 'Leo, get in the sidecar.' He didn't see them. He said, 'Get the hell over there.' I said, 'No, look!' So he jumped in and we took off. They chased us. We were nearly to Madison before we lost them. I drove like hell. Them days cars didn't go so fast. Plus we could ride! We took that sidecar around corners with the wheel up in the air. My wife wanted to try that once. She got the wheel up but couldn't get it down again."

*   *   *

As the Great Depression strengthened and production fell, Harley-Davidson found itself in dire straits. Joseph Borgen, hired in 1925 and who worked in the riveting department said this, "After a while there wasn't much work. I'd come in Monday and they'd say come back Fri-

day. If the foreman gave you a job you'd go around the different departments trying to get parts. If you found them you could work. If not you went home. My paychecks kept getting smaller and smaller until finally it got down to ninety-two cents for two weeks work. I'd have framed the check if I didn't need the money so bad. But I still had a job. In thirty-six years I always had a paycheck."

Joe Borgen was one of the lucky ones. As times got worse departments were combined and cost cutting measures put into effect. One old timer recalled Arthur Davidson going around turning off lights during lunch hour to save on the light bill. Times were bad. There were major layoffs. Bill Davidson did what he could to spread the work around, but more layoffs were inevitable. Some of the men thrown out of work had families. One worker in the office remembered a day when Arthur Davidson sat down next to him and with tears in his eyes said there was going to be another layoff.

John Gadwood, who started in the mailroom in 1927 and later worked in purchasing, remembered the Great Depression years at Harley-Davidson, "Things were going smoothly until the Depression. Then it sure dwindled. They knew they had to cut expenses to stay in business. Pretty soon it was just Horn and me in the department. They laid off the big pay people. That's where Horn and me came in. We were the lower paid guys. They never closed the factory. Some machines were sold, but they got very conservative."

These were hard times for Harley-Davidson, where the workforce had in some ways been like a big family which might sound inappropriate when speaking of a large corporation, but there was truth to it according to the people who worked there. A close feeling between the men and management existed at Juneau Avenue. The family metaphor is often used by retired employees from that era. They'll tell you right out that the pay wasn't the greatest, but it was a good place to work anyway. They did their job and did it well, but rarely felt under pressure. Even in later years the bosses' door was always open—according to one guy even if you wanted to pop in to tell a joke.

The family connection was real. Men were often hired because their father, uncle, or brother already worked there. This tradition went back to the earliest days when three Davidson brothers joined Bill Harley in the motorcycle building business. In 1911 five Beckers worked there. John Behrs began working at H-D in the teens and today his descendants can count more than one hundred and sixty combined years of working for H-D. That's the way it went. When guys were hired at Harley-Davidson they stuck.

If you didn't have a relative to get you in, enthusiasm might do the trick. When Al Henrich rode up on his JD in 1923 looking for work he was turned down flat by Leo Connors, who said, "Sorry, we ain't got a thing for you." Squibb pleaded, "But I need a job." Connors was adamant, "Nothing doing!" Then Squibb hit the right note. He said, "I sure would *love* working for Harley-Davidson." Connors shot back, "You're hired!"

Sometimes divine intervention seemed to play a role—take the case of John Nowak, who prayed for a job the night before. In 1936 a total stranger—never seen before that day or afterwards—rode up on a motorcycle and told John's mother they wanted her boy down at Harley-Davidson for a job. John gladly went. But it wasn't true. They hadn't sent anybody out. Sorry. Somehow Nowak managed to get hired anyway. He started out lacing wheels and finished by setting up the factory at York, Pennsylvania. What's that you ask? Who came by that day? You got me. Maybe fate. Maybe a guardian angel riding a motorcycle. If you find out go tell John. He still wonders about it.

John Nowak (right rear) with his father, mother, siblings, and Two Cam (28JDH12590). Photo from about the time he was hired by Harley-Davidson. Divine intervention seemed to play a role. *Courtesy of John Nowak.*

Much of the closeness between management and employees was due to the personality of works manager William A. Davidson. He knew the men by their first names and wasn't above asking about their families. One employee from the thirties remembered, "Old Bill Davidson would come around every morning. If you were working on a machine he'd pat you on the shoulder, 'How's it going there young fella?' He was a friendly guy."

But it wasn't just Bill Davidson. Otto Resech recalled when he was the new guy in the accounting department. He lived downtown in the old Martin Hotel. One day after work he was waiting outside the factory for a bus. Walter Davidson pulled out of the garage with his LaSalle automobile. "I didn't even wave at him," Resech told me. "I

didn't think he'd know me from Adam. Just some guy standing on the corner. But lo and behold a little while later he came around the block and gave me a ride. For the president of the company I thought that was pretty damned good."

Another time during a bus and streetcar strike the founders in their own cars took office workers home who were stranded without transportation. There are many stories like that.

But as the Depression dragged the company down, the future of the once busy Juneau Avenue factory grew uncertain. The founders might have called it quits at that point and few would have blamed them. The company was dead on its feet. Even without the Depression the market for motorcycles simply wasn't there anymore, and with the Depression it seemed hopeless. Why not just throw in the towel? The founders had made their fortune. The workforce was already cut to the bone. Why not just close the doors at Juneau Avenue—forever!

But however tempting that course of action might have appeared it wasn't their way. Harley-Davidson wasn't run by men who would lay down without a fight. Far from it. These four individuals had started with nothing but a dream in the first years of the century. Through efficient management, good engineering, excellent manufacturing skills, sound sales policies, and a dedicated dealer network, Harley-Davidson had become the leader of the American motorcycle industry. But that was when they were young men and when an insatiable demand for motorcycles existed. Things were different now: the founders had grown old, the once booming market for motorcycles was gone, and even before the Depression the American motorcycle industry had been sick. Under these conditions how could the founders possibly repeat their past success? Facing the odds they did it almost seems impossible. Yet the founders had one last card up their sleeve: dedication. As long time H-D employee Art Kauper put it, "Money was important for them like anyone in business, but making motorcycles was more important. That was their life."

Could the founders and their people possibly rekindle the once vibrant motorcycle scene and give it new life? As already shown Harley-Davidson had adapted to changing times with the sporty new 45 and 74 side-valve models. But H-D had another strategy as well. One they had been pursuing for some time. This was an attempt to revitalize the organized motorcycle club scene.

Motorcycle clubs had fallen on hard times after the First World War. But from their extensive knowledge of the early pre-war club days the founders saw new potential in that direction. But Harley-Davidson couldn't do it alone. That's where the dealers would come in. Yet during such rough times were the dealers up to the task? Would the riders respond? Was it too late? These were unanswered questions. But the testing ground for H-D's new tactics was no mystery. This could be done right at home in Milwaukee.

In 1924 the Milwaukee Harley-Davidson dealership was relinquished by Louis Peterick. The new dealer was an ambitious young salesman from Jim "The Motorcycle Man" Clark's Indian agency on Fond du Lac Avenue. The new man who got the nod from Arthur Davidson to handle the country's most scrutinized H-D dealership was one William C. Knuth.

Bill Knuth had learned the trade from a master. R.L. "Jim" Clark had been in the bicycle and motorcycle business in Milwaukee for eleven years. By 1923 he was doing $150,000 of business annually in Indian motorcycles. The Indian Motocycle Co. couldn't resist crowing that Clark was their "most aggressive dealer" in the country.

"Jim" Clark's secret was to start the customer young. He had everything in his shop from small tricycles for little kids to heavyweight motorcycles for big ones. The theory was that as the child grew to adulthood he or she would graduate up the retail line. It worked like a charm. Clark told *The Retail Journal* in 1923, "I sell the small child a kiddiecar...later he needs a bicycle and when he gets older he buys his motorcycle from me."

Clark claimed a monthly mailing list of 13,000 customers. While attending the Indian dealers' convention he mailed 18,000 personally signed postcards from New York City. He said, "Personality helps to

Bill Knuth outside his shop in the fall of 1932. According to the late William H. Davidson Knuth was an outstanding dealer in every respect. *Courtesy of Frank Matheus.*

sell motorcycles and bicycles. Six thousand children in Milwaukee know me by name and I have made my store the meeting place for motorcycle fans."

Clark accomplished this from a salesroom twenty-two feet wide by twenty-seven feet long. And all this within twelve blocks of the Harley-Davidson factory.

With this background it's no wonder that Arthur Davidson tapped Clark's top salesman as the new Milwaukee H-D dealer. By mid-1925 the Knuth Cycle Co. was established on Fond du Lac Avenue on Milwaukee's north side.

Bill Knuth was a big, jolly, fatherly man who had been around the Milwaukee motorcycle scene since the teens. Early on he had shown better organizational and sales talents than skill in the saddle. In the twenties he tried one of his own hillclimb machines and dislocated his shoulder in the process. On the first day of January 1919 Knuth and "Jim" Cark left Milwaukee riding solo Indians in the company of three H-D sidecar rigs for a hundred mile "arctic" endurance ride. Anyone who's been in Wisconsin in January might call them crazy, but they weren't—around the time of the First World War there was considerable interest in proving the motorcycle was suitable for combat conditions. The Harley-Davidson riders were all factory men: Frank Stark, Ed Kieckbusch, and experimental boss Frank Trispel. The presence of rival machines made things a little more competitive. The temperature was frightfully cold. The wind blew hard. Snowdrifts blocked roads. At Becker's Hill near Menomonee Falls Bill Knuth decided that riding in Stark's Harley-Davidson sidecar made more sense than freezing his ass off on an Indian. Six years later he jumped ship again, and this time for good—Knuth would be Milwaukee's Harley-Davidson dealer until the day he died.

A major part of Harley-Davidson's success was an outstanding dealer network. The credit for this goes to the early work of Arthur Davidson. In the belt-drive, single-cylinder days he barnstormed the country on a Silent Gray Fellow. His mission was to convince bicycle men to handle this new proposition of mechanical two-wheel horsepower; this at a time when there were hundreds of would-be motorcycle builders, few of which were based upon more than a dream. Where Art Davidson

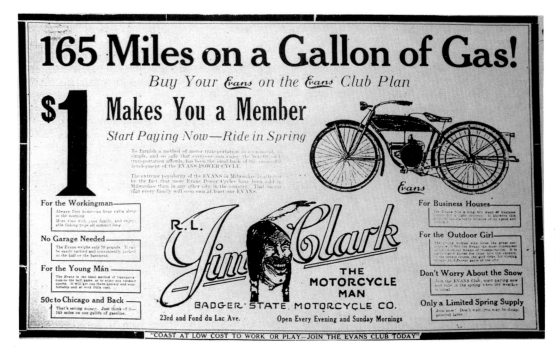

Jim Clark "The Motorcycle Man" was an outstanding Indian agent right in the heart of Harley-Davidson country. Clark's methods are evident in this 1923 ad: Get them started young. In this case with the Evans motor-bicycle. *Author's Collection.*

25

differed was the promise of total backing by the Milwaukee factory. It was a promise well kept. It was just as true for small one-man operations run out of barns to large dealerships in ideal climates or made rich through police motorcycle contracts.

All H-D dealers had one thing in common. It was part of Milwaukee's unwritten philosophy that dealers had to make money first. Then the company would worry about its own profits. This may not have been written down in black and white, but it was always there. The factory might make the bits and pieces but the dealer sold, serviced, and kept the motorcycles running. In the eyes of the public, the dealer not only represented the company, he was the company.

Harley-Davidson treated dealers as their number one customer. If a dealer found himself in trouble the factory would try to help. As the Depression worsened such help was needed. Sometimes it was simple honest advice. In late 1933 assistant sales manager Joe Kilbert penned the following to a midwestern dealer whose business was on the rocks, "When I told Arthur Davidson that your selling expense was 42% and is running 28% this year, he said that the average for the retail motorcycle business was about 17%, so you can easily see that a drastic change in conducting (your) agency is absolutely necessary if you are to be saved...To cut your sales expense, a reduction in wages and salaries is imperative. Your business simply can't stand the load...You can therefore understand why we are so insistent for your own good that the help be cut down to a man who can handle sales, a combination bookkeeper and parts man and only productive help in the repair shop...everyone feels that (this) plan...offers a real opportunity to put your business back on a profitable basis."

In return the factory expected total loyalty from the dealers, and this cannot be stressed enough. It stemmed from the earliest days when dealers were recruited from the ranks of bicycle men. Back then some dealers tried to handle several makes at once. These were usually weak sisters of the industry: Eagle, Dayton, Jefferson—to name a few of dozens. When these vanished—and all did—so too these dealers. H-D drew its own conclusions. Because a motorcycle dealership represented a large investment in time, expertise, floor space, tools, and parts inventory, H-D considered it essential that a dealer concentrate exclusively on a single

Small photo shows a portion of the well-equipped repair department in Knuth's north side store. Knuth gave his rebuilt used bikes the same guarantee as did nearby H-D factory. *Courtesy of Stanley McClintock.*

Dealerships came in all sizes such as this small one in Manitowac. Dealers fortunate enough to hold the local police contract were especially blessed during the Great Depression, although in many places this might consist of a single machine. *Courtesy of Mary Kakuk.*

make. A dealer either represented Harley-Davidson or he didn't. The only deviation from this policy was the case of small time operators who H-D wanted to gather under its corporate wings. Harley-Davidson would tolerate the double dealership until the dealer became established, then quietly suggest the other brand be dropped. Usually the dealer agreed because with H-D he was making money.

Motorcycle companies were highly competitive. The racing scene was part of it. Because most riders were young and obsessed with speed, it was easy to play off the rivalry between different makes. Young guys think nothing of risking their necks to prove their brand of iron fastest and a declining industry made matters worse. Old timers remember hearing how they cheered at Harley-Davidson during the teens every time a rival motorcycle company went out of business, thinking these slices of the pie would go to them. Under such conditions it would never do for a dealer to sell one brand and be caught riding another. By the early 1920s it had settled down to just three: Indian, Excelsior, and Harley-Davidson, and by then most dealers were single brand exclusive. Finally it came to just two. Like punch-drunk heavyweights, Indian and Harley-Davidson kept up this hereditary feud until one finally lay down and died.

In later years this exclusive dealer policy would become controversial. But between the world wars it was standard business procedure. Some dealers may have bitched but most did not. They had a good thing with Harley-Davidson and knew it. A decent dealer made an adequate living—better in fact than a factory worker—including those at Juneau Avenue. One old time dealer recalled being at the factory during the Second World War where he "accidently" saw some secret army parts. The army rep got mad and said, "Now you have to hire that guy. He knows too much!" When the dealer heard the pay he hollered, "What? I make twice that much in my dealership!" Harry Devine was there and whispered, "Sshh! Sshh! The men will hear you."

By the late-1920s Harley-Davidson was pushing its dealers in a new direction. After years of neglect the motorcycle club scene took on new significance. Emphasis on the club scene started before the onset of the Great Depression. The original impetus was the unhealthy reliance on exports and the decline of motorcycling as a sport in the U.S. Once the Depression sunk in the club scene became a life preserver to a drowning man. It was no coincidence that Bill Knuth's first order of business was to put the moribund Milwaukee Motorcycle Club back on its feet because that's exactly what Harley-Davidson wanted him to do.

*   *   *

Bill Knuth's north side mechanics in the early thirties. From left: Johnny Spiegelhoff, Frank "Stinky Davis" Matheus, and Bill Manz. This last guy had been around Harley-Davidson since about day one. *Courtesy of Frank Matheus.*

Before the First World War the Milwaukee Motorcycle Club had been a live-wire proposition. It was filled with guys who worked at Harley-Davidson, women motorcyclists, and within its ranks were a wide variety of American built motorcycles including several types made in Milwaukee. Even the founders of Harley-Davidson joined in the fun and competition events.

After 1918 the club scene declined countrywide. In 1919 the sport's national governing body, the Federation of American Motorcyclists (FAM), went belly up. An industry group called the Motorcycle & Allied Trades Association (M&ATA) stepped in to handle competition duties. In 1924 the M&ATA's Registered Rider Division was reorganized as the American Motorcycle Association (AMA). This signalled an upturn in organized club activity in the United States. But unlike

Members of the Milwaukee Motorcycle Club in the early 1930s. Knuth sponsored this group out of his north side store. Early club uniforms beginning to take shape. *Courtesy of Joe Simandl.*

the independent FAM, the early years of the AMA were dominated by the big motorcycle companies through their financial backing.

Harley-Davidson took a leading role in organizing new clubs and reinvigorating old ones. A booklet, *Suggested Constitution and By-Laws for a Motorcycle Club* was distributed free by the factory. After a couple of short-term secretaries the AMA "boss" with staying power was E.C. Smith. This may have been—as revealed in a letter written on Harley-Davidson stationary in 1930—because, "[Smith] is a YES MAN and says he is."

But the object was to get the club scene moving and Smith accomplished that job with great efficiency. This success was due to endless boosterism and countless worn-out tires on his H-D sidecar rig as he criss-crossed the country injecting club enthusiasm wherever he went. Rousing talks and movies were his forte. He stood ready to help iron out club problems as they arose. By the early thirties the formation of new motorcycle clubs was increasing rapidly, and many which had disbanded after the First World War were back in action. In Milwaukee, organized club activity was the bailiwick of Bill Knuth. He transformed the local club from nothing to two separate chapters with a national reputation right in the face of the Great Depression.

The Depression may even have helped. Even a poor guy could afford to buy a second hand motorcycle—old timers tell of buying their first machine for a quarter or fifty cents. Gas was dirt cheap. As long-time rider and retired H-D employee Royal Beguhl said, "We went into Kasten's shop. We went into Knuth's. Another guy had a place on Wells Street. That was Ingold. He had anything he could get hold of. Old stuff. Acetylene bikes. Those were the days if you had a quarter in your pocket you were feeling rich."

Belonging to a club was a way to find camaraderie, friendship, and fun with very little money. If you bought your machine from Knuth you were automatically put into the club for a year. During that time Knuth covered your dues. When a nearby building became available Knuth rented it for the Milwaukee Motorcycle Club as a meeting place. When he opened his south side store he sponsored the Badger Club over there.

Knuth sponsored the Badger Motorcycle Club out of his south side store. From left: unknown, Johnny Spiegelhoff, Harvey "Shorty" Lindstrom, Joe Simandl, Paul Chilli, unknown. Tilted wings was a common practice during 1930s, but the meaning is unknown to author. *Courtesy of Joe Simandl.*

Knuth was the ideal motorcycle dealer—he was friendly, gregarious, sympathetic, and generous. Yet all the while he remained a shrewd businessman. As William H. Davidson described him, "Bill Knuth was an outstanding dealer in every respect."

Knuth's right hand man was Frank "Sidecar" Werderitsch. A tall irascible man, some of the riders called him "Water-bitch" behind his back. Werderitsch was Knuth's chief salesman in the north side store. He was also an AMA district referee and a hard-core rider in his own

Bill Knuth and his hillclimbers. Knuth was said to sponsor the only dealer team in the country. *Courtesy of Albert Henrich.*

right. He was known for his short fuse and tenacity. H-D test rider and thirties club member Harold "Hal" Deckert recalled one occasion: "Once I rode in Werderitsch's sidecar on a Goose Run. All I did was help push when we got stuck. The clay got under the front fender and we couldn't go anywhere. Finally we took the fender off. The guy insisted on finishing. I would have quit but he insisted. Nobody was at the finish when we got there. But he was an old timer. He had to finish that run."

Another Knuth employee who'd been around the Milwaukee motorcycle scene forever was head mechanic Bill Manz. In this case forever means forever. A circa 1907 photo of Bill Harley and Walter Davidson with some employees and admirers includes a young Bill Manz.

Eddie Axel was parts man. He was related to Bill Knuth by marriage. Wise guys called him Eddie "Axel-grease." Others who worked for Knuth during the thirties included Frank "Stinky Davis" Matheus, Frank Tamus, Fred Sadowske, Carl Knuth, Bill Nadler, "Hal" Deckert, and Johnny Spiegelhoff. When Jim Clark dumped the Indian franchise Knuth hired his salesman, Harvey "Shorty" Lindstrom, to manage the south side store. Later in the thirties Lindstrom took the H-D franchise in New Orleans.

Part of Bill Knuth's success throughout the Depression was his contract with Milwaukee County law enforcement agencies. These were big users of Harley-Davidson motorcycles and sidecars. Between the police and sheriff's department there were over one hundred and twenty-five H-Ds on roads and city streets in Milwaukee County. Knuth sold and serviced each one.

But Knuth didn't neglect the sporting side of his business. Far from it. For a time in the late twenties and early thirties he was the only dealer in the country to sponsor a hillclimb team. He was assisted in this endeavor by the factory, the idea being that Knuth's example would

Knuth's Lone Star Riders at a Slinger hillclimb in the early 1930s. From left: Herb Reiber, Al "Squibb" Henrich, Stanley McClintock, Norm "Tubby" Syvertsen, and Don Jaffke. *Courtesy of Stanley McClintock.*

28

inspire other dealers to follow. His first group was called the "Lone Star Riders" after member Herb Reiber's home state of Texas. Other members included "Squibb" Henrich, Norm"Tubby" Syvertsen, Art Earlenbaugh, Don "Tiny" Jaffke, and Stan McClintock. After Reiber left Milwaukee the group became "Knuth's Klimbers." This bunch included McClintock, Earlenbaugh, Henrich, Russell "Kid" Fischer, "Swede" Anderson, Frank "Stinky Davis" Matheus, the Gettelman boys, and others. Knuth provided a hillclimb machine and in turn received a percentage of their winnings. In 1931 these riders entered twenty-four events. They took seventeen firsts, nine seconds, and ten thirds. McClintock led the pack with seven first place wins. That year "Kid" Fischer took the National Championship Hillclimb at Rochester, New York. Knuth's Klimbers dominated the Midwest hillclimb circuit for several years.

Knuth fielded hillclimb machines with "Homebrew" engines. These consisted of 21 ci OHV single "Peashooter" heads and cylinders grafted onto Forty-five side-valve bottom ends. This was serious medicine even after Harley-Davidson came out with a 45 OHV competition engine of their own. No doubt the factory had a hand in Knuth's Homebrews and they may have been built in H-D's racing department. Connections like that didn't hurt. If Knuth needed something he'd send one of his boys over to see Tubby's brother Hank Syvertsen in the racing department—which is how Stinky Davis saw the Sixty-one Overhead two years early.

While hillclimbing was popular during the late twenties and early 1930s it was largely a professional sport. In endurance and reliability runs, however, ordinary club members could compete. The premier event of this type was the Jack Pine National Enduro held each year in Michigan. Many clubs put on similar events of their own in varying degrees of difficulty. Some were tough, others relatively mild, but all offered a challenge. "Runs" of all types became extremely popular during the 1930s.

Lone Star Riders with a 21 ci OHV hillclimber. From left: Al "Squibb" Henrich, Herb Reiber, and Stanley McClintock. *Courtesy of Stanley McClintock.*

Bill Knuth sponsored several each year: the Junior Jackpine, Midnite Mystery Trial, Badger Derby, and annual Goose and Turkey Runs. These were anything from fifty to five-hundred miles long and all variations on the same theme: a race against time. The route was laid over a predetermined marked course, the object being to maintain a steady speed over the route while hitting the checkpoints according to a set time schedule. If you were early or late at a check you'd lose points from your initial score of one thousand. The winner was the rider who stayed closest to schedule and whose score was highest.

This sounds easier than it actually was. Over good roads on a well-marked course the schedule wasn't hard to maintain but inevitably there would be rough stretches: sand, mud, swamp, woods—you name it. In the dark, markers were hard to see—or missing—and guys got lost. Over bad ground delays were inevitable, then they'd try to catch up. There were also secret checks thrown in to catch riders off guard, but it was high adventure. The prizes weren't much: a leather jacket or rainsuit maybe, but all it cost to enter was gas and oil the willingness to accept a challenge.

"Hal" Deckert, who belonged to the Milwaukee Motorcycle club, described what a more difficult endurance run was like. "We'd start at midnight," Deckert said. "A guy left every minute. Those first hours we'd ride the highway and backroads. Around Fond du Lac we'd stop for breakfast. After that it got rough. They'd send us over trails through the woods. It was up in that sand country around the Dells. Sometimes it was swamp. Unbelievable! One time I had a flat tire in the sand. I took the rear tire off, patched it, put it back on, pumped it up and only lost eighteen minutes. One time the Henderson club laid out the route. Maybe they were trying to stick it to us Harley riders. We came to a woods where the marker said go straight. But there was no trail. Nothing! It was a matter of whoever got through first would win. I told myself, 'Just turn it on and go!' It seemed like some guys were in there for

Stan McClintock on one of Bill Knuth's "Homebrew" machines. Engine was custom built on Forty-five side-valve bottom end with OHV "Peashooter" heads and barrels. Transmission was from the Big Twin. This was potent medicine before H-D came out with a factory 45 OHV competition engine and paved the way for later overhead-valve twins. *Courtesy of Stanley McClintock.*

A "Two Cam" as hillclimber. Such machines continued to be popular in hillclimbing due to their large displacement and light weight until phased out under AMA rules in 1936. *Courtesy of Peter Ulicki.*

days. Sure I could have wrecked the machine. But we didn't worry about that. It was our sport. Our life."

The Badger Derby was first run in 1931 over a course 370 miles long. Carl Griesbacher, riding a new VL with his girlfriend Jean Welton in the sidecar, won the gold plated derby hat for first place. The new Kenosha H-D dealer Frank "Uke" Ulicki—one point behind—was second. Griesbacher apparently had the right stuff as he won the event again in 1932 when Art Stauf, Joe Ryan, Al Kieckbusch and Walter Davidson, Jr.—all factory guys—joined the forty-seven entrants. In 1933 Griesbacher did it again and kept the gold-plated derby permanently. He gave the credit to his pretty sidecar passenger Jean Welton and was so grateful that he married her.

As the number of clubs increased, so did the number of derby-style reliability runs. Hank Sawaske, the dealer behind the Wisconsin Rapids Club, found an old First World War German army helmet, had it chrome-plated, and created the Silver Derby. It was no cakewalk. This contest led through some of the worst swamps and deepest sands in central Wisconsin. The first time only two riders out of twenty starters finished: Sawaske and Herbert Nieman. Two guys made a wrong turn and went twenty miles in the wrong direction. "Ev" Lambert got pinned under his machine in the mud.

The Green Bay Club countered this by adopting an American doughboy's helmet for their "tin hat" run. They called it the Northwoods Derby and the prize was an old musket. The Janesville Club deviated from the derby theme when they offered the "Little Brown Jug" as their prize. Whether or not it contained moonshine during those thirsty prohibition years was left unrecorded.

These prizes had little actual but great symbolic value, taking their inspiration from the famous Jack Pine Enduro whose prize was the

beat-up but eagerly sought "Cow Bell." What they did represent was an increase in club activity and hard-core enthusiasm during the early 1930s brought on by factory support and the sleek new side-valve models. Paradoxically, this increase in club activity was occurring at a time when motorcycle sales and registrations continued to decline.

By the early 1930s over three hundred clubs were registered with the AMA yet 1933 saw the lowest number of motorcycles registered in the United States since the early years of the century. In Wisconsin annual registration dropped below three thousand. This was the lowest figure since records were first kept in 1911. As contradictory as it seems, while numbers were dropping motorcyclists were having more fun than ever!

Juneau Avenue dreamed up several new devices to boost enthusiasm and—hopefully—sales. One device was the Enthusiast Trophy which was offered to the club that fielded the most members and racked up the highest mileage over a season's worth of events. The factory also used contests to sell motorcycles. One 1931 example encouraged riders to bring newcomers into the fold. Club members who brought his dealer two sales would receive a bronze medal. Four sales got a silver medal. Eight sales a gold medal. This effort may have helped but there's no record of the factory appealing to the U.S. Mint or opening gold mines in northern Wisconsin to fill the demand for medals.

Like any new and rapidly expanding movement, all was not quiet on the rejuvenated club scene and this went beyond an occasional fist fight over somebody's girl. The club scene was growing too fast and there was jealousy between various groups and factions. One problem stemmed from the long rivalry between riders of various makes. As new clubs sprang up the situation was confused by some being comprised of a single make while others contained a mixture. The manufac-

Art Earlenbaugh unloading at a Cary, Illinois, hillclimb in 1932. Startled on-lookers watch as Earlenbaugh shows perfect form. He appears to have landed on his feet. Earlenbaugh was also an experimental Harley-Davidson test rider. He died prematurely in 1941. His death was curiously foreshadowed during a hillclimb back east. *Courtesy of Stanley McClintock.*

turers—Indian, Harley-Davidson, and before 1931 Excelsior—cooperated behind the scenes through the AMA and tried to calm the waters. As one old timer from H-D told me, "Harley and Indian worked hand-in-hand before the war. They weren't enemies. They were friends. If one went out so would the other. They worked together."

There is evidence that such a policy extended right down into the club ranks—at least for a time. Apparently E.C. Smith was given in-structions from the big boys to reconcile disputes in mixed clubs. Here the natural antagonism between Harley-Davidson and Indian riders couldn't be suppressed. When such friction disrupted a club—and thus began to hurt a dealer's business—the club often split along brand name loyalties.

In 1930 one club in a large midwestern city found itself under the sharp gaze of E.C. Smith when the Harley riders—led by the dealer—broke away and formed their own club. One well-placed individual at Harley-Davidson—who didn't like the mixed club concept in the first place—wrote the following to the H-D dealer involved, "(Smith) will naturally try and...put you right BACK where you were before. I know. And that is just what you don't want. The first thing that Smith will

preach is to ALL JOIN HANDS, brothers in the Jewels of the Crown, to have ONE 'mixed' club. He'll tell you how Walter Davidson and Pop Schwin [sic] swim in the same lake, live in the same hotel and eat at different restaurants. And so on. Anything to B.S. the big shots WHO put him in the Secretary's chair."

This raises as many questions as it answers. It appears that the AMA—thus the factories—were trying to overcome past hostility among the riders. The logic of mixed clubs was sound. Anything that disrupted the club scene like fights and turf wars would be detrimental to motor-cycling in general. In practice, however, it didn't work as planned and the push for mixed clubs petered out after a time. Nor was it pressed if the rebels held their ground. The reason being that the mix could be as explosive as gasoline and air. Quoting again, "Karl, (you're) in business for profit...And if there is something that interferes with (that) busi-ness; then the A.M.A. or Harley-Davidson have no business butting in. We are still creeping with this A.M.A. thing, for the simple reason that it is a FACTORY proposition, run and dictated by FACTORY offi-cials. A rider's organization? I ask you? I'm for an A.M.A. organization that IS something, something for all riders and all dealers, but I'm not for BullShit and politics. And that's what we've got."

As time went on, Harley-Davidson gained more influence with the AMA through greater financial backing. At that point H-D found less advantage in cooperating with Indian and the policy for mixed clubs was dropped. It was doomed to fail anyway, for the rivalry between makes ran too deep. No doubt there were successful mixed clubs—some guys liked both brands, but these were exceptional. Bill Knuth's two clubs were an example of how touchy this could be. His north side club, the Milwaukee Motorcycle Club, was exclusively Harley-Davidson while his southside club, the Badger Club, was a mixed club. This was the deci-sion of the members and tolerated by the dealer so long as it didn't create hard feelings. When one Henderson rider was turned down by the north side club Bill Knuth told him, "You want to be in that club? I'll get you in. That's my club." But after thinking it over the Henderson rider decided that discretion was the better part of valor and he joined the Badger Club instead.

It was probably an impossible dream all along. How could the AMA or the factories expect riders to accept their opposite numbers after rivalry had been encouraged for so long? Harley-Davidson didn't pro-vide a sterling example of brotherhood: after the mid-1920s you'd be hard pressed to spot an Indian even in large group photos of bikes in *The Enthusiast.* The very words "Indian," "Super X," and "Henderson" were taboo when reporting competition results in that same publica-tion. A blank space was provided instead.

"Two Cam" hillclimber used by Russell "Kid" Fischer. Mechanic Dick Trauch stands behind machine. Heavy climbing chains can be seen on rear wheel. *Courtesy of Russell Fischer.*

Herb Reiber on an H-D factory 45 OHV hillclimber. Both Reiber and Joe Petrali were factory racers until Depression worsened and only Joe was kept on. *Courtesy of Stanley McClintock.*

Swastika Motorcycle Club hillclimb June 1932 at LeMont, Illinois. For all its rough and tumble appeal "slant artists" were rarely seriously hurt. *Courtesy of Stanley McClintock.*

Slinger hillclimb in early 1930s. Slinger Hill was the premier climb near Milwaukee. After a few runs hills were badly mauled and climbers had to carefully pick their course. *Courtesy of Stanley McClintock.*

Johnny Spiegelhoff prepares to ride at Cary in May of 1932. Spiegelhoff was colorful figure who first rode Harley-Davidsons and later switched over to Indian. AMA referee in photo is Noel Floistad of Chicago. *Courtesy of Stanley McClintock.*

Indian riders were vastly outnumbered at most Midwest events. Here Claude Smith of Rockford, Illinois, shows excellent form but probably lost anyway. *Courtesy of Stanley McClintock.*

In time Harley-Davidson's control over the AMA and all aspects of organized motorcycling became an iron rule. Some resented it. But at the time it was necessary. Indian was growing ever weaker under the effects of the Depression and rotten management. Only H-D had the strength—minimal as it was—to provide direction through the AMA by controlling club charters, granting sanctions for events, and establishing rules that restricted AMA members to sanctioned events only. This organization kept the naturally boisterous motorcycle scene under control. It coordinated events and made sure that competition stayed honest, it weeded out the bad apples, and it worked for years. But it also sowed the seeds of discontent and reaction which later resulted in the outlaw motorcyclist, outlaw motorcycle club, and—it might be added—the outlaw motorcycle historian.

To those who toed the line plenty of fatherly advice was handed out to keep tempers down and clubs on an even keel. Troubled clubs were counseled not to turn minor grievances into a battle royal. Clubs were steered into harmless and profitable avenues. Successful clubs were singled out as models to be emulated. One was the Pittsburgh Club whose headquarters was a floating barge said to be "as classy as a yacht," another was the ill-named but highly regarded Swastika Club of Chicago. In one day the Swastika boys put $1000 into the club treasury, and this during the worst year of the Depression.

Clubs were urged to appoint a publicity manager to get press releases out to the local paper because a good club image was the number one goal. Being Depression years it was stressed that a club need not be rich to have fun. Some with ten bucks in their treasury were doing fine—usually by attending neighboring clubs' events. Being a broke club, how-

33

Bill Dallmann (left) and "Hal" Deckert on 1930 Big Twins at Castle Rock. Dual headlights on VL only lasted one year. Deckert has been a rider since 1934. He has over one million miles on H-Ds as a factory test rider and still rides today. *Courtesy of Harold Deckert.*

Getting assistance in the Badger Derby. Such reliability trials grew more difficult as the thirties progressed in spite of bigger bikes with more horsepower. *Courtesy of Ray Griesemer.*

ever, wasn't the suggested path to success; after all, penniless members couldn't buy new motorcycles.

Yet there were many broke riders in the early 1930s. That was reality. When they could scrape together a few cents for gas and hot dogs a favorite pastime for Milwaukee riders was to find a quiet place down by the lake or out at Lannon stone quarry. There they could swim, gather around a campfire, roast wienies, and sing songs. Although beer was scarce moonshine was readily available. For the most part motorcyclists of the 1930s were law abiding types. They made a little noise and rode too fast but it was mild stuff by today's standards.

Yet the signs of rebellion were there. A non-AMA group sprang up in Milwaukee. They had no name or clubhouse and oldtime riders remember them vaguely as the "lakeside bunch." They rode various motorcycle types—Indians, Hendersons and Harley-Davidsons—and didn't cultivate the clean-cut image that Juneau Avenue liked so much to see. They didn't always shave, they looked swarthy, they wore studded leather and not the preferred white uniform, and once in a while they'd show up at motorcycle events and try to cause trouble. But they were vastly outnumbered and made little impression at the time.

Milwaukee club member during a spring Goose Run. Bike is 1930 Big Twin. Notice dinged front fender. Damage to extremities led to practice of removing headlight, front fender, muffler, and rear fender tail. *Courtesy of Ray Griesemer.*

But even among AMA clubs there were hints of that irrepressible daredevil spirit that motorcyclists seem drawn to like moths to flame. These took the form of club names like the Swastika Motorcycle Club of Chicago, Hell's Harley Riders of Chicago, the Demon Motorcycle Club of Des Moines, and a little later in the 1930s a Detroit club called the Hell's Angels Motorcycle Club. This last—however similar in name—is believed to have had no connection with a later group bearing a similar title.

While renewing the club scene was a good way of strengthening motorcycling in general, it also had its dangers. From the origin of the invention the public at large viewed motorcyclists as loud, reckless, and

Harry Devine, Jr. running the Badger Derby in 1934. Harry, Sr. was manager of the parts and accessories at the Harley-Davidson factory. Son was member of Milwaukee Motorcycle Club. *Courtesy of Ray Griesemer.*

Frank "Stinky Davis" Matheus during a spring "mud" run. Clay gumbo in Milwaukee area was one reason Harley-Davidsons were built rugged from day one. Bike is 1933 Forty-five. *Courtesy of Ray Griesemer.*

Green Bay Motorcycle club. Early 1930s. Club sweaters were popular item. H-D dealer "Jib" Arndt on right.
Courtesy of Fred Process.

Appleton Motorcycle Club members. By the 1930s leather jackets, flying helmets, and goggles had become standard riding apparel. Cool Wisconsin climate was good model for rest of country outside South and southern California. *Courtesy of Max and Edna Kroiss.*

Opposite Page:
Not all riders were men. Margaret "Mugs" Pritchard of Appleton on her 1932 Forty-five. She got the bike when she was just sixteen. *Courtesy of Margaret Pritchard.*

The MOTORCYCLE MYSTERY

JIMINY! TEN TO NINE AND TONIGHT'S CLUB NIGHT! I'VE GOT TO HUSTLE TO MAKE IT!

THIS OLD CEMETERY ROAD WILL SAVE ME SOME TIME! -WHAT A DISMAL PLACE! -GOSH! -I'D HATE TO PICK UP A NAIL HERE AND ___ HUH! WHAT WAS THAT! CLATTER!!!

WHEE! WHAT IN THUNDER! I'M GETTING THE CREEPS!! GULP! - GULP !!

GULP! I DON'T BELIEVE IN GHOSTS - BUT.. HARLEY-DAVIDSON DO YOUR STUFF! KLANK!

AND JUST AS I GOT ALONGSIDE THE OLD CEMETERY GATES - SO HELP ME HANNAH, FELLAHS - BLOOD CURDLING MOANS AND THE CLANKING OF CHAINS LET LOOSE AND STAYED WITH ME CLEAR TO THE COUNTY LINE! BOY! DID I PERCOLATE! - THE EIGHT MILES IN SIX MINUTES!

GHOSTS, HEY- JERRY! HA! HA! THERE'S YOUR GHOST! YOU LOST YOUR OIL TANK CAP AND THE WIND BLOWING ACROSS THE TOP AT A CERTAIN ANGLE AT HIGH SPEED CAUSED THE MOAN!! -AND THE CLANKIN' CHAINS WERE YOUR TOOLS SCATTERING ALL OVER THE GEOGRAPHY - YOU FORGOT TO LOCK YOUR TOOL BOX!

Several themes are present in this short-lived but excellent comic strip from the early 1930s. Club life is primary focus of this installment. *The Enthusiast.*

potentially dangerous speed freaks. Such perceptions are nothing new. A renewal of organized clubs could be viewed with trepidation by the non-riding public. Thus as H-D felt its way along trying to bring fresh excitement to motorcycling they also sought to create a better image for motorcyclists. As the thirties progressed this new image included great emphasis on clean motorcycles, neat riding costumes, and peaceful behavior. The ideal motorcycle event was one you could bring your wife, girlfriend, or kids to without fear of a riot breaking out. Motorcycle clubs were encouraged to be model citizens who performed good deeds and in some cases semi-official duties. The Beloit Club, for example had several of its members deputized. These riders performed minor traffic control duties and warned autoists when they broke laws. In time this disciplined approach would lead to club uniform contests and drill teams, these later assuming a para-military flavor.

The club scene also brought increased emphasis on a better line of parts and accessories offered by the factory. Perhaps the most significant invention coming out of this time period was the introduction of the Buddy Seat in 1933. Here was an accessory that changed the very nature of motorcycling.

Before the Buddy Seat came along the only way to take a passenger was in a sidecar or on a separate tandem seat over the rear fender. The tandem had never been very popular and the sidecar was losing its former appeal. The Buddy Seat changed all that. With this new invention, rider and passenger shared the same saddle which offered exciting new possibilities when the passenger was of the opposite sex. This was the saddle that riders had been dreaming of and it would be one of H-D's best selling accessories ever.

The Buddy Seat was the dual invention of Bill Harley and Frank Trispel. The latter man was foreman in H-D's experimental department for many years before Ed Kieckbusch took over that position around 1933. What Harley and Trispel developed was an elongated saddle that was narrow in the front and flared in the rear. When used by a single rider the spring seatpost took care of bumps. With a passenger a set of

Opposite page:
Frisky Forty-five pictured on cover of 1932 accessory catalog was new concept for the thirties but golfing style hat was hold over from previous decade. In spite of a difficult marketplace H-D offered ever more accessories. Reduced prices was sign of hard times. *Author's Collection.*

The Buddy Seat was the joint invention of William S. Harley and Frank Trispel. It became one of Harley-Davidson's best loved accessories. Reasons are obvious. Rider is Frank "Stinky Davis" Matheus. *Courtesy of Joe Campbell.*

PRICES GREATLY REDUCED

1932 *Spring & Summer* CATALOG

HARLEY-DAVIDSON
Accessories

auxiliary springs mounted to the frame were clipped to the rear portion of the seat and gave increased suspension for the combined load. It was an ingenious invention and added considerably to the pleasures of motorcycling; it gave female passengers new confidence and rider and passenger were now in close physical proximity. Although the passenger was provided with separate handholds, many preferred holding onto the rider and the passenger could now get into sync with the rider's sense of balance instead of bouncing around on a separate tandem seat. Few inventions provided so complete a feast for the senses. There's no better experience in life than a ride with one's favorite girl holding on tight when the day is summer warm, the road good, and the V-twin running smooth.

Another innovation to strengthen the club scene in Milwaukee was dreamed up by Bill Knuth with support from the factory. This was the wildly popular "Knuth's Kollege." This event was run every year from the 1930s until Knuth died. It was a series of informal lectures held during the winter months that covered all aspects of motorcycle maintenance and repair. Because times were rough and many young riders had little money some ignored regular servicing or tried their own hand at fixing the machine; neither of which was desirable from the dealer's viewpoint. A poorly serviced machine was likely to fail and could cost the rider more than if he brought it to the dealer in the first place. To counteract this trend "Hap" Jameson was borrowed from the factory to entertain and educate riders about the precision equipment they were riding.

Knuth's Kollege was an instant hit. Club members, independent riders, prospects, and the curious were invited to attend. The real object of these lectures was to teach riders how *not* to work on their motorcycles. How effective the message was is unknown, but there were seldom empty chairs. It helped cement loyalty between riders, dealer, and factory. While covering technical subjects, the lectures were anything but stale; the reason being they were given by two of the most colorful figures ever found around Harley-Davidson: "Hap" Jameson and John Nowak. Much of the success behind Knuth's Kollege lay in the humor and inimitable personalities of these two men. In 1932 about a hundred "graduates" dressed in their Sunday best attended the "Bank-Wet" held upon conclusion of Knuth's Kollege. Out of town dealers were invited and shown Milwaukee methods. The success of Knuth's Kollege was evident in the many smiling well-scrubbed young faces in attendance.

The instructor at Knuth's Kollege during the 1930s was "Hap" Jameson. Already encountered on these pages working in Harley-Davidson's "fountain pen" department, Hap had been a fixture around Juneau Avenue for decades. He officiated at nearly every Midwest motorcycle event for over twenty-five years and played the roll of referee, announcer, entertainer, and "benevolent despot." He wrote much of *The Enthusiast* during the1920s and 1930s under the pen names "Hap Hayes" and "Uncle Frank." He wrote the book on motorcycle maintenance entitled *Questions and Answers*. Hap's book has gone through nineteen editions and contains service information on American motorcycles from the 1920s to 1960s. The book is still in print and still useful today.

Like many guys around H-D in the early decades Hap was a self-taught mechanical genius. He was born in 1891 near Springfield, Illinois. At a young age he talked the village blacksmith into building him a motorized bicycle. By 1909 he was riding and racing an Indian. This lasted a year when he crashed hard.

The year 1910 found Hap in a new career: aviation. Going to New York he enrolled in the Moisant flying school, the first of its kind established in the United States. With enough money to pay for the two-phase course, Hap went to Georgia for flight lessons. There—flying a French Bleriot machine—the engine stalled and the plane crash-landed. Hap wasn't hurt, but repairs to the plane cost him the remainder of his tuition. In the words of his son Bob, "That ended a short but colorful career in aviation."

Returning to the Midwest Hap found a job only slightly less stimulating than flying: working for Harley-Davidson.

Starting there as a test rider, Hap progressed through the electrical department, posed on new models, trained soldier mechanics during the First World War, worked in sales, advertising, and parts and accessories. For a time he ran a dealership at Bridgeport, Connecticut. He flipped a coin with Joe Petrali to see who would get Number 13 when the AMA was founded.

As usual Joe won.

Under the name Uncle Frank, Hap carried on a long running banter with readers of *The Enthusiast* not matched before or since. His column "Frank's Mail Bag" covered all aspects of normal maintenance along with special problems. It was done in a folksy, down-home style. The suggestive rumors that appeared in print about "Unc' Frank" and his "Steno" were probably a little too risque for the time and soon dropped. Yet Uncle Frank got away with jokes like this one called "Motorcycle Sex." It went, "Frank said: I get so many letters from fellows and they call their machines a 'she' or a 'her,' and for the life of me, I can't figure it out, unless it is because the pistons have skirts."

While the language sounds corny to modern ears it shows Hap's ability to entertain. When one rider asked about a smoking engine and addressed the letter to "Franklin" Hap waxed eloquently about everything but motorcycles. He wrote, "Hot diggety dog, brother, do you refer me to Benjamin or just the air cooled automobile? Anyway Franklin is highbrow and I'm going to drink my next bottle of home brew to your good health. Al old socks, take my advice and stick to motorcycles (now all the ladies are peeved at Frank). You can at least get hot under the collar at the motorcycle and cuss it out or tell it something, but no man ever lived that told a woman anything and got away with it. Of course there are exceptions, Al, because my Steno has to lissen' to me without saying anything back. That is, of course, during working hours...I'm going to help you Al, 'cause I don't like to see a girl smoke—especially my cigarettes."

If you were a rider and visited Juneau Avenue in the 1930s chances are it was Hap you'd ask for. As one old guy remembered,"We loved Hap. When we visited the factory he always gave us a free quart of oil."

But Uncle Frank could be serious too. In 1932 Hap wrote several articles similar in theme to what he taught at Knuth's Kollege. They covered the essentials: lubrication, fuels, carburetion, compression ratios, spark plugs—all from Hap's vast knowledge of motorcycle innards. Besides providing good technical information, these columns drove home certain themes: be sure engine timing is accurate; use only good high-octane fuel; periodically scrape the carbon from the combustion chamber; keep the valves ground properly and compression correct; make sure the carburetor is set a little on the rich side; and be careful when running wide open with sidecar and windshield. Phrases like "very hot," "detonation," "one-way ticket to the repair shop," "serious damage," and "excessively hot" jump out at the modern reader. It doesn't take a genius to read between the lines. Frank's many warnings reveal that something wasn't quite kosher with the top-o-the-line Seventy-four side-valve VL.

When we last left it, this motor had been corrected of its faults, or so we thought. By H-D standards the big side-valve could be expected to carry Juneau Avenue's flag for many years to come, decades maybe. Its old F-head predecessor had lasted twenty-seven years. The flathead had supposedly solved the problems of the earlier engine. It was ultra-modern. Many expected the side-valve to have a long and profitable career.

Trouble was the lovely predictions weren't panning out in the world of hard knocks. While the VL's initial woes had been ironed out there were other problems not so easily solved. These were fundamental to the basic design of the side-valve engine, especially in Big Twin form. Some of the blame could be placed at the hands of the riders. They didn't always heed Uncle Frank's warnings; they didn't watch their timing, they tampered with the carb, they let carbon build up. Being young and wild they beat the living piss out of their machines. Whether this was done on smooth highways or back in the boonies didn't matter. To the factory's dismay many were finding that the VL engine was surprisingly easy to break. No matter how many warnings and subtle propa-

Factory paint schemes became more artistic after 1931. This "bird's head" design was unique to 1933. Here seen on that year Big Twin. *Courtesy of Fred Process.*

ganda Hap gave the boys not to push the VL too hard or suffer the consequences, it did little good. Bill Harley, his engineers, and the other founders were hearing enough complaints emanating from the service department to realize that the side-valve was not the ultimate motorcycle engine after all.

* * *

The year 1933 was memorable in several respects. For the first time since the end of the First World War Harley-Davidson broke from its standard olive green paint job. This long running color was either inspired by lots of war surplus paint or Bill Harley and Bill Davidson's love for the duck blind. For the first time, flashy colors were offered as standard along with new and exciting gas tank decals. If the side-valve engine wasn't bullet-proof at least the VL and its smaller brothers were as good-looking and striking as the multi-hued Indians of the time.

Yet brilliant paint could not alone sell motorcycles during this worst depression year. To the riders, Harley-Davidson put on a good public face. They continued to portray the club scene as a haven of friendship and camaraderie during tough economic times, that motorcyclists were free of the worry, doubt, and fear plaguing the average citizen. The reality at Juneau Avenue, however, was quite different.

Additional layoffs and more cost-cutting had trimmed H-D's operating expenses to the bone. Here the boss was taking the same medicine he was asking dealers to swallow. Departments were combined. Office and shop pay was cut. Yet sales continued to be dismal and motorcycle production out of Milwaukee in 1933 dropped to the lowest since 1910: the day of the Silent Gray Fellow.

Think of it. A factory capable of turning out 35,000 motorcycles a year operating at thirteen percent of capacity. When the balance sheet was tallied up that year it showed a large operating loss. Things were so bad that entire departments were operated by a single man. In 1933 the once extensive experimental department was cut down to just one guy: Art Kauper. Occasionally Rudy Moberg came down to check up on him. Things got awfully quiet and ghostly around the once thundering halls of Juneau Avenue. Of that time William H. Davidson remarked, "That was an ugly thing. Not just for motorcycle companies, but also for individuals. People without a place to stay or enough to eat. That sort of thing. It was gruesome."

A few lucky ones did odd jobs for Bill Davidson. Louis Thiede remembered working at Old Bill's summer cottage on Pine Lake and cleaning up the Davidson's basement at their Milwaukee home. He recalled, "Old Bill put a quart of beer on the table and said, 'Hey Louis, take a drink once in a while.' They were very nice people."

But while the economy dragged and Juneau Avenue continued to wither away the riders continued to have fun. One reason was the AMA's adoption of Class C competition.

Before this time motorcycle competition had been conducted on a professional basis (Class A and Class B). Outside of reliability and endurance runs most events emphasized special racing machines using exotic fuels. Race bikes were trailered to events. This usually meant dealer or factory backing. But with the upsurge of organized clubs and a new crop of younger riders there was a growing demand for events where anybody could compete. This was especially true for dirt track racing and hillclimbing where the pros pretty much had things tied up. Some rebellious dealers defied AMA rules and staged hillclimbs of their own. One of these renegades was Uke.

In 1929 Frank "Uke" Ulicki was an ordinary rider. He worked part-time for Harold Haggerty the Harley-Davidson dealer at Kenosha, Wisconsin. One day Uke was in the shop and Haggerty was pacing up

Frank "Uke" Ulicki became Kenosha H-D dealer in 1930. He was an early proponent of Class C competition. Here Uke is shown getting ready to ride at an early thirties hillclimb. *Courtesy of Frank Ulicki.*

and down. He was slated to take an Ohio dealership and needed a reliable replacement. He turned to Uke and out of the blue said, "How would you like to take over my dealership." This came as a surprise to Uke, but he was eager to try it. Later Arthur Davidson talked to Uke and liked his style. Uke got the franchise. But around 1932 Uke pulled a fast one that almost cost him his dealership, and it may also have changed the course of history. Uke credits it to one of his heroes—Joe Petrali.

"We were putting on a Class A hillclimb," Uke recalled one day while sitting in his newly remodeled dealership. "Things were going fine. The people were coming. I was selling tickets. Then the rain came and the crowd quit. We had $140 collected. I told the hillclimbers, 'You guys can divide the money up any way you want.' Mr. Petrali said, 'No, we'll come back for a rain meet.' But I was pissed off with Class A competition. All those factory guys. Alcohol-burning machines. You'd wait a half-hour between each climb. The people got bored. I analyzed things. I watched the crowd. So I told them, 'There ain't gonna be no rain meet.' I sold my sanction to Squibby's gang and never ran a Class A event again."

Uke gambled on what his instincts told him was right. In the process he defied AMA rules. Obtaining a sanction for a reliability run, he brazenly put on a hillclimb for ordinary riders instead.

"I went to a farmer near Lake Geneva who had some hills, "Uke revealed. "I made it milder than a regular hillclimb so the riders wouldn't be falling down too often. We charged a nickel and took in thirty-two dollars, but a lot of people watched for free from the railroad tracks. There were about fifty entries. The people went nuts over it because it had fast action. Everyone had a good time: the riders, the crowd. There were no dull moments. I speeded everything up. Before that people were broke and there was nothing going on, but the crowd showed the mood fast."

The people may have liked it, but when the word got out what Uke was doing other dealers warned him to watch out. One was Bill Knuth. "Knuth and them guys thought I was pushing things too fast," Uke said, "but I took the chance. Later the AMA began to see my viewpoint. Most likely it was the Davidsons. We had to go to E.C. Smith for a sanction and most likely he went to Arthur Davidson. They were the guys who sponsored the AMA."

For a while, however, Uke was in hot water. Some guys predicted he'd lose his dealership for breaking the rules. The moment of truth came at a 1933 dealers' meeting in Milwaukee. Smith got up and told the crowd there was an announcement about the Kenosha Club which Uke sponsored. For a moment Uke thought he was all washed-up as a Harley-Davidson dealer.

"I was a smart-ass kid," he recalled, leaning back with a sigh. "Then Smith started to speak, 'We're going to—' Then there was a noise and he didn't finish. An arm came out from behind the curtain and waved him over. He came back with a trophy for the Kenosha Club for putting on the best events. That was the original Harley-Davidson behind the curtain. Oh yes!"

As it turned out the very "corrupt practices" that Uke and others were engaging in pointed the factory and the AMA in the right direction. Class C competition was first authorized under AMA sanction in 1933. Class C mandated that contestants had to ride their own motorcycle, use pump gas, and leave the machine stock except that headlight, front fender, and muffler could be removed. Any AMA registered rider could compete. Class C threw open the gates for a new world of owner participation in dirt track racing, hillclimbs, road events, and special Class C only competition like TT racing and field meets.

Norm Zietlow of Wausau blazing up Junction Hill during a Class C hillclimb event. Class C rules allowed head-light and front fender to be removed. *Courtesy of Mel and Emma Krueger.*

Bob O'Neil on an Indian participating in a Class C event near Wausau, Wisconsin. Indians put on brave show but were always the underdogs in H-D's home state. *Courtesy of Mel and Emma Krueger.*

Not only did Class C boost rider interest to fever pitch, but it let the factory off the hook when it came to spending money on racing machines and professional riders. In 1933 *The Enthusiast* offered this challenge, "Now, Mr. Private Owner, you can get out and into competition without worrying about the specially built homebrews or 'hopped-up' crates built by some dealer for the local flash. Boy, you better get your hack in shape and get out in the old gravel pit and do a little practicing because private owner competition should thrive like a weed..."

But 1933 saw another event that appealed to the average motorcyclist even more than Class C racing. Franklin Delano Roosevelt was sworn in as the nation's thirty-second president that January. One of the first orders of business for the new administration was the repeal of the despised Volstead Act—the Eighteenth Amendment to the U.S. Constitution—the prohibition of alcohol. On April 7, 1933, the Cullen Bill went into effect legalizing 3.2 percent beer and wine. Complete repeal legalizing other spirits occurred in December. Beer was back in Milwaukee—with a vengeance!

Not that beer had been ever totally gone, not if you had the right connections. One of Bill Davidson's cronies was "Fritz" Gettelman of the "Get-Get-Gettelman" brewery—later bought out by Miller. One of the senior Davidsons lived next door to the Gettelman household and one second generation Davidson recalled as a boy handing an empty pitcher over the fence to Mr. Gettelman, who filled it with real beer and passed it back. This was certainly a luxury during those long thirsty years.

The legal return of the "amber suds" to Milwaukee was a highly anticipated event but none were more eager than the city's motorcycle clubs. With three Gettelmans in the Milwaukee Motorcycle Club it was fated that one of the first legal half-barrels was ear-marked for Bill Knuth and the gang. Frank "Stinky Davis" Matheus was dispatched with Bill Knuth's sidecar to pick it up. The historic night was celebrated with a spanferkel dinner and all the beer they could drink. Some had never tested the stuff before. Afterwards, in the wee hours of the morning, the club members paraded around town with red running lights blazing on their motorcycles while others stayed at the clubhouse and got drunk.

Up in Green Bay the city held a "Mardi Gras" celebration to honor the amber necter of the hops. H-D dealer "Jib" Arndt became so excited he rode a motorcycle in the parade wearing a tin-robot-man costume. This stunt baffled everyone. But good-natured Arndt was probably too loaded to care.

Nowhere was the return of legal beer more happily received than in Milwaukee. A "beer celebration" was held in April, but that only whetted the whistle of most Milwaukeeans. In July city fathers hosted a great "homecoming" for Beer City's favorite son. It ran a full week with activities every day: parades, dancing, nightly fireworks, air races, boat rides, singing clubs, horse and German police dog shows. There was an authentic Indian village with forty Chippewa. A grandstand to seat 25,000 was built. Mayor Daniel Hoan (who worked beside Bill Harley as a waiter when the two were in college during 1904-1908) gave speeches until he was hoarse. There were tours of local industries including breweries and a motorcycle factory. Milwaukee motorcycle police officers put on formation drills at the Merril Park recreation field while their comrades marched in formation behind the Chief.

To quench the thirst from all this activity, an outdoor tavern in the layout of a German beer garden was constructed. The bar itself was sixty feet square with twenty bartenders on duty day and night. The busty waitresses were dressed in Bavarian costume. There were five hundred tables and two thousand chairs. The place was mobbed day and night. Breweries worked overtime to satisfy Milwaukee's pent up thirst.

On "Wisconsin Day" a big motorcycle hillclimb was held at Bradford Beach. For once nobody minded roaring motorcycle engines even in this select residential neighborhood. Over fifteen thousand spectators picnicked on the beach and watched as contestants flung their machines up the 142 foot high, seventy-two degree Bradford Beach bluff.

Thirty riders from all over the Midwest attacked the hill, but Milwaukee boys dominated the event. The stars of the day were Al "Squibb" Henrich who took two first place wins and Bob "Boppo" and Bill

The return of beer to Milwaukee was celebrated in high style. Motorcycle hillclimb at Bradford Beach kicked off a week of activity. *Courtesy of Laura Decheck.*

Program cover of Milwaukee Homecoming reads like a who's who in the Milwaukee motorcycle scene in the 1930s. *Courtesy of Stanley McClintock.*

Al "Squibb" Henrich was big winner at Bradford Beach hillclimb taking firsts in both the 45 Professional event and the 80 Class B event. Here calm determination marks Henrich's blasting uphill progress and secret of his racing success. *Courtesy of Albert Henrich.*

Left:
Frank "Stinky Davis" Matheus took second place at Bradford Beach in the 45 Class B event. He was riding a 21 ci OHV "Peashooter." *Courtesy of Frank Matheus.*

Right:
Bradford Beach Hill. Indiana rider Ralph Moore in foreground wearing number six. *Courtesy of Stanley McClintock.*

45

Russell "Kid" Fischer on "Jinx No. 13." Jinxed or not, Fischer took third place in the 80 Class B event at Bradford Beach. *Courtesy of Russell Fischer.*

Stan McClintock took second place in both the 45 Professional and 80 Class B events at Bradford Beach. Behind him is a Two Cam hillclimber. *Courtesy of Stanley McClintock.*

McClintock going over backwards at Bradford Beach aboard Bill Knuth's "Homebrew" OHV machine. Notice that his foot is caught by the kick start pedal. This made it difficult for him to unload causing this predicament. *Courtesy of Stanley McClintock.*

Photo from a slightly later date than 1933, but the message is the same. Ken Bryne of the Milwaukee Motorcycle Club downs Milwaukee's favorite refreshment. Return of amber suds was greeted with great joy in "Beer City." *Courtesy of Harold Deckert.*

Gettelman who took two other firsts. Stan McClintock took two second place wins. Frank "Stinky Davis" Matheus also took second place in a different event. "Kid" Fischer took a third place win. Others Milwaukee boys who rode that day were Art Earlenbaugh, "Swede" Anderson, and Wilbur Mellantine. Len Lauby from Marshfield and Len Sawaske from Wisconsin Rapids also rode and Jack Pine champion Oscar Lenz from Michigan and Syl Polacek from Chicago were there too.

Stanley McClintock had an "artistic" mishap that day which was caught on film. The photo was widely circulated. McClintock recalled the occasion, "We started from the parking lot across the street from the bathhouse, rode up the hill and landed on the street on top. What happened was the guy who started my machine forgot to turn the pedal in and I caught my leg and couldn't get off. I would've stepped off otherwise. Instead I went over backwards with it. That picture was shown all over. In fact it won a prize."

After the terrible economic hardships people had endured during the previous few years the worst was now over. The country had fresh hope in Roosevelt's New Deal legislation which created millions of government jobs for out-of-work Americans. This was the beginning of the road back to prosperity. For many the reappearance of beer in Milwaukee was the first real sign of better times to come.

Once again race meets, rallies, and hillclimbs could be enjoyed while sipping a cool brew. Paradoxically the return of beer would erode the new image for motorcyclists that the AMA and the industry were trying so hard to instill. At once the squeaky clean image so carefully cultivated began to deteriorate from the moment beer made its reappearance and guys and gals with no previous drinking experience now tried to make up for lost time. In 1933 bikers resumed their love affair with the amber brew that has carried down to the present day.

The club scene was booming. In 1933 Milwaukee clubs were awarded an AMA trophy for the largest Gypsy Tour attendance in the country. Milwaukee dealer Bill Knuth was awarded a bound volume of *The Motorcyclist* for having turned in more AMA memberships than anyone else in the country. In honor of the occasion E.C. Smith was on hand for a big party with movies, beer, and food donated by a grateful Harley-Davidson Motor Company. Their hunch about Bill Knuth was paying off handsomely. A more ambitious or live-wire dealer would be hard to find anywhere.

In spite of hard times, most riders were happy. They were young, their girlfriends were pretty, they could drink beer again, and they had their motorcycles—mostly Forty-five or Seventy-four flatheads. What more could they ask for?

Yet by late 1933, something else was making the rounds in Milwaukee. There was a rumor circulating among club members and riders that had filtered out of the Harley-Davidson factory—guys in the know claimed that Bill Harley was working on a new motorcycle. They said it was going to be unlike anything H-D had ever offered in a road bike before. It wasn't going any 45 or little single-cylinder job either, this was going to be a full Sixty-one cubic inch twin. And it wasn't going to be a pocket-valve or flathead either—this Big Twin was going to be full overhead-valve!

CHAPTER THREE:
A Secret Weapon

Thunderbolt steers all things.
Herakleitus of Ephesus, 500 B.C.

One day in 1934 Bill Knuth sent one of his mechanics over to the Harley-Davidson factory for some racing parts. The mechanic was Frank "Stinky Davis" Matheus. The real Stinky Davis was a comic strip character who Matheus slightly resembled. One day at a Gypsy Tour he was doused with cologne and the fragrance—and nickname—stuck. Many years later at a dignified gathering of Milwaukee businessmen a voice boomed across the room: "Hey Stinky Davis!"; it was William H. Davidson using Matheus' nickname from the 1930s.

So Stinky Davis rode over to Juneau Avenue that day. At the time, racing was located in the rear of the big south building down in the basement—you went straight ahead past the guard house where Juneau Avenue turned left into 38th Street and then between the two big buildings. Near the "oil house" you'd turn left to the west side of the south building, there was an outside door and a ramp where bikes could be

"Stinky Davis" and Bill Manz operating a small lathe at Bill Knuth's motorcycle shop. Stinky was sent over to factory to pick up some racing parts. While there he saw prototype 61 OHV. *Courtesy of Frank Matheus.*

ridden in from outside. At that time racing directly adjoined the experimental department. The only thing separating them was a row of low workbenches so when you were in one you were essentially in both.

Although racing and experimental were located in this remote part of the factory where most ordinary visitors didn't go, it wasn't the bastion of secrecy behind locked doors you might expect. If you were known around the factory, like Stinky Davis was, they didn't care much where you went or what you saw. That's how Stinky saw the prototype Sixty-one Overhead two years before the rest of the world.

While waiting for Bill Kasten or "Dutch" Becker to get the parts, Matheus walked over into experimental. Sitting off to one side was a partially assembled motorcycle. There was a frame with engine, transmission, and oil tank installed and that was about it. There were no wheels or fenders on it but what Stinky saw was electrifying.

"There were rumors about a new Sixty-one Overhead," Matheus told me, "but nobody had seen it. Right away I figured it must be the new model they were talking about. A guy come over—not Kieckbusch—and I asked him about it. He said, 'Yeah, that's our new Sixty-one.' Right away I knew I had to have one. That was the big thing then. Overhead-valve. And that was a beautiful engine."

Overhead-valve in 1934? How could that be? A few short years earlier Harley-Davidson had redefined their approach to motorcycle technology with the side-valve engine. In retrospect it seems incredible—almost illogical—that with motorcycle sales in the doldrums, with millions out of work, and the future uncertain, that conservative Harley-Davidson would expend precious resources on a radical new engine type and a totally new Big Twin when by H-D standards the VL was still new.

What was going on at Harley-Davidson?

Unfortunately, the men most intimately involved with these decisions are long dead. These included the founders of course, but also guys like Ed Kieckbusch, "Hap" Jameson, Joe Ryan, Joe Kilbert, Orin Lamb, and Bill Knuth. All the real old timers from Harley-Davidson have been gone for many years.

As this is written (1995) a few "youngsters" on the fringes of the Sixty-one Overhead project are now very old men. One has just died in a Milwaukee nursing home of a fatal brain disease. Another, while providing much important information, wasn't placed closely enough to recall certain critical details. Some guys who would have known the facts—like Joe Geiger—the author just missed. Others—like Wilbur Petri and second generation Bill Davidson—passed away before the author's research was complete. Unfortunately, sometimes the important questions only arise as time passes and you think stuff over but by then it's often too late.

Luckily the reasons for the early demise of the VL are not difficult to infer. Two major factors were at work: one was the mood at Juneau Avenue in the 1930s and the other involved technical developments of the day. Together these pushed the overhead-valve engine to the forefront and hastened the flathead towards oblivion.

For all the original promise of the side-valve engine, the VL never met the expectations Juneau Avenue held for it. As early as 1931 Bill

Herb Carlson with a 1935 model Big Twin. With full valance fenders side-valve models took on classic look, but problems still remained with flathead engine. *Courtesy of Ray and Ellen Frederick.*

Bill Dallman (left) and "Hal" Deckert on 1930 model Big Twins in 1934 Milwaukee. Motorcycles were tickets to freedom in worry-haunted Depression years. *Courtesy of Harold Deckert.*

Wausau Motorcycle Club at the local brewery in 1934. Note appearance of "Harley Hat" on rider at far left. *Courtesy of Mel and Emma Krueger.*

49

Harley was back at the drawing table and it was no secret why. Even with the original bugs worked out the VL had failed the most important test of all: the one at the hands of the riders.

In spite of simplicity, ease of maintenance, and favorable manufacturing costs, the side-valve engine had several strikes against it. It possessed a Jekyl and Hyde personality. In moderate use the side-valve engine was quite acceptable, reliability was not a problem, but putting the VL through its paces as a high-speed, high-performance mount was asking for trouble—and you usually got it.

*   *   *

The flathead's worst faults were due to the layout of the side-valve, air-cooled engine design. Poor thermal efficiency is inherent in this type. The combustion chamber is poorly shaped for maximum output per cubic inch. The fuel charge is forced to make two complete changes of direction getting in and out of the cylinder. Due to its "clumsy" shape, the combustion chamber cannot be properly filled by the piston for high compression ratios. The valves are placed off to one side in a big chunk of iron with the heat in the wrong place. The hottest part—the exhaust valve—lies next to the cylinder where it causes local overheating in the area of the weak and vulnerable piston skirt. These things all conspire against the flathead, but especially in the air-cooled engine where the devil of overheating is always scheming to break loose and run wild.

Some claim Indian had better luck with the side-valve engine than Harley-Davidson did. But where is Indian now but face up in the Happy Hunting Ground? Where's the side-valve engine today? We all know the answer to that. One might point to H-D's long success on the racetrack with the side-valve WR and KR models. True. But racing engines are a special case. Trained mechanics hover over them like mother hens. Everything is dialed spot on. Your typical motorcyclist is something else—he neglects the oil level, and is quick to tamper with the carburetor. Set the points? Sure. What? No thin dime? Two nickels then—they've got the same value.

Get the message? No? Consider this. One day you're tooling down the highway on your VL with its slick Art Deco paint-job. The mercury's topped out the thermometer and you're in a rush for a cool one so you're pushing real hard. Lately the mill doesn't have the pep she once did. This morning you fiddled with the carb and now it's adjusted too lean and your timing's off, too. Who knows when you last scraped the carbon out of the combustion chamber, and if you're hauling a passenger, sidecar, or windshield—so much the worse. A combination of small things like that and you might well experience that sickening loss of power through the seat of your pants even as you crack the throttle wide. Or smell the hot sharp stink of overheated metal just before something breaks. And then you and your VL are sitting along the road as you damn the faithless crate to hell. If you're lucky you might thump home on one cylinder. If not you just start pushing.

If you press old factory men from Harley-Davidson they'll admit it. Some are more candid than others but it all amounts to the same thing. Arthur Kauper, who worked for years in experimental, put it this way, "That (VL) motor improved, but we did have problems. Piston trouble. The flathead wasn't a bad motor, but what happened was that hot spots would develop and occasionally weld a piston."

That's diplomacy. John Nowak is more blunt, "I'll tell you. Really. That VL wasn't very good. You couldn't keep pistons in it. Suppose you wanted to go from Milwaukee to California. You wanted to head up to seventy-five, eighty miles an hour. Chances are you'd stick a piston. At high speed they'd score. From here to California count on bringing a couple spares. There used to be a tire ad in *Harper's* magazine saying how you could drive from New York to California with four tires and four spares. The VL was like that too—with pistons."

When it came to high-speed reliability, the VL wasn't up to the aggressive rider of the day. By the 1930s good paved highways offered more speed potential than motorcycle engines could deliver without risking a costly detour to the repair shop. If Joe Ryan were around he'd tell us and probably quote chapter and verse from stacks of irate letters along with a few fried pistons as proof. "Hal" Deckert said this when asked if his VL ate pistons, "It sure did. Even after they came out with

the T-slot piston one time the whole rear part fell off and into the crankcase. But I came home with it—slapping like hell all the way!"

There was also dissatisfaction with the VL's total loss oiling system. The auto world had never put up with this anachronism. On the motorcycle it was an archaic leftover from the original drip-feed days—oil took a one way trip from tank to crankcase and one result was that oil ran hotter than it should have. At high-speed or when slogging in sand or mud riders were advised to give the mechanical oil pump a booster shot from the hand pump, but overuse of the hand pump was no good either. Too much oil caused spark plug fouling, overheating, sticky valves, and carbonized the combustion chamber and this would play hell with compression and lead to loss of power, detonation, overheating, and engine damage.

In many ways the VL with its side-valve engine was a nice motorcycle (said as past owner of 31VL1403). But the VL was a temperamental and fragile mount that did not meet the demands of the hard-core 1930s rider.

*   *   *

William S. Harley was a smart man. By the early thirties he had more experience designing motorcycles than anyone else in the country. Early greats like Oscar Hedstrom, Joe Merkel, Arthur Feilbach, Andrew Strand, and Perry E. Mack were long gone from the scene. Still, what they and countless others had accomplished was part of Bill Harley's vast knowledge. He kept abreast of technical developments in England. The mature Bill Harley rivaled anyone in the world in knowing what a motorcycle should be. In practical experience and technical expertise the other founders and their top people weren't far behind. At no other time in history has there existed so formidable a group devoted to the single purpose of designing and building motorcycles.

For all its agony, the Great Depression may have been a blessing in disguise for Harley-Davidson. The years of coasting on the export market while neglecting the American enthusiast brought the chickens home to roost. In the fullness of time H-D had seen the error of their ways. They had come back with the side-valve VL and 45 models as their best offerings for a new generation of riders. The trouble—and it didn't take long for Bill Harley and rest of the crew to figure it out—was that the VL wasn't good enough. But by then it was almost too late.

The Depression scared Harley-Davidson and shook Juneau Avenue to its legend-haunted foundation, it made them lean and hungry, thoughtful and nostalgic for the glory days of yore. As the founders looked back to the past and ahead towards the future they must have realized the profound responsibility that was their's alone. Nothing less than the future of the American motorcycle lay in their hands. A once great industry had been swaged down to just two actors and one—Indian—was slowly dying.

Were the ghosts of the past watching? Ghosts that went back to Pennington and his impossible yet wonderfully prophetic "Motor Cycle"; to the riders of the pioneer days when hundreds of would-be American motorcycle builders came and vanished like flashes on the horizon; to the racers who risked all and sometimes died senseless deaths just to prove their machines were faster by a few lousy fifths of a second and whose sacrifice must have weighed heavy in the founders' hearts; to the countless riders who just rode and suffered in the rain and heat and sometimes went down, but who loved it anyway. The combined legacy of all these lay in the hands of the founders. The only survivors with enough resources, skill, resolve, and maybe just plain luck to justify what came before and what must need follow if all was not to be lost.

Many had tried and ultimately failed. During the Depression it seemed like Harley-Davidson's turn to leave the game. This spirit was often heard and felt at Juneau Avenue during those terrible years. As the machinery ground to a halt and the presses grew silent, Harley-Davidson's own death-mask grinned as the clock struck midnight—where else came the inspiration to build what they did?

The Depression brought the great collective talents within Harley-Davidson to bear upon the simple yet profound task of survival. The

Joe Simandl's well-equipped Big Twin: 30VL11301. A country ride with one's girlfriend was and remains a popular pastime. *Courtesy of Joe Simandl.*

A happy motorcycle couple: Gus Stenmark and Elsie Toplak. Stenmark was a consistent winner of Milwaukee area endurance and reliability runs. *Courtesy of Harold Deckert.*

A well-dressed rider of the mid-1930s. Pete Johnson of Mosinee and his 1935 Forty-five. Riding clothing was formal by today's standards, but set apart by Harley wings, multi-buckle riding belt, and breeches tucked into high boots. Bikes looked good. Riders looked good. *Courtesy of Ray and Ellen Frederick.*

Riders of the 1930s seem to have had an affinity for taking their bikes into the water. Here a member of the Milwaukee Motorcycle Club shows how it was done. Note unusual check pattern paint job on front fender similar to some First World War aircraft. *Courtesy of Ken Bryne.*

boosting of the club scene, the introduction of Class C competition, and the dictatorial takeover of the AMA—a move most bitterly scorned in some quarters—all these were necessary if Milwaukee were to exist at all. In that desperate time there was no more loafing, no more, "Hey, Davidson's coming, better get to work." As Roosevelt's policies began to spread money around and people could buy a little more again, one by one the men were called back but the feeling was different now. The easy ways of the twenties were gone. Everyone—from top to bottom—wanted to get back to what they knew best: building motorcycles.

As the men returned they heard what others soon heard. An entirely new model was on the stocks—a machine designed to be everything riders dreamed of in a motorcycle. A machine of great speed to fulfill every desire for the open highway. A mount with an iron heart and endless endurance. An object of ineffable beauty to bewitch and beguile the eye.

From the inception of the "motor-cycle," riders had been dreaming of a super-machine—one that moved like lightning, was unbreakable, and stirred the senses while standing still. The founders of Harley-Davidson—mature men at the peak of their powers—now decided to play their last hand. There was no guarantee of success, but there never had been. Once before they had bet all and won, back when they started on a shoestring and rose to be the world's greatest motorcycle company, when the books showed a balance of ninety-nine dollars one year and a few years later they were talking millions. Now they set upon an equally improbable task. This was nothing less than fulfilling their own hearts' desire and that of every true rider: to create the world's ultimate motorcycle.

This machine would embody the spirit of motorcycling itself: freedom, elemental power, and the lure of adventure. One look at its sleek lines would wash away the worry, doubt, and fear of "Old Man Depresh." This new model would be symbolic of everything lacking in peoples' lives and the life of the nation. It would carry none of the gloom of the past. This new machine would break the psychological barrier of hard times and provide a glimpse of a brighter future to come.

Clearly the side-valve engine did not possess the mechanical genes for the powerplant the founders now wished to build. But what was there to take its place?

Maybe H-D was stuck in a rut of sorts in the twenties, but they wouldn't coast now. Milwaukee would take the bull by the horns and leap ahead of the competition. Not only in the motorcycle industry but also when compared to contemporary automobile practice. H-D would pick and choose among the best and most advanced engine technology of the day. Everything on this machine would be new—and right, incredibly right. Even today many marvel at the flawless beauty of the first EL models. With this new machine Harley-Davidson would redefine the *gestalt* of the American motorcycle. To propel this new Big Twin into the future there was only one answer: O-H-V. Overhead-valve.

From the earliest years of the internal combustion engine the overhead-valve layout was known to be superior. In 1906 Enrico Giovanni, chief engineer at Fiat, demonstrated that OHV engines would produce twenty percent more power than other types. Writing in the *Horseless Age* in 1911 P.M. Heidt stated, "The nearest approach to an ideal combustion chamber is obtained when both inlet and exhaust valves are located in the cylinder head at an angle of 30 to 45 degrees, the cylinder head being made of the hemispherical form."

In England, J.A. Prestwich & Company (JAP) produced OHV V-twin racing engines as early as 1906 using two separate pushrods and rocker arms. By the 1920s, Germany, Italy, France. and Great Britain

were all hotbeds of OHV motorcycle engine technology. In this country, however, things were somewhat different and after a promising start early in the century the OHV motorcycle engine fell by the wayside, except in special racing engines.

In 1905 a young machinist named Perry E. Mack was working for the infant Harley-Davidson company. Riding one of their first motorcycles that summer Mack set a new Wisconsin state speed record. He soon left H-D and set to work on ideas of his own. By 1910 he had designed and was building the OHV Mack motor in Milwaukee. From that date until 1914, when the company went bust, the Mack motor in single and V-twin form was used in a series of production road bikes including the Kenzler-Waverley, Waverley, P.E.M., and Jefferson. During its meteoric career this pushrod overhead-valve engine was the terror of Midwest dirt tracks with the single cylinder job often beating Indian and H-D twins.

In 1912 and afterwards Indian fielded OHV racing machines with good results. In 1913 the Pope company introduced an OHV road bike with possible engineering ties to Perry E. Mack. For a year or two in the teens Pope overheads gave the big boys a run for their money on the race track but the advanced Pope motorcycle died in 1918 when Colonel Pope threw in the towel and went back to his bicycle roots.

The most famous of the early overheads was the legendary and myth-haunted Cyclone. This motorcycle was built in very small numbers at St. Paul, Minnesota, circa 1914-1915. The Cyclone engine was designed by Andrew Strand and came close to blowing the competition off the track at the famous Dodge City 300 miler in 1915. The secret of the Cyclone was its overhead-valve, *overhead-camshaft* engine that was probably the fastest V-twin motorcycle of the time but rarely held together long enough to win a race. The Cyclone was over-engineered for the technology of the day and especially for the resources of the company building it. Eighty years later old guys from H-D remember hearing about the fabulous Cyclone in their youth.

Milwaukee Motorcycle Club members gather to talk. Young women were not intimidated by powerful motorcycles and many loved to ride. Third person from left is Harry Devine, Jr. *Courtesy of Harold Deckert.*

Little beauties on a 1934 sidecar rig. What kid doesn't like to climb all over a motorcycle? Small girls included. *Courtesy of Margaret Pritchard.*

Harley-Davidson wasn't a stranger to the overhead-valve engine in those early years. By 1916 Bill Harley and Bill Ottaway had developed a pushrod OHV engine utilizing four valves per cylinder. That year Milwaukee boy and H-D employee Irving "The Youngster" Jahnke beat the field at the Dodge City 300 Mile National riding a new OHV Eightvalve. These H-D OHV racers enjoyed good results well into the 1920s. In that same decade H-D designed an all-aluminum pushrod OHV twin but never seemed to have raced it. In the 1920s both H-D and Indian built competition OHV singles—H-D's OHV "Peashooter" was famous. In 1930 H-D began building a 45 ci OHV twin for hillclimbing and a few experimental road racers, but for the ordinary American motorcyclist the only overhead road bike was the 21 ci single which only sold here in small numbers, intended mainly as an export machine to overhead-hungry British markets where singles of that type had a strong following.

In this country no large demand for overhead-valve engines existed. Both Harley-Davidson and Indian had steered clear of the type in their big road bikes. The OHV engine didn't seem necessary, results had been adequate with big F-head and side-valve engines.

In the late 1920s, however, new anti-knock gasolines such as Ethyl and Esso greatly improved the ability of designers to fully utilize the advantages of the OHV engine. These new fuels allowed higher compression ratios with less concern for overheating and uncontrolled combustion. While anti-knock gasoline was helpful in side-valve engines it was pure ambrosia for overheads, bringing out their full potential. With the OHV's ideal valve placement and combustion chamber shape the piston could squeeze the fuel charge right down tight for higher compression ratios—hence more power—than any side-valve. As a result overhead-valve engines produced more horsepower per cubic inch at higher

Members of the Marshfield Motorcycle Club. Wings were a common theme and showed motorcycle's exhilaration akin to flight. *Courtesy of Ray and Ellen Frederick.*

engine and road speeds than the flathead without the bugaboo of "hot spots" and piston failure.

One event that helped bring the OHV engine to the public's attention was the trans-Atlantic flight of Charles Lindbergh in May of 1927. Lindbergh's plane the *Spirit of St. Louis* was powered by a Wright Whirlwind aviation engine, Model J-5C. This nine-cylinder, air-cooled, radial engine was the ultimate in lightness and power output. It was full overhead-valve with perfectly shaped hemispherical combustion chambers. After his return from Paris, Lindbergh embarked on a nationwide tour promoting aviation to a captivated public. Before long the terms "overhead-valve" and "OHV" were synonymous with high-performance.

*   *   *

During 1931 Bill Harley and his designers mapped out their strategy. General specs for the new machine included new forks, double-cradle frame, and a four-speed, constant-mesh transmission. The engine would be a V-twin—the American standard—no fooling around with anything else. Bore was 3-5/16 inches and stroke 3-1/2 inches. This yielded 60.32 cubic inches (987.9 cc)—making the new engine a "sixty-one." Following aircraft engine practice lubrication would be dry-sump type. Most importantly the new engine would be full overhead-valve.

In spite of this broad departure from VL practice there was no deviation from the classic Big Twin lay-out of 1916. Dual chain drive was retained. Seat post and rigid frame remained as before. Controls and service points would stay where they belonged. While new and radical, the machine would be instantly familiar to veteran riders and it was this blend of old and new that was the genius behind the new model.

An Indian in trouble. His bike mired in sand this rider struggles while crowd looks on passively. Indian riders were a heroic minority at most Midwest competition events. *Courtesy of Joe Campbell.*

Ruth "Smitty" Smith on her own 1932 Forty-five. This was first year of the horizontal generator. Bike is clean and looks brand new. White was popular color option throughout the 1930s. *Courtesy of Margaret Pritchard.*

At that point in Harley-Davidson history there was no separate styling department. They did, however, have a locked room where they built mock-ups for modeling purposes but there were no individual stylist—styling went to whoever had the idea. They put him in the design room to develop it. Normally the engineers and designers had the strongest influence on styling. The chief engineer might suggest it look one way, the assistant chief engineer might suggest another. It happened more or less on a "catch-as-catch-can" basis, yet these guys knew what looked right and nothing proves that better than the 1936 EL model.

Several new features first produced on the 61 OHV were already in prototype form when work on the overhead-valve engine began in 1931. In mid-year the founders saw a mockup flathead in the design room that included a double-cradle frame, teardrop gas tanks, tank-mounted instrument panel, and experimental tubular forks. Thus some of the most important bits and pieces were already there, the major components yet to be developed were engine and transmission.

Even here past practice was a guide: the basic flywheel and crankcase assembly could be adapted from previous models, the traditional ways of handling carburetion, intake and exhaust porting, and gear-driven generator would be retained. The overhead-valve mechanism and lubrication system would prove most challenging. When still in the paper stage a number of engine designs were drawn, considered, and abandoned. Art Kauper—a young guy in experimental at the time—put it this way, "There were a lot of things they considered and laid out in the design department. Some of which they eventually tested. Some of which didn't get that far."

Harley-Davidson may have also studied air-cooled aviation engines of the day. Indeed there is a resemblance between the heads of 1930s aircraft radials and the heads of what later generations know as the Knucklehead. It's unlikely, however, that Harley-Davidson seriously copied any aircraft engine for reasons that will later be discussed.

A more direct influence may have been contemporary English OHV practice. It's no secret that throughout their long history H-D has studied the competition, but then so did everyone else. In the 1920s they bought, tested, dismantled, examined, then scrapped numerous

Arnold Boehmer rests during an Oshkosh TT race. Empty bottles most likely a prank by friends. Limburger cheese smeared on cylinders and chewing gum plugged gas cap vents were others. *Courtesy of Euella Trapp.*

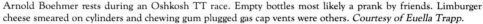

"Hal" Deckert up to his hubs in mud near Lyndon Station. Deckert said, "Sure we could have wrecked our machines, but that was our sport. Our lives." *Courtesy of Harold Deckert.*

Norm and Bertha Zietlow at a Class C hillclimb. Distinctive dress, activities, and mannerisms made motorcyclists a distinct subculture by the early 1930s. Low slung side-valve models helped interest a new generation in motorcycles. *Courtesy of Ray and Ellen Frederick.*

English overheads. There's a nice photo of "Squibb" Henrich sitting on a 1927 BSA OHV single in Milwaukee when foreign bikes were unknown in that city.

The late Christy Spexarth, who worked in engineering during the Sixty-one's development, recalled the English connection: "Indeed we did study other motorcycles at that time. They were mainly English bikes. I believe we evaluated the Brough-Superior. That was a sixty cubic inch engine I believe. Some parts of it were distinctive. Some were not. We picked up what appealed to us. But overall we didn't pay much attention to English designs."

Foremost of the men responsible for the radical new engine and subsequent motorcycle was William S. Harley. As chief engineer and company co-founder, Bill Harley called the shots in the design and engineering department. He pointed the way ahead and approved or disapproved what others came up with. Much of his own work on the Sixty-one went into designing the lubrication system, the combined oil-tank battery-holder, and integrated instrument panel. His name appears on patents for these items. Of course Bill Harley could not design an entire motorcycle by himself; working under him was a skilled team of designers and engineers. Among old time H-D employees interviewed for this work were named several other key players in the original design of the Sixty-one Overhead.

While second generation Bill Davidson was not directly involved with engineering or design, he recalled one of the top men working under Bill Harley. Davidson remarked, "Alf Kuehn was given the job of laying out that 1936 overhead under Mr. Harley's direction. Kuehn was

Another happy and good-looking motorcycle couple, Fred and Margaret Process of the Green Bay Club. Note cute little running lights. *Courtesy of Fred Process.*

in our engineering department at that time. He had a lot to do with designing that thing."

Alfred "Alf" Kuehn went back with Harley-Davidson to at least 1916 as a draftsman. By 1930 his job title was designer-engineer. Kuehn was a tall, raw-boned man with the lank, lean look of a cowboy. His features were sharp, his hairline receding, and he possessed a high intelligent forehead yet he wasn't above a laugh now and then. He was a cautious individual who carefully planned every move and his work on the nearly perfect 61 OHV bears this out. Old timers remember Kuehn's son as a member of the Wauwatosa Motorcycle Club. Around 1935 Alfred Kuehn left Harley-Davidson. The reasons for his departure are not known but Kuehn's last big job at H-D was accomplished with a flourish. The design he originally put down on paper would be famous long after his name was forgotten.

It was Kuehn's job to make a general layout of the new model. He then assigned individual components to various other designers. Depending on skill and experience each man was given some aspect of the machine to work on. Later the individual parts would be drawn in detail in the adjacent drafting department. There Ed Pfeffer was in charge of a half-dozen draftsmen, the most experienced of whom were Sam Lehmkuhl and Walter Foley. Both of these men later went into business for themselves and did very well.

Several designers worked under Alf Kuehn. At that time Charlie Featherly was one of their crack designers. Featherly was a good-natured guy with a perpetual smile, about five-nine, a little on the heavy side, and also very talented. He was especially skillful with valve arrangement, porting, cooling fins—anything to do with head work and cylinders on air-cooled engines. It may well be the distinctive style that came to be known as the "Knucklehead" was the creation of Charlie Featherly.

Another designer at that time was Ed Toma. He was a short, heavy man with an Edward G. Robinson build. He was especially skilled at transmission work and was given the job of designing the new constant-mesh, four-speed gearbox. What Toma came up with was a true masterpiece. Toma may also have worked on the double-cradle frame and redesigned spring fork.

These guys had been around Harley-Davidson for many years at the time of the 61 OHV project. Taken together they had an incredibly deep grasp of motorcycle engineering and design experience to draw upon. New guys at the time were Christy Spexarth and Wilbur Petri, both of whom went on in later years to top positions in the engineering department. Young Bill Harley joined engineering in 1935 when the 61 OHV project was pretty much in the bag and while he didn't get in on the design phase, he played a role in testing it.

Outside Fischer's Cycle Shop at Wisconsin Rapids in 1934. Dealers provided a meeting place for riders during Depression years. *Courtesy of Ray Wheir.*

Another individual with important connections to the Sixty-one Overhead project was Lothar A. Doerner. According to several old timers, Doerner was just under Bill Harley and over Kuehn in the design-engineering department. The late Wilbur Petri—hired in 1934—stated that Doerner also spent time at the drawing board. Anything that Kuehn and the other designers came up with had to meet with Doerner's approval or modification before going on to Bill Harley, thus Doerner held a key position to influence the new design.

Doerner is an interesting case. His background may help explain why the early Sixty-one Overhead models are so striking even to modern eyes.

A native of Germany, Doerner had served as a naval engineer in the Kaiser's U-boat fleet during the First World War. He survived that conflict and emigrated to the United States. He went to heavily German Milwaukee where he found employment at Harley-Davidson. He wasn't unique in that regard—H-D liked to hire guys right off the boat if they were skilled workers—even if they couldn't speak a lick of English. Doerner, however, must have been extremely talented to have become number-two man under William S. Harley. It may never be known how much of Doerner's influence was stamped on the 61 OHV, but considering his position and skill it may have been an important factor. Over

Milwaukee Motorcycle Club officers, 1934. From left: Carl Griesbacher, Harvey Boettcher, Joe Simandl, Tony Raymond, and Al Kieckbusch. This last guy was son of Harley-Davidson experimental boss Ed Kieckbusch. *Courtesy of Joe Simandl.*

A crumpled 1931 VL wearing a 1935 paint job. Identities of 1930s bikes are often complicated by riders up-grading machines with latest decals and paint schemes. *Courtesy of Mel and Emma Krueger.*

the years many have pondered what design influences shaped the magnificent lines of the early EL models. Could it have been the German U-boat?

Doerner was a perfect example of Teutonic efficiency and discipline. He was about five-foot seven, wore glasses, well-built and well-proportioned, and was handsome with a distinguished, manly look. He retained his Prussian reserve and bearing—he was strict and stern; there was no fooling around with Doerner, he was all business. He was also intelligent. As one guy from H-D who remembered him said, "Doerner was a top notch engineer. An engineer's engineer. He was about the smartest one they had over there."

While Doerner may have put his mark on the 61 OHV he didn't live to see it develop. Wilbur Petri told the story this way, "In those days our management in engineering would ride motorcycles on test trips. Bill Harley was too old by then to go, but a half-dozen top guys would take off. This was common. You do something new and when it's still in the engineering phase—even before the test riders get it—the engineers would take it out. Anyway around 1939 a half-dozen of these guys were north of LaCrosse on the Mississippi River. Doerner was

with them. On the way back he hit a real deep hole and went over the handlebars. He was dead right there. Doerner had a young wife and small child and just like that he was gone."

Art Kauper was supposed to go on that trip. In fact it was his machine Doerner was killed on. He gave the following account, "It was a strange thing that happened. Although I wasn't a test rider I sometimes went along on those trips. I was slated for that one. I wanted the motorcycle to be in top shape and went over everything on it. They usually went on Saturday and came back Sunday. On Friday Spexarth informed me that I wasn't going on the trip and that Doerner was going to ride my machine. That bothered me. But I was kicked off and Doerner rode the machine I was preparing. As I understand it Doerner hit a hole in the road and dumped the motorcycle and was killed."

While the men in the engineering-design department had the largest input on the new overhead-valve model, others also played a role. Some writers have claimed that Bill Ottaway, Hank Syvertsen, and Joe Petrali contributed heavily to the design. This may be true, although no old timer from H-D this writer spoke to mentioned them as playing major parts. By the 1930s Bill Ottaway no longer worked in the racing

Ed Bruskewitz and pal at a mid-thirties event. Bruskewitz was original owner of 36EL1816. *Courtesy of Joe Simandl.*

Milwaukee Motorcycle Club at their Friess Lake clubhouse in 1934. According to one member it was meant for just the guys but this photo suggests it didn't work out that way. *Courtesy of Ray Griesemer.*

department, but held a position "off to the side" under Bill Harley and did what was assigned to him. Old timers thought Ottaway's input on the 61 OHV was relatively minor.

Petrali was there during that period, sometimes working with Syvertsen in the racing engineering department. Petrali knew engines and what made them go. Stanley McClintock—who had close factory ties and played with "Shinky" (William H.) Davidson as a kid in Miller Woods—remembered Petrali and Syvertsen from those years.

"Joe was a guy with a lot of good ideas," McClintock told me. "One time on the track they were having trouble with the 21 single racing engine. If you came around and cut off coming for the corner and your pit crew didn't see a little smoke come out of the rear of that machine next time around they'd hold up a sign: 'Oil,' so the engine wouldn't tie up. That was a problem in that engine at first. Joe talked to Hank Syvertsen. He said, 'Our problem is this way: we got to put bigger fins on these engines so the heat dissipates better.' That's what it was. I don't know why Hank didn't think of that. It was Joe's idea. After that we didn't have any more trouble."

What specific input either Petrali or Syvertsen had on the Sixty-one Overhead is not known. Old factory men didn't mention them as key players, although men with racing engine experience would certainly play a role in this new high-performance engine.

Christy Spexarth—hired in 1931 and who later took over Kuehn's job—summed up the development of the EL model best, "That Sixty-one was so intertwined it would be hard to say that any one man was the originator of it. But you could say that Bill Harley took us out of the side-valve engine and into the overhead engine. He was a great man."

Rumors began leaking out that Harley-Davidson was working on an overhead-valve twin. Favorite dealers visiting the factory with access to the engineering department saw things. As time passed word got out through various avenues. Guys in the shop told what they knew, the younger Harley and Davidson boys who had free run of the factory and sometimes hung around the local motorcycle clubhouse probably talked. Concrete details were sparse—the only sure thing was that it was a Big Twin engine with overhead-valves. As one old time Milwaukee rider recalled, "We heard rumors. People were wondering when it was coming. Rumors of a big O-H-V coming out. Everything was supposed to be different on it. Everything."

As time went on the rumors spread around the country, reaching amusing and even ridiculous proportions. There were also doubters—some predicted H-D would never build the machine at all and become just another experiment never to see the light of day. Others—Indian riders and die-hard flathead fans—scoffed at the notion of a big overhead-valve road bike. Overhead might be okay for racing machines, they said, but unnecessary in a road machine. You couldn't blame them for thinking that way. There hadn't been an American OHV big twin since the Pope and Jefferson went out in the teens. They could point to the elegant simplicity of the flathead motor and its mighty locomotive-like appearance. It was a logical point. Overhead valves did not have a sterling reputation, the old JDs still clattering around with their overhead intake valves proved that. Better to stick with the flathead. Today—sixty years later—a few die-hards still remain unconvinced yet the majority of dealers and riders enthusiastically awaited the new model with the only question being: when?

Harley-Davidson wasn't being rushed. Here was a cautious, conservative company attempting the radical. There was certainly discussion of aluminum cylinders—patents on which had been granted in 1923 and 1925—which they hadn't built then and wouldn't build now. Other

Lauby Cycle Service near Marshfield in 1934. Operation was similar to hundreds of smaller H-D dealerships. Marshfield bunch was noted for their hard drinking and rowdy behavior. *Courtesy of Mel and Emma Krueger.*

Joe Simandl, Harvey "Shorty" Lindstrom, and friend during a summer outing. Originally a salesman for Knuth, Lindstrom later took a Harley-Davidson franchise in Louisiana. Rig is a 1934 Big Twin model. *Courtesy of Joe Simandl.*

designs toyed with different angles between the cylinders—some sported unusual cooling fins, and one guy told of seeing oddball crankcase parts he described as an experimental "drip" lubrication system where oil was carried on little "trays" then dumped on the camshaft. In a 1990 interview with this writer, the late William H. Davidson shed some light on this unknown but fascinating developmental design period of what ultimately became the 61 OHV—the Knucklehead.

"I would say," Davidson remarked, "that it was a combination of experience and luck in this sense. We had designed a number of layouts at that time. They were all overhead-valve. But some were Mickey Mouse type designs. Some of them had freak valve mechanisms. I remember one that had a transverse pushrod. They were not good designs. Leave it go at that. Groping for something new you reach in many directions

Indian Joe (kneeling) poses with friends. Rivalry between H-D and Indian riders didn't exist for some guys. But if your club was militantly H-D (or Indian) or you worked at the factory you were bound to take some flack. *Courtesy of Joe Campbell.*

hoping that one will be right. And one was right. We finally froze on that one as the best of the lot."

By late 1932 the engine design was fixed upon—as Bill Davidson called it—"the best of the lot." At that point H-D's ace pattern maker, Walter Slottke, made patterns for new crankcases, cylinders, heads, and other cast parts. Prototypes were procured from Eck Foundry in Manitowac and Badger Malleable in Milwaukee. At the same time prototype engine parts were being fabricated in the tool room where Wilbur Petri's father Bill Petri was foreman. In mid-1933 these parts were turned over to the experimental department where they would be assembled into complete engines and transmissions.

As noted previously, the experimental department had been closed down during the austerity measures of the previous winter. For several months there was no experimental department at Harley-Davidson. Even Art Kauper, the only guy not laid off, was transferred to the repair department for three months. Now a few men at a time were called back and these were the guys who put together the first 61 OHV prototypes. First back was Art Kauper to run some gear tests. John Mooney, Ray Hackett, Paul Pudleiner, and Vic Hepfinger soon followed. It would be a while before the test riders were called back but in time there'd be about ten guys between bench mechanics and test riders in experimental.

Before 1933 the experimental boss was Frank Trispel, then a new man took over that position, another of Harley-Davidson's unsung heroes: Edward H. Kieckbusch. History will probably never know the full extent of Kieckbusch's contributions to the Harley-Davidson motorcycle. Before taking over as experimental foreman he had been set up in an area of his own in the electrical department where he could develop things. The 32E three-brush generator was one of his inventions, as was the ignition timer that first appeared on the 61 OHV. The "square" coil was also his design. He also invented a wheel that could be removed without tools, but which the company didn't adopt. He cast and machined pistons right in the experimental department, and he invented a successful wheel-weight for motorcycle spoke wheels. This split-sleeve design was granted a U.S. patent in 1941 and the Kieckbusch wheel-weight is still used by H-D today.

Like many others around H-D in those years Kieckbusch was not educated in a scholarly sense but what he lacked in formal schooling he made up in other ways. Kieckbusch was a motorcycle workaholic. John Nowak remembered him this way: "When I seen Kieckbusch coming I'd run and hide. Once he got hold of you he'd talk shop for two hours. But that guy had ideas." Art Kauper worked with Kieckbusch for years and took over his job when the older man retired. He remembered Kieckbusch this way, "He was always inventing. He was a very bright man. Very inventive. A mechanical genius."

Carl Griesbacher on cycle and Ray Griesemer in sidecar as Badger Derby winners in 1935. Griesbacher took the sidecar division for several years running. For the first three years his girlfriend Jean Welton rode as passenger. "Hap" Jameson is timer at right. *Courtesy of Ray Griesemer.*

Kieckbusch was about five-eleven, a big man who probably looked bigger than he really was due to a demonstrative personality. He had an unruly shock of salt and pepper gray hair that seemed to fly in all directions and his face was dominated by a large hook nose and piercing light blue eyes. They were beautiful eyes, but they didn't match the face—they belonged to a more handsome man, but not a more intelligent one.

Around the factory Kieckbusch was considered a character by those who didn't understand him or the difference between eccentricity and genius. Art Kauper recalled one example, "Some people thought Kieckbusch was eccentric. I didn't. He had an unusual way of explaining things. One time he said to me, 'You know Art, if you're working on something and you have trouble with the piston for example, you've got to go inside that engine and become that piston.' When he said that he illustrated what he meant by bending his knees and going up and down at the same time rotating his hips to imitate the crankshaft. How many guys would think of that? But if someone saw it they might think him strange. He wasn't. That was just his way."

Kieckbusch was the man in charge of getting the new 61 OHV prototype up and running. Under his supervision the bench mechanics would assemble the parts and modify them as necessary. They would test the engine on the dynamometer. His men would assemble the prototype motorcycle. His test riders would put the prototype over the hurdles and their findings would help develop the experimental machine. Their reports would go back to engineering and lead to additional improvements until there existed a motorcycle ready for production.

Kieckbusch's assistant was John Mooney. Here was another fellow who had been around Harley-Davidson forever. As early as 1907 Mooney was racing H-D motorcycles in local events. His other claim to fame was an attempt to go into the motorcycle building business (Mooney-Hoye, 1913). Royal Beguhl, who worked with Mooney in experimental after the Second World War, said, "John Mooney was our supervisor. He was a nice mild guy. He never balled anyone out. If you were doing something wrong he'd just say, 'I wouldn't do that.' Way back in ought something he and his brother built a motorcycle. They called it the National. He had one in his basement. It was sitting in one corner. It looked like one of those early bikes. He said, 'Oh, I'll keep it a while yet.' When I came back in 1963 he was dead. The wife got rid of all the junk and that was the end of that."

Mooney assigned the work to the bench mechanics and test riders, taking care of the experimental department records. He was a meticulous sort of guy. He kept a small notebook where he recorded each

A rare occurrence. "Hap" Jameson presenting Badger Derby prize to Indian mounted John Chasty. Year is 1935. Place Milwaukee. *Courtesy of Ray Griesemer.*

day's weather—no small matter to motorcyclists in Milwaukee's unpredictable climate.

Ray Hackett had been an experimental road tester in the 1920s when he rode the V-twin shafty with "Squibb" Henrich and now worked as a bench mechanic and machinist. Vic Hepfinger had a similar job. He was a die-hard rider—even in the hard times of the Depression he owned three or four motorcycles. His brother Louis was even more fanatical—no winter weather kept Louis off two wheels.

Vic Hepfinger was a bench mechanic in the experimental department at Harley-Davidson. He helped assemble the prototype 61 OHV engine and motorcycle. Hepfinger and his brother Louis were also hard core riders. Photo taken when Hepfinger was member of the Milwaukee Motorcycle Club. *Courtesy of Ken Bryne.*

"Hal" Deckert negotiates the edge of a gravel pit during the 1935 Junior Jack Pine. This Milwaukee area event was on a smaller scale and shouldn't be confused with the longer and more rugged Jack Pine Enduro held in Michigan. *Courtesy of Harold Deckert.*

Bill Nadler and Ted Jones on way to Yellowstone Park in 1935. Nadler was seventeen at the time. Photo taken at Albert Lea, Minnesota. Condition of VL suggests why they didn't make it. *Courtesy of Bill Nadler.*

Erwin Martin and Francis Schiller practice stunt riding near Wisconsin Rapids on a 1934 Big Twin. This skillful pair were hired by the factory to perform at race events. *Courtesy of Erwin Martin.*

Art Kauper was a bench tester in experimental at that time. Paul Pudleiner was the dynamometer man. There were five dynamometers to test engine output. A little while later Ed Maronek and Eddie Sikowski were called back. This was the crew that assembled and tested the first Sixty-one Overhead engines and later assembled the prototype motorcycle.

The target date for the new 61 OHV was the 1935 model year. Also on the table was a 30.50 ci single-cylinder version. This meant the new motorcycle would begin production in late-1934 giving H-D somewhat less than a year to built a running prototype, work out the bugs, make necessary changes, and tool up for production.

In any experimental department things don't always work out the way they're planned, there are always unexpected surprises. Nothing invented by human hands ever works just right the first shot out of the bag—there are always things to be modified and small last-minute details that get overlooked. And of course, a company is in business for profit with a schedule that must be adhered to and for that reason there is always the feeling of crisis in the experimental department. Time grows short and the men grasp at straws. Sometimes the schedule is met, other times not, but a day must come when the product is either put on the market or abandoned.

This crisis atmosphere would be greater with the 61 OHV due to its revolutionary nature. Harley-Davidson was treading the path of new technology for the engine that was first bench tested in 1933 differed in important respects from any motorcycle engine ever built in America, and by far the most ambitious powerplant ever attempted by Juneau Avenue. Not only was this H-D's first production engine with a recirculating dry-sump lubrication system, it also possessed features unique in the history of American motorcycling.

Early in 1934 the first Sixty-one engine was installed in a frame. It was to be the first working 61 OHV prototype. This is what Frank "Stinky Davis" Matheus saw that day he was running an errand for Bill Knuth. Recalling the sight sixty years later, Matheus could hardly restrain the excitement in his voice, "The engine was mounted in the frame. The transmission and oil tank were in there but no oil lines yet. The forks were on it. But no fenders. No wheels. I think they were trying different gas tanks that day. Seems they had more like a VL style on it. They were trying different things to see what they liked best. But it was the Sixty-one Overhead motor. You couldn't miss it. There was just one of them down there. Maybe some other parts too, but no other motor that I saw. It was a beauty. When I got back to Knuths' I told Bill and he said, 'Aww, that's not coming out for a long time yet.' From what I saw it was a damned nice engine and I wanted one. I didn't see it again until I got mine two years later."

Another guy who saw the Sixty-one early was H-D dealer, Erwin Martin of Wisconsin Rapids. "I got to know 'Hap' Jameson," Martin said. "He was quite a guy. That's where I learned about it. Hap said that a sensational new machine was coming out in the sixty-one category and that it was going to be a full-blown overhead-valve. Then I got into the engineering department and saw stuff. You could sort of put things together and figure out what was going on. I saw the engine when it was pretty well assembled in 1934 when they were in the preliminary stages of getting it up. Being interested in engines I'd compare it: 'Hey, this one has got something.' It was out of this world. It really was."

* * *

Joe Simandl during a field meet at a 1934 Gypsy Tour. Big men threw big machines through a variety of conditions that can only amaze modern riders. *Courtesy of Joe Simandl.*

These experimental activities were only vaguely known outside of the Harley-Davidson factory. The riders of 1934-1935 continued to buck the Depression with countless events and activities aboard their machines. Up in Wisconsin Rapids Lyle Rockwood took the one hundred mile Silver Derby. Francis Schiller finished second and Erwin Martin also placed among the top four. Over in Green Bay club president Fred Process laid out the annual Turkey Run but some contestants got lost and covered a hundred miles instead of fifty-two. "Jib" Arndt came in the winner.

The Milwaukee Motorcycle Club's Turkey Run covered seventy-four miles including some previously undiscovered "badlands." Most of the course was over muddy rock-strewn hills and slippery, leaf-covered trails. Riders got so far behind schedule that whenever a straight appeared throttles were twisted wide and the endurance run looked more like a TT race. Stinky Davis took a fall. Frank Tamus took first in the sidecar class and Jack Markowich won the solo class. For the second year running the combined Milwaukee, Badger, and Wauwatosa Clubs were awarded a prize for the largest Gypsy Tour in the country.

In September 1934, Fond du Lac's Ray Tursky became the country's enduro champion when he won the National Jack Pine Run in Michigan. Tursky covered the 511 miles of wet clay, deep sand, rocks, gravel, swamps, mud gumbo, overgrown logging trails, river crossings, ruts, and forests riding a 1934 VLD. He was only the second non-Michigan rider to win the coveted Cow Bell trophy in the Jack Pine's twelve year history, the first being William H. Davidson in 1930. The Fond du Lac Motorcycle Club team was comprised of Tursky, Harvey Haase, and Adam Beyer who took the Club Team Prize as well. Not long after this double win Ray Tursky obtained the valuable H-D dealership in Madison, Wisconsin.

Gypsy Tours were often the high point of the year and 1935 was no exception. The destination of the Milwaukee riders that June was Tichigan Lake. This impoundment of the Illinois Fox River lay about thirty miles southwest of the city. Weather was perfect when three hundred riders lined up along Lincoln Memorial Drive for a group photo before setting forth. They rode out of the city in perfect formation. On the "whoppee grounds" there were dozens of activities at this giant motorcycle picnic. Frank "Stinky Davis" Matheus won the *Popular Mechanics* neat rider award and huge trophy for solo riders. Carl Griesbacher took the prize for sidecar riders. The event was so successful in the eyes of the factory that they began forming plans for an even bigger statewide gathering the next year.

It was a good summer that year 1935. There were signs of the economy coming back. Employment was up. More tales were emanating from the factory about the new motorcycle under development there. But the machine remained a mystery except to a very few insiders. The Milwaukee boys continued to run their events with VLs and Forty-fives. That year's Badger Derby was won by Carl Griesbacher and Ray Griesemer in the sidecar division. In the solo class, Willard Bold blew a tire and was stranded. His father came pounding on Frank Werderitsch's front door early the next morning shouting, "Ver ist my boy, Villie?" That year the unthinkable happened at the Badger Derby. An Indian rider from the Wauwatosa Club—John Chasty—was the top scorer in the solo division. Hap handed over the prize, but his smile—caught on film—seems a little forced. However, Hap was amptly rewarded: in 1935 he was given an honorary life membership in the AMA for his many contributions to the sport of motorcycling. After the award ceremony some movies of the Jack Pine were shown and old veterans like Hap

Wausau Motorcycle Club members in 1935. H-D dealer Mel Krueger in white coveralls. Club uniforms not yet standard but unique motorcyclist garb much in evidence. *Courtesy of Ray and Ellen Frederick.*

Side-valves and F-heads line up at a 1935 Marshfield hillclimb. *Courtesy of Mel and Emma Krueger.*

"Hal" Deckert with his 1930 Big Twin, probably 30V10664. Tanks sport the 1933 "bird's head" motif and rims appear to be cadmium plated—one dollar extra on order blank. *Courtesy of Harold Deckert.*

Another sharp looking motorcycle couple, Ray and Ellen Frederick of Mosinee. Ray was original owner of 36EL2091. *Courtesy of Ray and Ellen Frederick.*

could be heard grunting aloud as the riders extricated themselves from the sticky clay of northern Michigan.

Hap was H-D to the core. After the Second World War Alfred Rich Child invited Hap to be distributor for BSA/Sunbeam. He could have made a fortune, but Hap declined and stuck with Harley-Davidson.

At Green Bay H-D service department instructor Johnnie Powers cleaned up at the half-mile dirt track races. Harry Mansen and Steve Kakuk were close behind. Farther north the newly formed Heart o' Lakes Motorcycle Club ran their Gypsy Tour to beautiful Copper Falls State Park. In September dealer Wilfred Dotter put on a motorcycle rodeo at Tomahawk. Riders from several northern Wisconsin cities showed up. Some of the prize winners included Norm Zietlow, Pete Johnson, and Mel Krueger. As Dotter wrote to *The Enthusiast*, "...we planted the seed of motorcycle enthusiasm in the hearts of many of the spectators..." This was the sort of thing Harley-Davidson loved most to hear.

That year the Jack Pine Cow Bell returned to veteran Michigan winner Oscar Lenz. But the Wisconsin boys were right up there: Ray Tursky came in second place behind Earl Robinson in the Class A solo division, Frank Werderitsch and Ed Bruskewitz came in first in the Class A sidecar category, and Johnnie Powers came in third in Class B solo. But the surprise rider was Fond du Lac native Harvey Haase, who had been aboard an H-D Forty-five the previous year, but who he came in fourth in the Class A solo division in 1935 riding an Indian Scout. One wonders if Ray's brother Erv, the Fond du Lac Indian dealer, had anything to do with Haase making that switch!

*   *   *

By the summer of 1934, the first prototype Sixty-one Overhead was ready for road testing. It was now the turn of Ed Kieckbusch and the test riders. John "Freckles" Bonneau was transferred from production testers to experimental testers. Art Earlenbaugh was called back as was Griff Kathcart. George Schlinder was another test rider around that time. So was Ed Safford, who later became an H-D stylist. Bill Klein came in a little later. In 1935, when young Walter Davidson joined the company, he worked in the experimental department for a time and did some test riding.

Freckles died a few years ago, just before I went looking for him. More bad luck. Guys who knew him said Freckles was a top notch engine man. He started at H-D in 1929 and finished his long career as chief test engineer. He was of French-Canadian ancestry and grew up near Rhinelander in a log cabin among Chippewa Indians. During the Second World War he worked on the XA and tested motorcycles in the desert before joining the navy. At war's end he wired to Bill Harley, Jr., "Need a boy?" Harley wrote back, "Come on home."

Art Earlenbaugh was a fearless hillclimber in the 1930s. He was a tall, handsome fellow who was popular with the ladies, so maybe that's how he got the nickname "the Shiek." Earlenbaugh died young in 1941 of a rare disease. His early death was curiously foreshadowed during a national hillclimb back east. Taking a practice run up an unfamiliar hill Earlenbaugh burst over the top. Spread out before him was a cemetery. He only had a glimpse of it before crash landing among the stones.

Pals "Stinky Davis" and Paul Chilli after running the Badger Derby. Note factory accessory memo pad on handlebars. Was used to keep track of mileage and time during event. I-beam VL style fork and wide handlebars show up clearly in this photo. *Courtesy of Frank Matheus.*

Here it gets a little eerie. Of all the gravestones in the world fate should bring him to rest upon it was the marker of Eddie Brinck, a Harley-Davidson racer killed at the Springfield (Illinois) National Championship in 1927. The story sounds apocryphal but Bill Knuth repeated it time and again so maybe it's true.

Griff Kathcart originally hailed from Texas. While still there he made quite a name for himself on local dirt tracks. Harley-Davidson liked his style so much they brought him up to Milwaukee and gave him a factory job as an experimental test rider. He became one of the top midwestern racers of the 1930s—not that Kathcart was unbeatable. One old timer recalled Kathcart losing a race whereupon in a rage he jumped up and down on his motorcycle. Later Kathcart became police chief in Shreveport, Louisiana.

Unfortunately we don't have that desirable first person account of the Sixty-one's maiden voyage. The principal men involved are gone. We do have a good feel, however, for experimental test riding at various other periods. We know that riders were sent out on daily two-hundred mile stints year round, regardless of conditions. Weather didn't matter, it was part of the test. That must have been some job in Wisconsin's harsh winter climate. "Hal" Deckert—a test rider after 1942—said "We'd come in and punch the clock. The supervisor would tell us which machine to take. We could go anywhere we wanted to as long as we put on miles. Where you went depended on how you felt once you got going. In the winter we ran a sidecar or third wheel, winter windshield, leg guards, and lap robe. We were out there every day in the rain, sleet, and snow. I know all about it. Oh miserable! I put my miles on honestly, but

there were some shady ones. Way back I remember catching a couple testers out by Highway 41. They were sitting inside a cafe with their machines kicked up on the rear stand—in gear—with the motors running. They were racking up miles while inside drinking coffee."

"Squibb" Henrich, who spent three months in 1924 test riding in the Arizona desert said this about that earlier period. "Just ride," said Henrich. "Ride! Ride! Ride! We had a secret base at Reedsburg. (note: Reedsburg is 125 miles west of Milwaukee and home of early H-D board of director member J.A. Stone). We'd take those twisting roads up into the hills. That's where we had that shaft-drive V-twin. One time they had me stay in Milwaukee. They said run it and run it but never add oil. They wanted to see how long it would go before tying up."

Initial road testing of the 61 OHV was handled in the same careful manner as the engine tests. The motorcycle's potential would be felt out slowly and in moderation—they wouldn't be out speed testing that first day, and they were always conscious of potential handling problems. As Art Kauper said, "Just because you put two wheels under a frame doesn't mean it's going to be all right." Detailed records were kept, some made on a Dictaphone machine. It was John Mooney's job to keep the records straight.

Ed Kieckbusch was in charge of the new motorcycle's development. His reports and meetings with engineering and production people soon led to the conclusion that the Sixty-one Overhead would not be ready in time for the 1935 model year. It was officially dropped from the new model line-up in late 1934. Nor was it ready for a mid-1935 introduction. The original high hopes H-D officials placed on the 61 OHV began to fade in the face of continuing developmental problems.

For this reason more testing was done on the 61 OHV than any other motorcycle at that point in H-D history. This included bench testing on the dynamometer, stand testing, and extensive road testing. Engines were run, torn down, reassembled, run again, and torn down again. This took place over and over to check for wear patterns. Everyone in experimental got a chance to try the prototype Sixty-one on the road. Art Kauper was one. "That was not specifically my job," Kauper recalled, "but I did ride with some of the test riders with that particular motorcycle. Being in the experimental department it was very convenient to do that. They were there and the opportunity was provided. But you didn't get that excited about it being new. You accepted those things and sometimes a new model came on so gradually with the mockups that there wasn't a brand new motorcycle one day to ride. You didn't say, 'Oh boy, I rode a Sixty-one.' Some of that excitement was lost because it was a job. You were looking for what might fail."

Through the winter of 1934-1935 and into the following summer testing was continuous. As noted this sometimes included the big boys in the engineering department. Young Bill Harley, who joined the engi-

The old and the new. An overhead-valve aircraft engine next to a side-valve Forty-five. By early 1930s "OHV" was synonymous with speed and power. This was helped by Charles Lindbergh's trans-Atlantic flight in 1927. *Courtesy of Ray Wheir.*

John "Freckles" Bonneau (left) about 1941. Freckles started working at Harley-Davidson in 1928. He was a test rider in the experimental department at the time the 61 OHV was being developed. *Courtesy of Aileen Bonneau.*

Harley-Davidson test rider and competition champ Griff Kathcart. This Texas native came to Milwaukee in the mid-thirties where he landed a job at the factory and continued his racing career at the same time. Kathcart was another experimental tester on the Sixty-one Overhead project. *Courtesy of Aileen Bonneau.*

neering department in 1935 went along on some of these trips. The late Christy Spexarth recalled the men and places involved, "Bill Harley, Jr. and I test rode that thing as well as the factory crew. Sometimes Freckles went with us. Walter Davidson, Jr. was also involved. There were different cliques you might say. Kieckbusch had his own people. On weekends we'd put on a couple thousand miles. Places like Iron Mountain, Rhinelander, Eagle River all strike a note. That's the way that Sixty-one got tested."

Occasionally these trips led all the way to Lake Superior. Art Kauper, while officially not a test rider, got to go along on some of these weekend adventures. While the company didn't pay for their time it did cover expenses. Kauper told of one trip in particular to the Lake Superior region.

"Kieckbusch would go down any old logging or mining road he could find," Kauper recalled. "He always thought he knew exactly where he was. One time he led us down a trail where there was a big ravine with a creek at the bottom. There was a shack with some old hunter or trapper living there. We stopped and Kieckbusch went over. He told him where we wanted to go. The old guy said, 'Well, if you can get them motor-sickles down this here hill, cross that river, make it up the other side with them, go through fifty miles of woods you'll get to where you want to go.' We turned back. But that's the kind of riding we did. A lot of riding was done up around Lake of the Clouds and the Porcupine Mountains. Beautiful country."

H-D's test riders had good reason for seeking out these remote environs. In that rough rocky country they could test the machine's ruggedness and the isolation kept the new model hidden from curious eyes. Experimental machines were always anonymous. They typically bore no company emblem on the gas tanks or any other identification. Everything was purposely kept hush-hush and secretive.

These trips were motorcycles only. Tools and spares were carried in saddlebags or sidecars. They avoided Harley-Davidson dealers like the plague. While this might have served some purpose near Milwaukee it was largely superfluous in the heavily timbered and sparsely populated region hundreds of miles north. Seeing a gang of motorcyclists emerge from the woods might have surprised the locals, but not for the reason you might think.

"We always caused a commotion," Kauper recalled. "Even among people who had no interest in motorcycles. They just wondered why a bunch of nuts were riding motorcycles where we were. It was a novelty. The local people weren't accustomed to seeing that. We drew a lot of interest that way. Not because they were secret models."

Spexarth told a similar tale, "We just barged in, filled up with gas, and went on our way. Sometimes we stayed at hotels. Sometimes at logging camps. We got fed better there. Some people were a little squeamish about letting a bunch of motorcyclists come in. It was all motorcycles. Nothing else."

High speed road testing of the prototype Sixty-one was done on stretches of new pavement outside Green Bay and in the central Wisconsin region around Big Flats and Friendship near a rock formation called Rabbit Ears.

These tests proved that the new overhead-valve twin was indeed the high-performance and spirited mount the founders had wished for. The motor proved rugged, with none of the piston eating proclivities of the side-valve VL motor. As numerous minor technical problems were overcome the motorcycle began taking on its final form. Yet in spite of the positive feedback by test riders and engineers alike the 61 OHV continued to be delayed from production by a few nagging problems—one of which would persist until it clouded the future prospects of the new model. Even after a year of developmental testing the new OHV twin designed for a super-motorcycle was behaving so perversely that it baffled the best minds at Juneau Avenue.

While the author cannot provide a definitive account of the events between 1933 and early 1936, the most perplexing difficulty they faced with the Sixty-one is known. What's hazy are the exact events and processes by which this problem was overcome and the roles of individuals involved. The surviving factory men who were interviewed during final

The reason for the Sixty-one's lingering developmental problems show up on this prototype engine's lack of valve spring covers and return oil lines on the detached head. This omission lasted until the eve of actual production. *Author's Collection.*

Opposite page, top:
61 OHV prototype was in final form by late 1935. But valve springs and rocker arms show no covering. Rear exhaust mechanism clearly shows snap ring and seal where rocker arm outer sleeve and inner fixed shaft enter backside of aluminum rocker housing. *Author's Collection.*

Opposite page, bottom:
This prototype 61 OHV was a experimental test rider's machine. Two things are evident. Signs of heavy wear on kick pedal end-plate and crank lever suggest bike has been dropped. More significant is the amount of oil and grime leaking out of exhaust pipes, covering engine, and spattered back over oil tank. *Author's Collection.*

research on this book were not close enough to the developmental work on the 61 OHV to recall the details. Art Kauper worked in experimental during that time but was not an engine man, plus he has forty-seven years of accumulated memories at Harley-Davidson to shift through. But Kauper did say this, "There were a couple false starts with that engine along the way. They wanted to bring it out as early as 1935. But testing turned up some things that had to be corrected." When later questioned about the "false starts" Kauper replied, "Only a general recollection of the normal difficulties you run into. Like I said that's how much of that development goes. You don't suddenly get a bright idea and put it on and that's it. You develop it."

Available evidence suggests that while the new overhead-valve mechanism in the Sixty-one was highly imaginative and reliable, it was also in one important respect a failure.

A universal practice in OHV motorcycle engines in both England and America at this time was the use of exposed valve springs and valve stems. There was no attempt made to cover them. The theory behind this now obsolete practice was the desire to obtain additional cooling of valve springs in high-performance, high-revving OHV engines. All previous H-D overheads followed this open valve spring style and H-D attempted to follow it now. As originally designed, the 61 OHV made no provision for covering the valve springs or stems. When coupled with Bill Harley's innovative lubrication system this open valve spring strategy would lead to great difficulties, frustration, and more delay.

In the early 1930s automatic lubrication of rocker arm bearings and valve stems in OHV air-cooled engines was still an infant technology. Even radial aircraft engines used simple pressure-gun grease fittings. For long-range service, standard grease fittings were replaced by a "magazine type" attachment. In all previous American OHV motorcycle engines lubrication of the overhead-valve mechanism had relied on manual oiling, greasing, or oil vapors rising up the pushrod tubes if so equipped. With a few exceptions English overheads used similar lubrication methods.

Advance literature for the November 1935 Harley-Davidson Dealers' Convention made no specific mention of the 61 OHV model, but years of rumor made the event standing room only. *Courtesy of Mel and Emma Krueger.*

But Bill Harley had developed a new and innovative lubrication system for the Sixty-one and its OHV mechanism. His method was original enough that a patent was applied for in 1936 and granted in 1938. One unique feature was an automatic oil supply to the rocker arms and valve stems. This was done through a separate pressurized oil line going to the heads. This oil supply was split up with each rocker arm bearing getting its share of the oil. From a orifice in the rocker arm pad, a small amount of oil flowed to the pressure point on the valve stem end. From there it dripped down to lubricate the valve guide proper. It worked well. By giving each rocker arm its own automatic oil supply, former problems of inadequate lubrication and premature wear were theoretically eliminated.

The system was designed so the amount of oil to each rocker arm was very small. Enough to lubricate the necessary parts but not a drop more. In theory this sounded reasonable but in practice it proved elusive.

Even a small amount of oil spraying on the open valve springs and guides proved messier than desirable. Early photos of test rider prototypes circa 1934-1935 (including the 30.50 ci prototype that never saw production) show open valve springs and oil-fouled engines that sometimes were a dripping mess. In essence the new twin's lubrication system was still in part a "total-loss" system. While crankcase oil was recirculated back to the oil tank, oil pumped to the heads was left to fly. It was similar in practice to how the front chain oiler worked. With no covers or return oil lines to catch and control this oil flow to the heads, Ed Kieckbusch was soon pulling his hair and the guys upstairs pulling some mighty glum faces.

During most of the 61 OHV's developmental period H-D doggedly stuck to this traditional open valve spring approach. No evidence found by this writer shows any attempt to cover the valve springs or fit return oil lines until late 1935 or early 1936—the very eve of produc-

tion. Until the last minute, factory strategy was to handle the OHV oil through metering the supply in order to retain the dubious advantage of naked valve springs.

By 1934-1935 prototype 61 OHV engines had an adjustable oiling feature incorporated into the rocker arms. An eccentric groove was cut on the outside of the rocker arm shaft. By loosening and shifting the position of the shaft the amount of incoming oil to the valve stems could be regulated. Turning the shaft to the right increased the oil supply. Turning it left decreased the supply. Each rocker arm was adjusted separately.

It's likely that early prototypes (1933-1934?) did not have this adjustable feature and utilized a non-adjustable supply. Evidence for this exists in the fact that patent records for the 61 OHV lubrication system describe a fixed, non-adjustable oil supply to the heads. When the fixed supply proved unsatisfactory the regulating controls were added, the idea being that by finely adjusting the rocker arm oil flow, a balance between too little and two much could be achieved. Too much and the engine exterior would drip, too little and the valves would squeak. This adjustable control was probably H-D's original developmental strategy to provide automatic oiling while retaining open valve springs. Either H-D was reluctant to drop the archaic feature of open springs or else the possibility of an alternative simply hadn't occurred to them.

But they couldn't have their cake and eat it too. No matter how much fine tuning of the OHV oil supply was done by the guys in experimental, test riders continued to come home with complaints that translated into negative reports going upstairs. If the adjustment was too liberal their pants would be sprayed with oil. High speed runs made things worse, for what was a sanitary amount at idle might be a nightmarish surplus at high rpm. Then the excess ran over the heads and down the cylinders where the oil would burn and stink. The rest would blow back over the machine. At the end of a high speed run the pretty new Sixty-one might be a dripping mess. No wonder they wore those high boots! On the other hand, if the supply was set too low, lubrication would be insufficient at high speed and the rocker arms would squeak. Reaching the necessary happy medium was nearly impossible.

One photo of a 1935 prototype is especially revealing. The machine shows signs of hard use. It's been dropped on the right side. There is no company logo on the tanks which marks it as an experimental road tester's machine. A winter windshield bracket shows year-round use. But the most striking feature of the photo is that the motorcycle is a stinking mess. The cylinder heads and other parts have been removed and laid out for inspection. There are no valve spring covers nor return oil lines. The practical result of this omission is a copious amount of oil spattered over the machine. Obviously Bill Harley's strategy of regulating the OHV oil supply was quite simply a failure.

Yet performance and reliability was there. The Sixty-one could hold top speed without melting pistons or blowing its guts all over the countryside even if it did piss oil on itself in the process. That motorcycle

Outside the Harley-Davidson service school dealers kill time. Orin Lamb was in charge here. He was issued 36ES1748 to test for early flaws. Early 61 OHV sits at left. *Courtesy of Mel and Emma Krueger.*

Photo from H-D's Convention News Bulletin dated December 16, 1935. Two young guys in front of camera are Ulicki brothers, Walter ("C.D.") and Frank ("Uke"). Circled couple at middle-right is Wausau dealer Mel Krueger and wife Emma. Earl and "Dot" Robinson are behind C.D. Los Angeles H-D dealer Rich Budelier is second man from bottom on far left. Guest of honor was 61 OHV in far left background. In spite of small image distinctive "knuckles" and pushrod tubes are visible. A similar photo appeared in the January issue of *The Enthusiast. Courtesy of Mel and Emma Krueger.*

Orin Lamb (lower left) teaches mechanics the fine points of the new 61 OHV four-speed transmission. Factory did have early problems with busted housings, but Rudy Moberg came up with a simple and inexpensive solution. After that transmission stood the test of time. Was standard in H-D Big Twins for decades with little change. *Courtesy of Frank Matheus.*

could move. "That Sixty-one sticks in my mind," Spexarth said, "because we cracked one hundred miles an hour with that one."

Among top officials at Juneau Avenue there was controversy over the new model. As late as mid-1935 there was talk of dumping it. They had already spent too much time and money on the thing with no payback: it leaked, it was noisier than the flathead models, and there was trouble with premature wear of sprockets and brakes. But the Sixty-one had staunch defenders too, and probably none more so than old Bill Harley himself.

It was natural that the man most responsible for the 61 OHV project should feel some affection for it. Yet there had been many brilliant experimental jobs in Harley-Davidson's past that were gathering dust in the garage loft or long since scrapped. The Sixty-one Overhead might easily have joined them.

Yet Bill Harley's belief in the new engine may have gone beyond mere affection. Mr. Harley was now fifty-six years old. Who could say how many more years he'd have at the drafting table? As things turned out the Sixty-one would be his last major creation, and maybe he sensed it. Christy Spexarth said, "Bill Harley thought the overhead was the way to go and he thought correctly. He often mentioned that to us. That the Sixty-one was the salvation of Harley-Davidson. He was right."

Because of continuing trouble with oil leakage, the factory proceeded cautiously with the new model. While the experimental and engineering departments continued to seek solutions for its lingering problems, it was decided to test the waters at the National Dealers' Convention held at Milwaukee in November of 1935. After several years of rumor and unrealized promises, H-D now let the dealers in on the secret.

Advance literature sent to dealers around the country promised a surprise at the upcoming event. Bill Harley was quoted as saying, "...we are offering a line of motorcycles that will set a new standard of styling, beauty and performance." In another place, "Boy, oh boy, oh boy—look what we have here...you'll have to come and see for yourself. It's a secret."

Early on the morning of November 25, several hundred Harley-Davidson dealers from thirty-seven states, Canada, and Japan assembled in Milwaukee's Schroeder Hotel. It was one of the largest meetings of its kind in Harley-Davidson's history. Attendance was boosted by the rumor that the new Sixty-one Overhead would be there. In spite of advance reservations a shortage of chairs developed on the morning the new 1936 models were to be shown. As the minutes ticked away in the Schroeder's luxurious Green Room the tension grew. There was standing room only, the crowd rumbled with conversation. The showing of new models was always a big moment, but this year the mood was electric. After years of rumor and waiting the dealers would finally see for themselves what this new overhead twin was all about.

Up front the stage was draped with a heavy curtain. Behind it the new models were hidden. Then Arthur Davidson stepped forth. In his folksy style he welcomed the dealers, cracked some jokes, told a story, then hinted that something special was about to happen. The dealers sensed the moment had come. Then William H. Davidson stepped forward. It was told to the author second hand that Davidson said something like this, "We're going to show you something that we have denied existed and after you see it, we're going to deny we ever showed it to you."

The new wonder of the motorcycle world: the Sixty-one Overhead. A machine with finer lines would be difficult to find. The evolutionary burst of creativity that began with the 21 ci singles in 1926 and then developed through the Forty-five and Seventy-four side-valve models found full expression in the 1936 EL model. Designers since that time have been hard pressed to match let alone surpass the mechanical perfection shown here. *Author's Collection.*

Below:
The new Sixty-one Overhead engine, transmission, and oil tank fit the double-cradle frame like the well packed innards of a U-boat. So called Knucklehead engine has a mystique difficult to match. Kick-start pedal is quaint reminder of the V-twin motorcycle's bicycle roots. *Author's Collection.*

While not as inspired as the "knuckle" side of the engine there's nothing slack about the new overhead twin from any angle. Nearly every piece on the machine was new. Only thing even close to the VL were fenders and seat. Bike was sleek. Ageless. *Author's Collection.*

At that point William S. Harley and "Hap" Jameson stepped onto the platform. Hap was dressed in a snappy new all-white riding outfit. There was a moment of hushed anticipation that added to the drama of the moment. Then the green velvet curtain was swept aside and there in all its magical glory stood a gleaming new two-wheeler unlike anything previously seen in the motorcycle world—the 61 OHV.

There was a moment of stunned silence. Every eye in the room—and there were hundreds—was transfixed by the sight. Here was a motorcycle whose style bordered upon genius—in front of their gaze was a futuristic engine unlike anything ever stuffed into a motorcycle frame before. Upon such moments history is made. It happened that day. There was no faltering, no indecision, no polite applause over a decal change and then a concealed yawn as in past years. Not that day. After a moment of stunned wide-eyed silence the throng of Harley-Davidson dealers jumped to their feet and broke out into prolonged cheers!

The day of the overhead-valve V-twin had arrived.

When the crowd quieted down—and before they rushed the stage—it was announced that a photograph would be taken. Pohlman set up his camera in the rear of the room. As a result the final photo would look out over a sea of faces with the stage—and the Sixty-one—a small detail in the background. This was purposely done to keep the new model obscure in the photo. As a result those sitting in the rear of this large ballroom were in front of the camera.

Prominent in the final photo are two dealers dressed in H-D riding outfits and notably younger than most others in the photo. By chance the camera had captured center stage Frank "Uke" Ulicki and his brother "C.D." (Walter). Uke—the oldest active Harley-Davidson dealer in the world today (1995)—told the story, "My brother and I were up late the night before and just got there. We had to sneak in and were way in the back. Then they announced a photograph would be taken. We turned around and there was the camera. We were so far back we didn't even know the Sixty-one was up there."

Like most dealers, Uke and C.D. had heard rumors of the new model but had never seen it. Uke was so excited at the prospect of the

new machine that he doesn't remember what speeches were given or what was said. But he does remember that motorcycle. He said, "They kept it pretty secret. The test riders weren't allowed down by us. But they had been testing it for quite a while. So we were thinking overhead-valve. When we got up there I fell in love with it. I said to C.D., 'That's my machine.' He said back, 'No, that's mine.' My enthusiasm for the Sixty-one was contagious. After that I put the flathead aside."

Many others agreed. The rest of the 1936 line was shown including the new side-valve Eighty. But the Sixty-one Overhead stole the show. What H-D heard from its dealers that day and those following was overwhelmingly positive. Like Uke and his brother the dealers were enthusiastic. For three days they pressed company officials with questions and for three days H-D did their best avoiding direct answers. They hedged by saying the machine wasn't quite ready, but it looked damn well ready to the dealers. The factory's former doubts were somewhat drowned in the dealers' enthusiasm and in foaming beer glasses, liverwurst on dark rye, and Milwaukee *gemutlichkeit.*

There was never a dealers' convention like that one. How could there be? Everybody was there! The two Bill Harleys. First and second generation Davidsons. "Hap" Jameson. Joe Ryan. Joe Kilbert. Walter Kleimenhagen. Harry Devine. Art Stauff. Jack Balsom. John Balmer. Herman Schuelke. And all the old time dealers who must have pressed the same question a hundred times each on the factory men: If not now, when?

An indescribable excitement hovered in the air. This went on for three days during factory tours, a rip-roaring bowling tournament, and lively evening banquets. It was a marvelous time with plenty of eating, drinking, and motorcycle talk. Arthur Davidson entertained everyone with his best stories in a variety of ethnic dialects of which he was a master. Somehow Detroit dealer Larry Unbehaum was bound and gagged. Arizona dealer "Cactus Bill" Kennedy emptied a six-gun at a crystal chandelier—luckily loaded with blanks—although the hotel staff nearly passed out at such high-jinks. The Wisconsin bunch—fully loaded on Milwaukee suds—led the singing of the German *schnitzelbank* song.

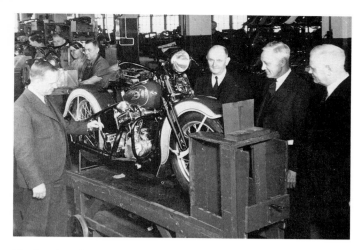

The founders of Harley-Davidson with their last combined effort at motorcycle building. Here it ended. Here it began. Genius of founders and their people created a motorcycle in the 36EL that formed the basis of all subsequent Harley-Davidson Big Twins including today's Evolution motor. Yet at time photo was taken the Sixty-one was no sure bet. It had serious teething problems and probably the reason for lack of enthusiasm expressed by founders in photo. *Author's Collection.*

Jack Pine multi-winner Don Raymond was there. So were transcontinental record breakers Earl and "Dot" Robinson. There was even a woman dealer in attendance: Mrs. Farrow of Columbus, Ohio. She received three cheers from the men. And through it all—running like an electric current—was talk of the brilliant new 61 OHV twin.

Most dealers went home enthusiastic, very few were luke-warm or doubtful. All knew that any first year model was bound to have troubles, but the brilliant execution of this new motorcycle dazzled them. Many would push the new model to favorite customers even before riding it. For during the three day dealers' convention there were no demonstration rides allowed on the Sixty-one, all they knew was the beauty of the glittering new showroom specimen. Few if any saw the oil-spattered examples safely tucked out of sight in the experimental department.

Many went away undeterred by H-D's evasions. Back home they told friends and customers, some sent in advance orders. But the factory wasn't ready to make a commitment. Shortly after the November convention H-D sent out a dealers' bulletin with the following statement: "For several years rumors have been current all over the country about a new Twin that Harley-Davidson was developing and would have on the market any day. The most incredulous and many time positively amusing fabrications have been spread about this model. True, our engineering staff has been working for a long time on a model of new and original design and their efforts finally reached a stage where such a motorcycle, a 61 cubic inch overhead, was shown to the dealers in attendance at the National Dealers' Convention. However, production on this model will necessarily be extremely limited and we are therefore in no position to make a public announcement at this time. Dealers will best serve their interest by putting their entire promotion efforts on the regular line of splendid models heretofore discussed in these pages. Under no circumstances should this model be ordered as a demonstrator!"

This language shows the doubt prevailing at Juneau Avenue. Here was a machine that was detail perfect in the looks department, one that had the performance and reliability the founders had hoped for. A machine the dealers were now clamoring for, yet a machine that H-D was seemingly afraid to release. That's how far this troubled child had sunk in the founders' estimation since the time they had planned it as the lead model for 1935.

Time for a fix was running out. In December 1935, a series of famous photos were taken on the third floor of the Juneau Avenue factory. They show the founders of Harley-Davidson: Arthur Davidson, Walter Davidson, William S. Harley, and William A. Davidson. These now elderly men were gathered around a spanking new Sixty-one Overhead sitting at the end of the assembly line. These were some of the last photos of all four founders taken together and the first of their legendary 61 OHV. Much can be inferred from these photographs.

Here the founders were together with their last combined effort at building motorcycles. This was to be their greatest achievement, one by which they would attain a sort of mechanical immortality. Yet the look of triumph that should have etched their expressions that day is oddly lacking. The photographs reveal a subdued, almost somber mood on each man's face. Something is missing. There's an uncharacteristic lack of confidence, no joy in this happy occasion. None of the all-consuming passion and enthusiasm they demanded so frequently from others and yet now seemed themselves unwilling to give. Little love for this new machine is evident—they're not grinning like you or I would be. All have tired expressions, just like the old men they had become.

In the photo Arthur Davidson is reaching out. His hand rests lightly upon the machine's kick-start pedal. What was probably an unconscious gesture is wonderfully evocative of the founders' status on that memorable day, for upon this glittering wonder Arthur has reached out to touch a remnant of its humble bicycle origins. These four men had begun an extraordinary journey over three decades earlier when they desired to take the work out of bicycling. They couldn't possibly have conceived the great distance between that first spindly razor-strap job and the fabulous iron horse now before them. Perhaps that in part explains why they themselves don't appear to be convinced. They were living a dream and they knew it.

None of the Davidsons reveal any sign of fondness for the machine. At best Arthur looks neutral. Walter looks grave. Thoughtful. In one shot (there were at least three) Walter stares at the camera with a slightly accusing expression. Bill Davidson doesn't look happy or well. His expression is gloomy—he had in fact a little more than a year to live.

Perhaps it's simple coincidence, or maybe the author sees what he wishes to see. But there's a curious feature in this photo. In one take Walter Davidson, Bill Davidson, and Bill Harley are standing behind the motorcycle on its left or chain side. All three men appear to be gazing at a common point on the motorcycle engine. They seem to be looking directly at the still uncovered valve springs.

Only Bill Harley shows a hint of fondness for his mechanical offspring. His is a thoughtful, even mildly inspired expression. Almost as if a light bulb had come on inside his head. But that's going too far. Or is it? Did Pohlman's photographer capture Bill Harley's moment of inspiration in this most famous of photos?

What is fact, however, is that of any men then living these four were most responsible for the future of the American motorcycle. The photo captured them at a crossroads between past, present, and future—all together, at once, at the same time. Yet for all their incredible experience at building motorcycles these same experts appear at a loss when confronted with this radical new mount. Almost as if asking themselves: What have we done?

We can't blame them if indeed they felt that way. Think about it. A mere seven years earlier the JD had been their top model. The JD was something they could understand, what they had grown up with, not this flashy futuristic knuckle-headed Buck Rogers style bronc. Maybe if everything had developed smoothly, but it hadn't. Now at the very last moment all bets were off. In spite of the dealers' enthusiasm this machine was no sure winner. If it failed there might not be another chance. They were reaching the end of their careers and their long collaboration together and they knew it.

It was now or never. Aesthetically the 61 OHV was ready. Mechanically—only time would tell. Dealers and riders alike were clamoring for it. The time had come. The decision was made to go ahead and release it. But this release would be quiet with no publicity. There would be no fanfare or the usual trumpeting hyperbole. This motorcycle would have to sell itself.

CHAPTER FOUR:
Soupy Sixty-one

Go ahead Harry.
William H. Davidson

When Harley-Davidson launched its advertising campaign for the new 1936 models the 61 OHV was nowhere in sight. Dealers blinked and looked twice in the January and February 1936 issues of *The Enthusiast.* Among the new road bikes and police motorcycles not a single photo or word was devoted to the Sixty-one Overhead. As far as H-D's official publication was concerned the 61 OHV didn't even exist. It was the new Eighty flathead that was given center stage. The VLH was described as the hot new "big shot twin" and a "cyclone on wheels." But a real cyclone would soon appear.

The 61 OHV did make a cameo appearance in January of 1936 although few probably noticed. It was there none the less. The same photo that caught Uke and C.D. sneaking in late at the November dealers' convention was published in the January issue of *The Enthusiast.* Readers had to look very close to see it but there was indeed a motorcycle in the background of this photo. The image was tiny and not helped through reproduction, but the distinctive aluminum "knuckles" and chrome pushrod tubes were clearly visible on the engine. The carburetor cover was on the wrong side for the machine to be a side-valve—clearly this was the new overhead-valve model so long rumored. Eagle-eyed readers around the world had their first glimpse of the legendary Sixty-one.

But this almost subliminal image was all H-D was willing to admit in the January and February issues. In March, however, the first hint of the new model came through a report on an endurance run held in the Pacific Northwest. *The Enthusiast* stated quite casually, "'Butch' Quirk, won the 350-mile endurance run sponsored by the Rose City Club of Portland, Oregon, on February 2, with the remarkable score of 999 points. Quirk was mounted on a new Harley-Davidson 61" overhead job to which was attached a sidecar outfit. Myron Wright teamed up as a passenger with 'Butch.' At the end of the run 'Butch' was mighty enthusiastic about the way the 61" model performed. Needless to say, the machine was the center of attraction all along the route."

Some readers must have asked: What Sixty-one Overhead job? Others, already waiting on old rumors or dealer's fresh promises, rushed down to find out. Some dealers had ordered machines already but few had received them. They did have factory supplied photos and order blanks. In Appleton, Wisconsin, three guys put in orders for new Sixty-one Overheads on the advice of Green Bay dealer "Jib" Arndt. In the Rapids six guys figured they'd try the new OHV model. By year's end twenty-seven would be running loose on Milwaukee streets and seventy-five in Harley-Davidson's home state of Wisconsin. Estimates vary on how many 61 OHVs were produced that first year. In November of 1936 H-D put the number at "nearly 2000" although this probably included some 1937 Sixty-ones. A more modern factory source says 1,704 were produced that first year. This was for the whole world, mind you, yet enough to set the stage for a whole new chapter in American motorcycling. But few realized that in 1936 as the first buyers came forward willing to try something radically new on the scene. Few of them would regret it.

First 61 OHV on the streets of Milwaukee: 36EL1307. Trend of serial numbers in 1936 registrations suggest that early (lower numbered) engines were held back for valve cover modification. *Courtesy of Harold Deckert.*

Edmund Kelly with brand new 36EL1307. Kelly worked at the H-D factory and knew EL was coming and what it looked like. Bike is heavily chromed for the day. While Sixty-one owners were usually crazy about their mounts others took a wait-and-see attitude while sticking with the side-valve. *Courtesy of Harold Deckert.*

Heart o' Lakes Motorcycle Club photo appeared in the May 1936 issue of *The Enthusiast*. The 61 OHV on left was first good look readers obtained of the new model. It was 36EL1226, the first Sixty-one registered in Wisconsin. Owner was Wilfred Dotter of Tomahawk the local H-D dealer. *The Enthusiast.*

Harley-Davidson continued to pursue a cautious line. In the March issue of *Motorcyclist* the 61 OHV model was pictured along with the rest of the 1936 model Harley-Davidsons, but with no attending hype. In April *The Enthusiast* printed two photos of Sixty-ones. One showed Quirk's winning machine, but most of it was hidden behind winter windshield and leg guards so readers saw nothing of the engine or overall styling. The other Sixty-one photo in that issue was more revealing. It was taken at Bill Thede's Oak Park, Illinois, dealership during his annual open house. Members of the Westgate Motorcycle Club were shown gathered around a brand new Sixty-one. The machine was positioned at an oblique angle, but the distinctive OHV engine was visible. For reasons of their own H-D choose not to identify the machine. The factory was acting mighty shy about the new model—first its very existence was denied, and now when they dared show it they seemed unwilling to admit it was their's!

But the 61 OHV was already proving its mettle. On March 1 in California's Gazos Creek Enduro at least three new Sixty-ones competed and Jim Young took first place riding one. "Windy" Lindstrom—a well-known West Coast hillclimber—came in fourth aboard a Sixty-one. Claude Salmon, the third 61 OHV rider said later that he surprised even himself with how good he did with the new model.

In Milwaukee the first Sixty-one hit the still snow and ice covered streets in early March. This machine—36EL1307—belonged to Edmund Kelly, who worked in H-D's inspection department. Kelly died many years ago, but his pal "Hal" Deckert remembered how it happened. "The Sixty-one was a big secret," Deckert said. "I didn't know much about it, but my friend Ed Kelly did. He was a parts inspector at Harley's and saw and heard things that I didn't. He put his order in early and got the first one that came into Bill Knuth's shop. It was red. Definitely red. We raced Kelly with our side-valves time and again. He always won. The thing I remember best about the Sixty-one was that everybody liked the way it looked."

While Kelly's machine was the first Sixty-one loose on Milwaukee streets one had been previously shipped north to H-D dealer Wilfred Dotter at Tomahawk, Wisconsin. In May *The Enthusiast* ran a photo showing the Heart'O Lakes Motorcycle Club. Front and center was a brand-new Sixty-one: 36EL1226.

For the first time readers obtained a really good view of the new overhead-valve twin. Once again H-D neglected to identify it, but unless readers were blind they couldn't miss it. Dotter kept this particular machine for himself and won quite a reputation in Class C competition on it where he gained the title the "Tomahawk Thunderbolt."

Early factory photo of a 1936 61 OHV engine. During AMF years boxes of photos and old documents were "ditched." Some managed to survive. *Author's Collection.*

Erwin Martin of Wisconsin Rapids—first owner of 36EL1341—said this about his machine: "That Sixty-one was a work of art. It was the best liked machine around. Everything about it was well done. I had more people come up to me on the street to admire it. The beauty of it. The workmanship. It caused quite a minor sensation. It was a little too fast for the riders we had then. It took them a while to get acclimated to that machine because of its speed and power. It really was outstanding."

Big Twin side-valve model shown here in its 1936 incarnation. These were pleasant looking bikes but lacked flash and inspiration of overhead-valve model. *Courtesy of Henry Seebooth.*

Along the road with 36E1943, Herbert Markwiese (left), and Walter Borer—all of Milwaukee. Identification of 36EL models is sometimes challenging when paint jobs were updated. Several 1936-only parts serve as guide. In this case "round" shift lever and "straight" shift gate are most obvious. *Courtesy of Royal Beguhl.*

Ray Frederick's Sixty-one: 36EL2091. "Burn" spots were on original photo but bike still looks good. *Courtesy of Ray and Ellen Frederick.*

William and Eveyln Swedesky of Appleton on 36EL1970. Appleton had four first year Sixty-ones. What appears to be another is fourth bike down the line. *Courtesy of Max and Edna Kroiss.*

That was the initial and lasting impression of the Sixty-one Overhead: looks and performance. From the moment of its wraith-like appearance these qualities took hold and stuck and its influence continues to the present day. Without exception original owners of Sixty-one Overheads recall their mounts as lightning fast and a machine that drew admiration and praise wherever it went.

In the saddle looking down at the cockpit (mixing our horse and airplane metaphors here) riders felt a new confidence and thrill. Here was a real motorcycle at last, the one die-hard riders had always dreamed of.

Even today the 36EL, Sixty-one Overhead, or Knucklehead—whatever name you choose to call it—has legions of admirers. From the beginning, riders were smitten by the looks of this machine. In the minds of many the 36EL and its 1937-1939 successors rank among the best looking motorcycles ever built. This machine reached an aesthetic peak difficult to match let alone surpass. This motorcycle was authentically handsome. It had perfect proportions, the design was compact and wonderfully integrated, and nothing appeared tacked-on or piecemeal. There were no jarring notes. This machine had a calm balance to it, there was no wasted space, nothing was left to hang. There was a slip-stream flair about it that made the VL hang its head in shame. Nothing was stodgy or disappointing here, nothing. Form followed function in the most tasteful and economical manner. Its styling was about as perfect as a motorcycle could be. The components of the 61 OHV harmonized like the well-packed innards of a U-boat.

Even at rest the 36EL exuded a sensation of dash and vigor with the look of a thoroughbred stallion at the starting gate. Part of this aesthetic force stemmed from the new teardrop-shaped gas tanks. Gone were the VL's soldered tanks with their middle-aged sag, replaced by tanks which exhibited a proud upthrust energy, giving the entire mount a wonderful illusion of defying gravity. Here was a machine that could lift the American rider from the gloom of the past and into tomorrow.

Part of the new gas tanks' appeal was the integral instrument panel. This patented feature located several control items in one compact and protected unit. A mounting base bolted directly to the frame and nestled in a cavity between the tanks. The speedometer, ignition switch, warning gauges, and wiring harness terminals were attached to this base. The speedometer cable ran down a hole in the frame between the gas tanks where it was protected and out of the way. The new ignition switch position allowed the wiring to converge to this same central protected point. The gas tanks could be removed without disturbing the speedometer or the wiring. An attractive shroud completed this innovative arrangement. This elegant and practical approach removed the former tacked-on appearance of the VL speedometer.

Appleton riders in 1936. (From left): Max Kroiss (36EL1973); "Windy" Glaser (26JD13280); and William "Swede" Swedesky (36EL1970). *Courtesy of Max and Edna Kroiss.*

The new double-cradle frame brought new proportion to the motorcycle. The engine, transmission, and oil tank now fit within the perimeter of the frame instead of hanging out beyond its natural lines as on previous models, giving the motorcycle a stable, rock-solid appearance. The classic rigid frame had come into being.

The VL style I-beam forks were superseded by gracefully tapering legs of a new oval tube design. The old I-beam fork instantly took on a prehistoric look when compared to the light appearance and enduring delight of the new model. Wheels and tires were 4:00 X 18 inch, an arrangement that may be the best size ever invented for motorcycle use,

Max Kroiss on 36EL1973. Note paint scheme details on front fender. *Courtesy of Max and Edna Kroiss.*

But what about the Sixty-one's fatal flaw—the one that left the founders frowning back in late 1935—that nasty propensity for slinging oil on machine and rider both? Why wasn't Joe Ryan fielding dozens of irate letters? On the contrary, from the moment of its quiet introduction, riders took to the Sixty-one like bees to honey. They were even wearing jaunty white outfits when riding their new Sixty-one Overheads and staying clean while doing so. Where were the laps of oil that myth tells accompanied the first year 61 OHV? In fact myth is an apt description here. For at the very last minute—possibly as the first engines were being assembled—Juneau Avenue had came up with a solution to the Sixty-one's dirty habits. That's why in the spring of 1936 riders were singing songs of praise for the Sixty-one Overhead instead of damning it to hell.

It was true, Juneau Avenue had pulled its own chestnuts out of the fire. There'd be no repetition of the VL episode. The fix wasn't perfect and armchair experts have criticized it ever since, but it certainly saved the Sixty-one from severe condemnation at the time. In fact, riders could hardly identify the repair parts as hasty last minute add-ons so well did they blend into the original design. The fix was good enough to change gloomy looks into winning smiles around Juneau Avenue.

As previously mentioned, the regulated oil supply to the Sixty-one's rocker arms had failed to keep the engine within acceptable levels of cleanliness. After two years of running naked valve springs with the inevitable mess H-D broke with its own tradition and sought to cover things up.

While past American and English practice was to leave the valve springs open to the wind, others—the German BMW for example—had covered up their OHVs from the mid-1920s on. But on the 61 OHV this was easier said than done. The cylinder heads—satisfactory in every other respect—had no provision to collect and return the OHV oil to the crankcase. But that's what they needed. The problem was obvious: how could the lubrication system be adapted to scavenge oil pumped to the heads? The solution wasn't so simple, however. No collection agency or drain-down scuppers had been included in the original design. Some-

creating a near perfect compromise between handling, ride quality, and looks. The fenders were similar to those first seen on the 1934 model VL and of new full valance type that provided excellent weather protection without the obese excess that Indian would later pursue. These remain the classic American motorcycle fenders, whose gently flaring ends bring to mind the style of certain early aircraft.

Ride control and horn were tastefully tucked out of the way below the headlight. The new slightly narrower handlebars gave plenty of leverage and a substantial feel but if you didn't care for their position this was easily remedied by a little bending. Bill Knuth bent hundreds to suit individual tastes—it's said that every motorcycle cop in Milwaukee had his own special fit.

But it was the engine that transfixed the eye. Riders couldn't get enough of it because the Sixty-one Overhead had just enough mechanical complexity to cast an aura of mystery and allure over it. The engine had an advanced, almost futuristic quality, and a smooth roundness emanated from its gently sculpted surfaces that lifted it far above the flathead's stubby ridges. This engine was fitted with a shining crown, giving it a *deus in machina* soul that few mechanical objects successfully achieve. The Sixty-one shouted to all the world that here was the new king of the highway.

No motorcycle ever combined function and looks like this one. Maybe this was a result of hard times, when people knew what was important and what wasn't. In 1931 Harley-Davidson had begun groping for something new, something exciting, something to put fresh spark into the motorcycle scene. Five years later they offered it to the rest of the world. This machine would roll down the decades like no other in history. In a quiet yet completely accurate way William H. Davidson said it best, "That was a good design from an eye standpoint as well as being one hell of a performer."

Edna Kroiss on 36EL1973. *Courtesy of Max and Edna Kroiss.*

Machine is 36EL1097. Original owner Woodrow "Woody" Ordscheid of Wisconsin Rapids. Buddy Seat looks large and ungainly compared to solo seat. Auxiliary seat spring is shown attached. For solo use it was clipped to rear fender. *Courtesy of Ray Wheir.*

how the oil to the head had to be retained then brought back to the crankcase while keeping faithful to the existing engine design. Any major modifications would mean additional time and expense. The solution needed to be quick and effective. And it was. The motor that saved Harley-Davidson itself had been saved.

It's unknown who came up with the solution; whether it was Bill Harley and his engineers, or Ed Kieckbusch and his crew in the experimental department, but considering the nature of the solution and how it incorporated Bill Harley's unique lubrication system, the nod goes towards engineering. In this case the parts may have been designed in engineering and fabricated in experimental. Whatever the case, it would have made a damn good story if someone were alive to tell it.

To understand what saved the Sixty-one Overhead it's necessary to look at the workings of its lubrication system. Considerable thought had gone into this first recirculatory oil system on a production model Harley-Davidson. The design was unique in several respects.

Previous H-D practice incorporated the oil tank within the gas tank. On the VL and earlier models the battery was located under the seat in a sheet metal container. Resultant battery spray was corrosive and anyone looking for original H-D battery boxes at swap meets knows this to be true.

The new design brought the functions of oil tank and battery box into one unit. The unique horseshoe-shaped oil tank was bolted to a platform beneath the seat. The oil tank included a receptacle into which the battery fit. This had several advantages: gas tank capacity was increased; the oil tank, separate and placed in the air stream, was better cooled; and the battery was protected on all four sides. This position also had another advantage—mist escaping from the oil tank protected nearby metal parts from corrosive battery acid spray. This practical but often overlooked quality is evident in the survival rate of horseshoe oil tanks and yet another example of old Bill Harley's genius.

On the engine side of the oil system were two gear pumps. One (feed) brought oil into the engine via a pipe from the oil tank. The other (scavenger) pump returned oil to the tank through a different line. Both pumps shared a common housing located at the rear of the right crankcase. Oil supplied by the feed pump was sent through galleys in the crankcase and gear cover into the pinion shaft where drilled passages led to the lower rod bearings. At normal road speeds a gallon of oil was circulated through the crankpin every sixty to seventy miles. Oil in the flywheel chamber splashed up to lubricate the cylinder walls, piston pins, and main bearings and then drained down to the scavenger pump, which returned it to the oil tank. Oil was also supplied under pressure through an external line to the overhead-valve mechanism. As already noted this supply was adjustable.

"Woody" Ortscheid with 36EL1097 and carnival midget Sam Draper. *Courtesy of Ray Wheir.*

In basic design the Sixty-one's lubrication system didn't vary too much from what Indian had introduced in 1933, but it also included additional features not found anywhere else. Bill Harley had gone to great lengths to adequately lubricate the new four-lobe camshaft in the 61 OHV. This was accomplished through a timed breather valve (patent descriptions call it a "trap valve")—a gear-driven cylinder that rotated in a closely mated aperture in the crankcase housing. The driven gear end of the breather valve was closed. The other end was open and in com-

Thelma Fischer, wife of Wisconsin Rapids H-D dealer Don Fischer with new 61 OHV in May 1936. Bike greatly resembles and could be 36EL1097. *Courtesy of Ray Wheir.*

munication with an elevated "sump" in the rear of the crankcase. During engine operation oil was scraped off the flywheels and collected in this sump. From there it drained down into the open end of the breather valve which was cut away over a portion of its circumference and timed to open during the downward stroke of the pistons. The resultant pressure blew the oil scraped from the flywheels through a screen in the breather valve onto the camshaft and roller tappets. This system delivered copious amounts of oil to the hard pressed camshaft and tappets. Now Bill Harley and his engineers were inspired to use it again, only this time in reverse.

The opposite effect of crankcase pressure caused by descending pistons is engine vacuum, or suction, created when the pistons moved upwards—this is simple physics. Just as pressure was used to blow oil onto the camshaft—Bill Harley reasoned—why couldn't engine vacuum be used to scavenge oil going to the OHV mechanism?

To accomplish this task an oil return system was designed. Small cup-like containers were fabricated to collect the overhead-valve oil. Each valve spring assembly received two cups, an upper and a lower. The cups enclosed the valve springs, except for a cut-away section in the upper cup that allowed access to the valve stem by the rocker arm. The lower cup was held in place by the pressed-in valve guide, and its job was to catch excess oil going to the valve stem. Each lower cup had a return oil line brazed to it with the other end plugged into the backside of the aluminum rocker housing (knuckle). These housings were hollow and held the upper ends of the pushrod tubes. Now what Bill Harley needed was a method of creating a partial vacuum within the pushrod tubes in order to suck the oil out of the cups and through the return lines, into the rocker housings, then back down the pushrod tubes into the breather valve where it would be blown onto the camshaft.

The solution blended perfectly with existing engine design. The breather valve's primary port was timed to close during the upstroke or vacuum period of the pistons. During this upstroke period vacuum was already utilized to draw excess oil from the separating chamber (part of the front chain oiler) and back into the breather valve through a smaller, secondary port in the breather valve wall. By creating a third port in the breather valve that was in communication with the lower end of the pushrod tubes, engine vacuum could be extended there as well. That's just what Bill Harley planned to do. It sounds

Roger Laabs, second owner of 36EL1973. Shown here with his son and sister. *Courtesy of Roger Laabs.*

81

Nice photo of 36EL1740 taken about 1941. Bike shows some wear and rear stand appears to be a replacement. Owner was Milwaukee rider John Birch. That summer a car pulled out and Birch hit it. He tucked into a ball and landed unhurt, but the bike was totaled. It was sold for $125 to a guy who wanted the unique engine. *Courtesy of John Birch.*

complicated, but in practice worked as simply as this: oil pumped to the OHV mechanism collected in the lower cups and on the pistons' upstroke the tertiary breather port opened long enough to extend a partial vacuum inside the pushrod tubes. This suction drew oil out of the cups through the return lines. As the engine was spinning this process was continuous and sucked oil out of the cups as fast as it could be pumped up there.

The hard-working breather valve was aptly named. The moving pistons and resultant pressure and vacuum acted like lungs forcing air and oil back and forth through various parts of the engine. It functioned similarly to a person inhaling and exhaling alternately through his mouth and nose. The breather valve's primary port opened and blew oil mist onto the camshaft like a person opening his mouth and exhaling, and like a person closing his mouth and inhaling through his two nostrils, the primary port in the breather valve closed while the secondary and tertiary ports opened and sucked oil out of the separating chamber and down from the OHV mechanism. It was this feature more than anything else that made Bill Harley's new engine unique because it delivered several times the oil to camshaft bearing surfaces than previously thought practical. This was a critical factor in an high-performance, air-cooled engine designed for the ages.

While not perfect, the OHV oil return system probably saved the Sixty-one from a bad beginning. It was a brilliant solution to a vexing problem and its elegance lay in the fact that no major changes were made to the engine. A few sheet metal cups, a little tubing, and additional passageways solved the problem which sounds simple in retrospect, but no doubt took time and brainpower to figure out. Incorporating it into engines was the easy part and that was the real beauty of the system. The existing engine could be used with very little modification, no major redesigning of heads or anything else had to be done. The

solution was so good that with some modification in 1938 it served through the whole run of Knucklehead engines through 1947.

Even engines assembled before the fix was ready could easily be retrofitted. It is the opinion of the author that no engines left the factory without the cups and return oil lines. The first engines assembled, however, may have been held back and fitted with them while engines assembled a little later—thus higher numbered—were built into complete motorcycles first.

Some indirect evidence for this possibility is found in Wisconsin motorcycle registrations for 1936. The first 61 OHVs registered in March were in the 36EL1200-1300 serial number range while the lowest numbers in the 36EL1000-1100 range (numbers began at 1000) were registered later in the year. This suggests the possibility that the first engines built were held back for repair and the slightly higher numbered engines were shipped out first. Original Wisconsin owners of very low numbered Sixty-ones all agree their machines had the cups and return lines and were not sold to them with open valve springs, including engines 36EL1011 (James Bukovic), and 36EL1083 (Willy Herbold).

For years it's been repeated so many times it's become gospel that first year 61 OHVs were plagued by terrible oil leaks and this writer has stated this "fact" in print himself. But after interviewing several original owners of 1936 Sixty-ones, I now believe such stories have been exaggerated. While some original 36EL owners recalled their motorcycles leaking from the heads all scoffed at the notion that this wayward oil ever amounted to "lap soaking" or "leg wetting" proportions and some recalled no leakage at all, while others told of minor leakage. Only one original owner described oil leakage as being excessive or in his words, "It leaked like hell." The irony here is that it was Willy Herbold who said that—the nephew of Bill Knuth—the Milwaukee Harley-Davidson dealer!

Fischer Cycle Co. and Wisconsin Rapids Motorcycle Club in early 1937. Two 1936 61 OHVs are forth and fifth bikes from right. *Courtesy of Florence Ortscheid.*

Close up of previous photo shows Henry Reiman with 36EL2632, and Les Landon with 36EL1981 (fifth and sixth bikes from left). Reiman was noted hillclimber. Note interesting examples of "bobbed" front fenders on 1937 and 1935 Forty-fives. This may have been a styling hit, but couldn't have added much enjoyment when riding in the rain. *Courtesy of Florence Ortscheid.*

Thelma and Don Fischer with a 1936 EL model. On right is Florence "Runt" Wheir with her bike: 36RLD1145. She was a rare example of a sister inspiring her brother to ride. *Courtesy of Ray Wheir.*

Records say this bike is 37EL1146. Several features suggest machine is actually a 1936 model. Rider is Robert Seebooth, who took machine to West Coast after Second World War. *Courtesy of Henry Seebooth.*

Norm and "Bert" Zietlow with 36EL1480. Sixty-one Overhead was answer to the dreams of hot-shot riders who promptly dumped the flathead and never went back. Zietlow was one. *Courtesy of Mel and Emma Krueger.*

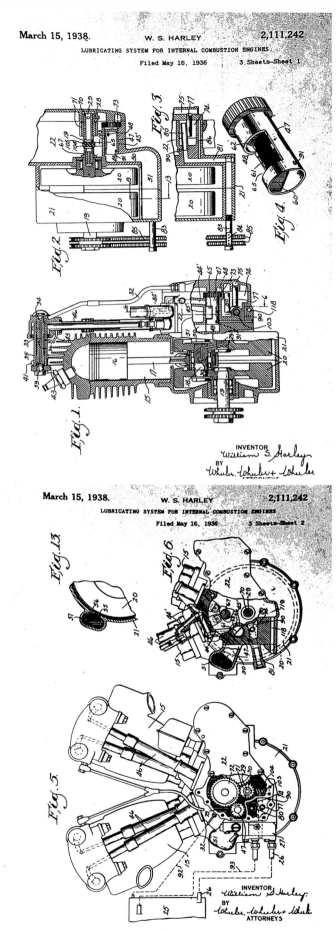

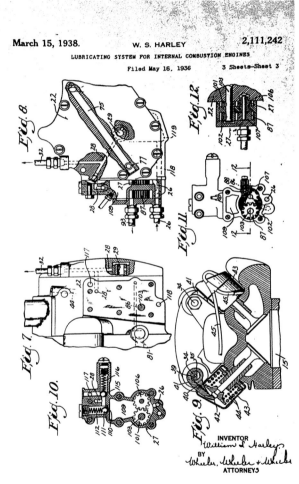

Patent drawing of 61 OHV lubrication system shows detail of breather valve at lower right. Patent description makes no mention of adjustable oil supply to heads. This suggests feature did not exist on early prototypes. *Milwaukee Public Library.*

"Cups" and return oil lines are shown on patent drawing but return line routing is different from production models. Patent was filed in May 1936. Note that combustion chamber in drawing deviates from true hemispherical shape. *Milwaukee Public Library.*

Elevated "sump," breather valve, and camshaft details are visible in drawing on right. Considerable thought went into Sixty-one's oil system. Basic design still in use today on H-D's Big Twin Evolution engines. Patent was taken out in William S. Harley's name and assigned to Harley-Davidson Motor Co. *Milwaukee Public Library.*

"Vern" Radke of Tomahawk, original owner of 36EL1880. Another well-chromed Sixty-one. Round air cleaner came with bike when new. *Courtesy of LaVern Radke.*

Most original 36EL owners told a story similar to Ralphie Heger, retired proprietor of West Side Cycle in Milwaukee and owner of 36EL1786, who said, "It leaked but not much. It ran backwards towards the rear. My pants never got drenched. Nothing like that. No drenching. No oil bath." Erwin Martin, original owner of 36EL1341 was more adamant when he told me, "When they say it sluiced oil all over someone is crazy as hell because that never happened."

If the oil supply to the heads was regulated properly there was little if any leakage out of the semi-open cups. If the supply was set too generously or a return line became clogged—a common occurrence—then a messy exterior could result. Even Bill Harley knew this fix wasn't perfect—this can be seen in the patent description where he states that oil collected in the cups would drain "preferably" through the return lines thus implying that oil might drain elsewhere. Maybe it worked better

than he expected. In any case the old stories about laps full of oil or drenched trousers are probably mostly false. The author now believes that these stories originated with the pre-cup prototypes when tales of the 61 OHV's nasty habits—so to speak—leaked out. Catastrophic leakage on production models occurred only if something wasn't right and, if the words of original owners are to be believed, happened far less frequently than in the fantasies or prejudices of certain motorcycle historians.

But enough gear talk—let's have some fun. Let's hear what original EL owners thought about their brand spanking new mounts back in 1936!

"That machine was quite hot," said James Bukovic (36EL1011), "The Sheboygan dealer—Eichmann—sort of convinced me and I went ahead and bought it. That was one of the best running machines I ever had. Never gave me trouble. Eichmann helped me soup it up. He was pretty smart about that. We took it to a hillclimb in Upper Michigan. Of three or four first places I took them all. A guy wanted to give me a brand new machine and some money to boot for that Sixty-one. I refused. On the highway I don't know what it wouldn't beat."

"That Sixty-one thrilled me," said Steve Kakuk (36EL1294). "It made you think you could do anything. It had instant power that was so smooth. I went to Milwaukee to pick it up and fell in love with it on the highway during the trip home. It felt like it was part of me. That engine was sweet. That bike was very well engineered."

Erwin Martin (36EL1341) knew the Sixty-one was coming. He had an order blank filled out early. He also had a sketch for an all-white paint job with special order red, gold, and black curls representing speed to be painted on the gas tanks. He put it this way, "Hap was right when he said it was going to be a sensational machine. I picked it up early in the spring at the factory. Damned cold ride back—ten below zero. I'd ride about 30 miles, stop at a filling station, warm up, then take another shot at it. When the other guys saw mine they wanted one. We had six (36ELs) here in the Rapids. The workmanship was about as neat as possible. The fins on the cylinders looked like they were machined on. The castings were perfect. Nobody could stay near me on that Sixty-one. No flathead could beat it."

Frank "Stinky Davis" Matheus (36EL1773) said this, "It was a very fine machine. Extremely fast. I loved that machine. I ordered mine in all-white and that took a little more time. I had to go to the factory that day and ride it home. What a wonderful feeling next to that other one (VL). The Sixty-one had terrific acceleration. It really went. It was

Radke's payment book for 36EL1880. He almost lost bike when he got in trouble with an officer in the Civilian Conservation Corps. Dealer's mother let him off the hook for a couple months until he straightened things out. Prices and monthly payments look ridiculous in light of today's costs. *Courtesy of Lavern Radke.*

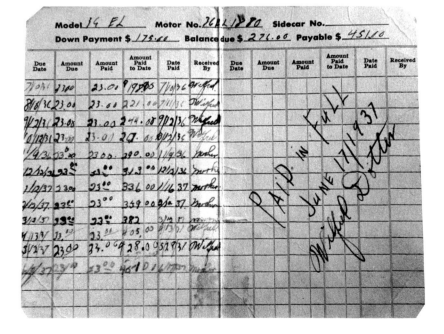

Mel and Emma Krueger with 36EL1480. Krueger was another early advocate of the Sixty-one. As Wausau dealer he sold them and as a rider hillclimbed and went through wall crashes with them. *Courtesy of Mel and Emma Krueger.*

quiet. Very trouble free. A little oil would come out of the valve covers but not very much. It was a pretty easy machine to keep clean. It was faster than the Seventy-four and Eighty side-valves. A fellow named Bob Stuth had a fast 80 flathead (36VLH2632). He and I would race for beers. We'd start on some new concrete west of Lambreck's farm. I'd take him every time. We'd start out pretty even, but by the time we got up in the gears I was leading. It used to bother the hell out of him."

Lavern Radke (36EL1880) of rural Tomahawk was then a young man in the Civilian Conservation Corps. He had this story to tell, "I was always on the tail-end and wanted something that moved. I bought that Sixty-one on time. Then I got in trouble with a smart-ass lieutenant and was court marshalled and busted. I nearly lost that machine before I got it. But Dotter's mother (the dealer) let me off the hook for a couple months. You wouldn't know what tough times those were. Dotter already had his Sixty-one and I liked it. I rode with Zietlow, Krueger, and Dotter. We all had Sixty-ones. We had a speed stretch on Highway 51 going north. You'd lay down on that thing and the speedo would run up over a hundred. I was going with my wife to be and would park down the street so her father wouldn't hear it. I didn't have a suit of clothes without chain grease on them."

Ralphie Heger, who bought 36EL1786 used in November of 1936 then rode it to Florida, recalled the new OHV twin, "A thirty-six in thirty-six for $200. A bargain. I couldn't go wrong. It was a unique bike. Different speedometer. Different frame. Different motor. Different everything. I liked it very much. A very nice bike. Very nice. It ran cooler than the side-valves. It got hot but not hot like the side-valves did. Side-valves used to burn pistons but the overheads not."

Ray Frederick of Mosinee (36EL2091) told it like this, "The Sixty-one was supposed to be a high speed job. Mine was red and black. There were two gas tanks. In one side I'd put aviation fuel in and get a few more miles an hour out of her. Every once in a while there'd be a guy in a souped up Ford or Chevy who'd challenge you. I'd switch tanks and put in the high octane gas. Then nothing could pass me on the road. I couldn't go fast enough."

At the first deliveries of Sixty-one Overheads the factory held its collective breath. William H. Davidson put it this way, "We purposely kept on the brakes and didn't push production. We let it demonstrate itself. Let it prove itself. Maybe we didn't want to strain our luck."

There were indeed several unknown factors—would this radical new bike take hold? Would the last minute fix to the oil system work? There couldn't have been much time to thoroughly road test the new oil return system before production began and the first motorcycles were shipped out, yet from the beginning feedback from the riders was overwhelmingly positive. Clarence Pieratt of Napa, California, wrote *The Enthusiast*, "Boy! This 61 is my idea what a super bike should be."

A super-bike! The epithet is fitting and perhaps the origin of the term. Ever since Pennington first scorched down Cleveland's Superior Avenue in 1894 riders had been dreaming of such a beast. Yet few production motorcycles in our two-wheel history had even come close. Without question the 61 OHV stands foremost among contenders for this title. As far away as England they paid homage; the *Motor Cycle* wrote, "There is an indescribable thrill about riding this machine."

By the middle of 1936, H-D's confidence in the radical new model was rising. The June issue of *The Enthusiast* portrayed six proud owners of new Sixty-ones. Jauntily dressed Mell Lenn said, "I'm the proudest and happiest guy in all Indiana except those other lucky riders who also have new 61's."

Advertising hype 1930s style? Not this time. The founders had outdone themselves. They couldn't possibly have realized the legacy they were bequeathing to the motorcycle world with the 36EL. They were probably satisfied that the new machine wasn't the failure they had feared it might be the day they gathered around their troubled child.

It had been a risky thing all along to embark on a totally new model of unproven design during the darkest days of the Great Depression and then to stick with it when problems plagued and threatened its existence, and all at a time when the market for motorcycles had sunk nearly out of sight except for the loyal few. But they had persisted and won.

Some of the men who worked alongside the founders remember the gamble. The late Christy Spexarth commented on the Sixty-one project, "We were considerably worried about it. We didn't know it would be as successful as it ultimately was. But there was a lot of help from many people. They all did their share and everything fell into place as it went along. In terms of engineering the Sixty-one's background was very good. It certainly has cut its niche in the motorcycle industry. The Sixty-one was a superior machine to anything that Indian had—or

Frank "Stinky Davis" Matheus at Shawano 1936. Matheus had seen Sixty-one two years early at Harley-Davidson. He knew from that moment he had to have one. Well-chromed bike is 36EL1773. First year Sixty-ones when set up properly were not the oil slingers of popular myth or guys with white bikes and white outfits would remember. *Courtesy of Harold Deckert.*

P R O G R A M

WISCONSIN'S TWO - DAY MOTORCYCLE RALLY AT SHAWANO, WIS.

ALL RIDERS REGISTER AT COMMUNITY HALL

SPONSORED BY
WISCONSIN MOTORCYCLE DEALER'S
UNDER SANCTION OF AMERICAN MOTORCYCLE ASS'N

MOTORCYCLING
"THE WORLDS GREATEST SPORT"

Program for the first Wisconsin State Rally at Shawano, 1936. In the Dairy State Shawano is a name that means motorcycles to old timers. Sleepy little resort village was transformed into a seething caldron of Harley-Davidsons in the late 1930s. *Courtesy of Mel and Emma Krueger.*

anything that Harley-Davidson had. It helped pull the company out of the doldrums."

When asked if he thought the 61 OHV helped save Harley-Davidson, Spexarth replied, "Yes, I think you could say that. I think you could."

The late Wilbur Petri put it in stronger terms, "I don't know what the management thought. I was brand new. The only thing I thought—

and still think—is that they were pretty damned brave spending their money on a new design when we were still in the Depression. It was very risky. But Harley-Davidson was a solid company. Apparently the management made the decision that if the company wanted to stay in business and prosper they had to do something new."

The late William H. Davidson described his feelings towards the landmark 61 OHV like this, "From day one it told hold. We had been ahead of Indian and this clinched it. A good design and a high-performance bike. They'd go like hell for that era. A ninety-five mile an hour bike. An *honest* ninety-five mile an hour bike. If I had to pick a favorite I think it would be that first 1936 model. But I imagine sentiment enters into that."

By mid-1936 things were definitely looking up at Juneau Avenue. Everywhere the Sixty-one Overhead was shipped it made new friends. In an H-D dealer bulletin dated June 15, 1936, veteran dealer Dudley Perkins of San Francisco wrote, "It is really surprising the sudden interest the 61 OHV machine has created. It seems as though the reaction from the riders who have purchased machines is beginning to become stronger all the time and they are advertising it to all of their friends in such a manner that the 61 has seemed to take hold all at once."

A dealer from Pennsylvania added, "This is the IDEAL machine of ALL motorcycle enthusiasts and we truly believe that in a year or two the 61 sales will by far exceed all other models."

Of course not everyone was convinced overnight, and some would never be convinced. But that spring something new took hold on the American motorcycle scene that has continued to the present day. Pretty soon the founders caught the fever too, and realized how right the Sixty-one Overhead was. Very few have disagreed since that time. Of course being an all-new model there were bugs to be worked out and improvements to be made but in the main the machine was proving its reputation every day. Under those circumstances the only thing missing was a celebration!

Nineteen thirty-six saw the first Wisconsin State Rally and Gypsy Tour. Previous to that year separate rallies were held in various parts of the state. But in 1936 the Associated Motorcycle Dealers of Wisconsin—with factory support—sponsored a two-day motorcycle party, rally, and races at the sleepy lakeside resort town of Shawano, Wisconsin. In effect it was a party for the new Sixty-one Overhead.

To this day the name Shawano (pronounced: "Shaa-no") is a word that means motorcycles among old time riders in Wisconsin and surrounding states. It conjures up images of classic Harley-Davidsons drifting in from all points of the compass, it means a great party, great races, and a great time. Sleepy old timers leaning on their canes perk up at the

Milwaukee Motorcycle Club members at Shawano with 1936 Big Twin side-valve. Not everybody took to the overhead engine that first year. Movement took years to build. Is still building today. *Courtesy of Ray and Ellen Frederick.*

word and grow excited. By today's Sturgis standards Shawano was small but 1,200 motorcycles at one gathering in 1936 was big stuff, especially when you consider the fact that only 2,841 motorcycles were registered in the entire state that year. In 1936 1,200 motorcycles nearly overwhelmed this sleepy little village 150 miles north of Milwaukee. Not that the town fathers minded—at least not at first. The red carpet was rolled out and a banner stretched across main street reading: "Welcome Motorcyclists." The American Legion held a welcome parade with dozens of American flags flying. This was a far cry from later decades when a motorcycle rally of big H-Ds would send a chill of terror through town fathers and an occasion to call out the National Guard. Things were a little different in 1936. The clubs present were predominately AMA affiliated. Riders were neat and well-dressed. This was Harley-Davidson's idea of a party and also a chance to see what their attempt to revitalize the club scene looked like in real life.

While some bikes arrived Friday the big contingents rolled in on Saturday. Bill Knuth's riders met at 7:00 A.M. at his shop for the three hour ride up Highway 41. Along the way other clubs joined their ranks from Fond du Lac, Oshkosh, and Appleton. The Manitowoc, Sheboygan, and Green Bay clubs came from the east. From the west came clubs from Marshfield, Wausau, LaCrosse and the Rapids. Others from the south included the Madison, Janesville, Beloit, Racine, and Kenosha Clubs. From the far north came clubs from Tomahawk, Rhinelander and Minoqua. There were also clubs from northern Illinois along with small groups of independent riders and loners.

By 10:00 A.M. Saturday a mere 125 cycles were in town but by noon the number had swelled to over a thousand. The townspeople had never seen anything like it before. If H-D's progress with the club scene was as successful nation-wide as in Wisconsin then its manipulation of the AMA must be viewed in a positive light, for here was motorcycling with new life. New spark. Some clubs came dressed in full uniform and all on well-polished motorcycles. The Wauwatosa Club held the distinction of being the first in the country to be one hundred percent in uniform. Their outfit consisted of all-white breeches and shirts with cuffs, collars, and pocket flaps jet black. High black boots, black belts, and black hats completed the uniform in a striking quasi-military effect. This trend towards uniformed clubs would skyrocket in the coming years. There was serious competition for the honor of being best-dressed club.

From the bikes in attendance there was no doubt that Wisconsin was Harley-Davidson country. For every Indian, Henderson, or Super X present there were two dozen or more H-Ds. The vast majority were stock machines although here and there could be seen the predecessors of later day "bobbers" and "choppers" in the form of cut-back fenders, straight pipes, and an occasional set of oddly bent handlebars. On the other hand some bikes were wearing additional and sometimes useless accessories. Although the choice was still fairly limited this was the start of the "garbage wagon" phenomenon. Interestingly enough these two movements which would find their full expression in the decades after the Second World War were beginning to take their separate evolutionary paths. Both would focus on the Harley-Davidson Big Twin as their primary object of affection.

Nor was there a foreign motorcycle in sight. Not one! Not unless it was driven in from out of state. Because in 1936 not one foreign motorcycle was registered in the state of Wisconsin. There was no source of supply and no demand.

Up and down Shawano's main street all you could see were Harley-Davidsons. The VL was predominant with lots of 45s and JDs. Many bikes sported Buddy Seats. Sidecar rigs were present but in fewer numbers than in the previous decade. Yes, there were also Sixty-one Overheads but not many that first year. Not when some were still sitting on showroom floors when the June Shawano Rally took place. But several were there. Most were from Wisconsin with a few ridden in from northern Illinois but they came, and they were the focus of attention. Within a few months of its appearance, a long-term love affair was beginning to unfold between American riders and this striking new motorcycle.

Imagine the scene: hundreds of stone-stock Harley-Davidson motorcycles, each one a valuable antique worth a small fortune today. Many were brand new or close to it. All were original H-D equipped. No freak customs in sight, no show bikes. These were riders each and every one. Honest stock motorcycles in this golden age of American motorcycling. But like most high points this too would be short-lived, ended like the first golden age by a world war.

But on that summer weekend in 1936 the future looked rosy. The economy had picked up considerably from its low point of 1933. During those two happy days at Shawano you might have forgotten the Depression existed at all.

At three o'clock the hillclimb began. "C.D." Ulicki took the 45 event. But the Sixty-ones were the focus of the crowd's attention.

Here modern "bikers" will marvel at their 1936 counterparts. Here were guys with big road bikes. A 61 OHV topped 500 pounds in standard trim. Yet riders on brand new machines attacked Lime Kiln Hill with a vengeance. The sight would be unnerving to modern eyes. Big Twins flung against the hillside as if they were puny dirt bikes. Who today would trust their skill or endanger the chrome or paint on their expensive mount in such a fashion? Not many. But riders of the 1930s did it without a second thought. As Steve Kakuk said, "Too big? That bike might have been too big for some people but not for me."

Lime Kiln Hill was several hundred feet of loose dirt, dust, and rocks. Al Campshure of Green Bay (36EL1436) roared skyward on his new all-white Sixty-one and made 189 feet to win the 80 Open Class. Steve Kakuk (36EL1294) took the 80 Final. One Sixty-one hill climber—whose identity is unknown—was shown in *The Enthusiast* unloading as the brand new OHV twin roared upwards with no rider.

After dark a motorcycle polo game was held beneath spotlights. The southern team—the combined Kenosha and Waukegan Clubs—beat the northern team. The ten riders dashed in and out while a large crowd looked on. The game was divided into four ten-minute quarters. Riders were only allowed to kick the ball. Touching it with a hand or backing up the machine resulted in a foul. It was actually more like soccer than polo but participants and observers didn't care. Everyone was having too much fun.

On Sunday morning a tour led by Roy Krietzer, president of the local North Star Club, went sightseeing at the nearby Menominee Indian Reservation. A visit was made to boiling Keshena Falls. Then another parade and a contest for best-dressed girl and boy riders. Another contest was held for the best-dressed club.

It was at Shawano that Joseph A. Campbell got his start announcing races around the Midwest (Note: there were two Joe Campbells who worked at H-D. Both are mentioned in this work, the one referred to here, and "Indian Joe" Campbell, H-D frame builder and original owner of 36EL1400). Campbell was then a young guy working in the parts and accessories department under Harry Devine when his natural talent to entertain was noticed. Campbell remembered the occasion, "One day Harry Devine told me, 'Arthur Davidson says we have to make better use of your talents. Go to these motorcycle events and tell them you're Joe Campbell from the factory. Be their friend. Do anything they want you to do. Find out what accessories they like and which ones they don't. Then come back and tell me.'"

That's what brought Campbell to Shawano in 1936. He remembered the event and the fame it later brought him, "The first day nobody talked to me. On Sunday a guy came up and asked, 'Are you Joe Campbell? Do you do anything?' I thought he was going to ask me to park cars, but he wanted an announcer for the races. I told him I'd never seen a motorcycle race. He didn't care. He said, 'Just get up there and do something.' So I did. They had a heat then I told a joke. They had another heat and I told another joke. During intermission I sang a song. Afterwards the dealer from Madison (Ray Tursky) asked if I'd come there. The dealer from Beaver Dam (James Trapp) asked if I'd go there. The next year I had twenty races to announce and they started sending me all over. Harry Devine said, 'That's a good idea. Take my sidecar. We'll fill it with sample accessories. Call on two dealers per day and sell the parts to the last one on the way home.' For the next thirty-

By 1936 the push for full uniformed clubs was in high gear. Increased accessory sales was part of reason, but also desire to improve public image of motorcyclists. Military styling is evident in this H-D ad. Entire outfit including boots cost $17.95. *The Enthusiast.*

five years I covered every event in the U.S. east of the Mississippi River from Maine to Florida."

At noon came the TT races. The American TT differed considerably from its British cousin. Instead of "Tourist Trophy" it might be called "Tricky Trials." As originally adapted by the Crotona Motorcycle Club of New York in the early thirties it consisted of a short course (typically 3/4 of a mile) with hairpin turns, short hills, ravines, and maybe a stretch of sand or a water hole thrown in for good measure. There were ten laps in each class with the three top riders in each event competing in a twenty lap final. At Shawano this final event determined the Wisconsin State Champion for 1936.

In the 45 Event Garth Lees took first place. But Johnny Spiegelhoff—whom we'll encounter later—was singled out as the "youngest and gamiest" contestant.

At least three new Sixty-one Overheads participated in the 80 Class: Steve Kakuk (36EL1294), Edmund Kelly (36EL1307), and Al Campshure (36EL1436). All three were in the thick of it. The preliminary heat knocked Kelly out of the running. Both Campshure and Kakuk went on to compete in the final with Garth Lees, Ray Van Hoogan, and "C.D." Ulicki. Here the winners in all classes went for the grand prize. "Galloping" Garth Lees of Green Bay shot out to take an early lead on his Forty-five side-valve. Lees held it through the entire course as he bounced through sand pits, slid through sharp corners, and roared over hills. Under such conditions the lighter and more maneuverable Forty-five had a natural advantage but Al Campshure was right behind him on his Sixty-one and held second place for three laps before losing it to Steve Kakuk who roared ahead to take second place just behind Lees.

"Indian Joe" Campbell (right) in 1936 with 36EL1400. This could be Shawano, but 1937 model in background suggests its later in year after release of new models. Joe had this Sixty-one for less than a year when he went back to the flathead. A second 36EL is among the other bikes. See it? *Courtesy of Joe Campbell.*

Harold Helms hillclimbing with 36EL1950. Note brace between front sidecar mounts. This was apparently used to stiffen fragile first year frame of which this is one example. Hard usage as shown in photo quickly pointed out areas of weakness in new model. Factory test riders didn't go quite this far. *Courtesy of Bernard Ernst.*

Kakuk's expert riding made spectators hold their breath. The tight squeezes, fast driving, and wonderful control Kakuk exhibited over his machine were described as remarkable. In the coming months Kakuk and his 61 OHV were prominent winners of hillclimbs and TT races as reported in the pages of *The Enthusiast.* He was hot on that Sixty-one—at one time he simultaneously held four state championships. His brothers Louis and Joe also raced.

Now living in Michigan, Steve Kakuk recalled his racing days. "That Sixty-one was a good machine for me," Kakuk said. "Like I was born on it. Guys at H-D told me that I was just right for it. My legs were fairly long and my weight was right for the horsepower. That thirty-six double

frame made a big difference in handling and balance. Once I took a hillclimb with a two hundred foot face in twelve seconds and rode on one wheel all the way up. They paid me thirty-five dollars to crash boards with it. In a good weekend I could clear a couple hundred dollars. Big money back then."

Harley-Davidson did their best to make Shawano a success. "Hap" Jameson and Frank Werderitsch were there to handle the races. Hap was riding brand new 36EL1531. Other factory men were sent to help out. Uke remembered one, "There was a guy from the office. He came over because I was in charge of the grounds work. He said, 'Mr. Davidson sent me over to help you.' I said, 'Fine, there's a barrel of beer. Sell beer.' Later we got to know him and his wife. Very nice people. But they were Catholic and I don't think selling beer on Sunday went over very big."

The top guys were there too, including some of the founders of Harley-Davidson. This was their party. Their presence was never loudly announced, but some at least showed up. There's a fine picture of a tipsy William S. Harley enjoying himself immensely with a beer in one hand and a pretty girl in the other. In truth he had something to celebrate: his troubled child—the 61 OHV—was gaining approval everywhere it went. Time would prove the Big Twin OHV the best motorcycle Harley-Davidson ever built. And while old Bill Harley wasn't riding one that day his oldest son William J. Harley was. If you old Harley-D enthusiasts can find 36EL1519 out there you'll have a real collector's item!

Like all motorcycle gatherings there were also high jinks at Shawano. After a few beers there were informal drag races down main street and a fight or two broke out. At one resort some guys hooked a rowboat to a sidecar rig and dragged it up and down the beach, which didn't thrill the owner much. When Johnny Spiegelhoff and his girlfriend disappeared into a hotel room a crowd gathered, started yelling, and broke down the door. There were the usual tricks like smearing Limburger cheese on another guy's cylinders or plugging gas cap vents with chewing gum. Tame stuff by today's standards. Even the bonfire and beer party that lasted until dawn didn't get out of hand.

But put young guys and gals together on motorcycles with plenty of intoxicants and somebody's bound to get hurt—like what happened to Ray Frederick and his future wife Ellen, although they got off easy. "On the other side of Shawano," Frederick recalled, "there was a line of big trees. We'd been drinking beer and on the way home we began acting up on the highway. Guys started zig-zagging. Some stood up. Some girls stood up too. Everyone could do something but me. So I said to Ellen, 'You drive for a while.' I laid down on the headlight. If I

Minocqua Motorcycle Club. Uniforms were popular and indeed looked good. *Courtesy of Ray and Ellen Frederick.*

"Hap" Jameson (center) at announcer's stand at 1936 Shawano races. Hap was everywhere during those years. He was probably the best qualified individual to give a true history of Harley-Davidson. He died in 1978, ten years before author began researching motorcycle history, otherwise you'd find his story here. *Courtesy of Joe Campbell.*

Three pretty motorcycle girls are all smiles at Shawano. Rosy complexions and sparkling eyes were free advertisements for the greatest sport on earth: motorcycling. *Courtesy of Ken Bryne.*

Three pals at Shawano. From left: Gary Koep, Leo Duffren, and Al Sharon. Courtesy of Royal Beguhl.

Shawano 1936. Girl on rear of bike is "Hal" Deckert's wife Anna. Girl on front is "Mel" Spindler, wife of guy who worked in H-D's parts and accessories department. *Courtesy of Harold Deckert.*

Joseph A. Campbell as motorcycle race announcer. Campbell was working under Harry Devine in H-D's parts and accessories department when Arthur Davidson noticed his talent to entertain. Campbell spent the next thirty-five years going from event to event all over the eastern United States. *Courtesy of Ken Bryne.*

Sticking with the side-valve. Here "Hal" Deckert on his new 1936 Eighty: 36VLH1060. By 1941 Deckert had two Sixty-ones. Flathead lovers were dying out although a few die-hards persist to this day. *Courtesy of Harold Deckert.*

didn't drink those beers I wouldn't have done it. When I looked up we were heading for one of those big trees. There was nothing to do but lay her down on the concrete at forty-five miles an hour. I flew off and didn't get hurt, but Ellen hung on and her one hand that was on the pavement every one of those knuckles were rubbed off bare."

Behind the fun and games of the Shawano Rally in 1936 were some very practical purposes. Here was an opportunity of getting hundreds of motorcyclists together and gauge their reaction to the new 61 OHV. Once recovered from their hangovers back at Juneau Avenue the big boys put their heads together and compared notes. The vast majority of opinion had been extremely positive. In a span of six short months H-D went from doubt and trepidation to confidence and near euphoria. From that moment on there was no turning back.

Shawano drove this point home. After that event the founders started believing it themselves. For the first time in *The Enthusiast* the factory saw fit to advertise the new OHV model. Listening to them you'd think they knew it all along!

"Sensation of the Motorcycle World," shouted the ad copy. "Minus fanfare and ballyhoo, a new motorcycle has come on the scene and has taken the world by storm. Wherever shown, wherever ridden and owned, the new 61 OHV Harley-Davidson has caused a sensation...As one owner writes, 'It's my dream come true.'"

Two illustrations accompanied this first ad for the Sixty-one. The small one showed Indianapolis Speed Classic winner Bill Cummings on an all-white new 61 OHV. The larger illustration, however, showed the uninspiring left side of the engine with its vestigial vertical fins. H-D still seemed to be holding back. Was this done so not to offend flathead riders? Was Harley-Davidson shy about this knuckleheaded motor? Or deliberately being coy?

No matter. The Sixty-one Overhead roared out of the Midcontinent with a force undreamed of by the founders. Wherever riders gathered or competition events were held the 61 OHV was in evidence. Just page through *The Enthusiast* from the middle of 1936 on and you'll see it everywhere, including a full page photo in the September issue showing speedboat racer Miss Florence Burnham on her fully chrome plated Sixty-one: chrome tanks, chrome fenders, chrome everything!

A year late perhaps, but Harley-Davidson finally tooted their own horn when the new 1937 models were released. Hap was apoplectic with ecstacy, writing, "What a 'line' of iron hosses...I've seen new models of motorcycles announced year after year since way back when—but the new 'stuff' on these '37 Harley-Davidsons really has got me down gasping...they ought

Here's a classic photograph. Walter Davidson, Jr. downs a cool one at Shawano as Fred Sherman looks on. Walter was known as a "sport" who partied with the club and joined in club runs. *Courtesy of Frank Matheus.*

zon. After years of rumor, it suddenly and quietly appeared...What an earthquake of excitement it caused!...The 61 brought a renewed interest to motorcycling. There was a rush to see just what this new and different motorcycle could do. And what couldn't it do! Wherever the 61 OHV appeared at hillclimbs, at race meets, at T.T. races, and at endurance runs, this super cycle just kicked up its heels and 'went places'. Boy! that baby sure did make a hit." And a little later, "I could fill a book with the peppy, enthusiastic letters I've received from 61 owners. They're absolutely sold on their sensational mount...Its speed, lightning acceleration and fine handling qualities have added a new chapter to American motorcycling."

The prose was a little purple, but for once the ad hype had some truth behind it. The big news was that the rest of the H-D line (45, 74, and 80 ci models) all received a Sixty-one style upgrading. All models now ran recirculating oil systems. All side-valve motors had been considerably reworked. Both 45 and Big Twin flatheads were upgraded to new models: the RL became the WL; the VL became the UL; and the big Eighty VLH became the ULH. The most classic Harley-Davidsons of all time had come into existence.

All machines now sported welded teardrop tanks and built-in instrument panels. The big flatheads were now built around the twin cradle frame, swaged forks, and the bulletproof four-speed transmission. The Big Twin side-valves and the Sixty-one shared so many parts in common they were virtually the same bike except for the mill. Engines could be easily switched and some guys did so.

Hap's text is entertaining and revealing. It doesn't take a genius to read between the lines. The 61 OHV was a road burner like no other. Hap admitted as much while giving the older models a slap when he said, "Gosh, when I wheeled some of my first gas chariots, there was only one way to try and keep a motor cool and that was to load up on oil and—trust to luck. Course, we weren't in much of a hurry those days anyway, so it probably didn't matter so much. But now'days the way some of you birds spank the saddle on our wide highways, it takes a real system like Harley-Davidson's to keep your power mills lubricated."

Harley-Davidson wasn't being shy now—they proclaimed the 61 OHV's magnificence with classic H-D enthusiasm. They certainly tried making up for lost time. But in fact the Sixty-one Overhead was a very good machine and even by modern standards it holds up pretty well, yet by no means was it perfect. During that first year several problems showed up, but none were life threatening. They were mere cracks in the road on the Sixty-one's run towards immortality. These problems, however, had to be tracked down and ironed out and from the way guys were flinging this brand new mount up rocky hillsides, over TT courses, and through endurance runs, any weaknesses would soon show up. Conceived and promoted as a high-speed, high-performance machine, this

to be started by nothing less than lighting a fuse....Yowsah, there's been plenty of high-class engineering, with a capital 'E'...They're far and away the most revolutionary, the sleekest, the most graceful motorcycles ever put together in America."

The EL model led the pack. In November the 61 OHV finally made the front cover of *The Enthusiast*. Inside, readers got the scoop on what most already knew. Hap wrote, "...what a sensation the 61 OHV created early in 1936 when it flashed across the motorcycle hori-

Don't forget the beer! Here members of the Milwaukee Motorcycle Club carry the keg to a spot in the shade. *Courtesy of Harold Deckert.*

Green Bay Motorcycle Club in new uniforms at Shawano. New 1936 Big Twin flathead on right. No overhead models in sight with this bunch. *Courtesy of Ray and Ellen Frederick.*

guaranteed a hard test at the hands of private owners, far more severe than any factory test rider would risk his neck for!

As a result, some things did break and faults showed up. One weak spot was the frame. As part of its high-performance design the Sixty-one's frame was fabricated of lightweight tubing. Hefted side by side with a 1937 or later frame, the weight difference is distinctly felt (1936 frame: 45 pounds; 1937 frame: 51 pounds). Because factory prototypes lacked sidecar mounting lugs this meant that no testing with sidecars had been done. When the Sixty-one went into production, sidecar mounting lugs were brazed to the front down-tubes. Another last minute addition. John Nowak, who worked on early Sixty-ones in H-D's repair shop recalled what happened, "That thirty-six was supposed to be a lightweight, high-speed machine. Light frame and all. But guys started hanging sidecars on them. That frame wasn't designed for that kind of driving. That's when frames started breaking."

Many 1936 Sixty-one frames were returned for repair at the factory. Some had the front down-tubes reinforced with brazed-on pieces so the diagonal slip joint is thirteen inches below the neck. During these factory repairs the frame bracket for the fifth mounting point on the transmission was added and the open brake anchor closed up. In spite of these repairs most 1936 frames proved too fragile and were discarded for the improved 1937 and later versions which utilized heavier tubing and forged sidecar lug fittings. These and later improvements made H-D frames the best in the business. As a result original 1936 EL frames are extremely rare.

There were also examples of transmissions locking up, resulting in broken housings. The problem was traced to a lock ring wearing through by contact with a rotating spacer. Without the snap ring two gears could engage and bust the gearbox to pieces. Rudy Moberg—liaison man be-tween engineering and shop foremen—came up with the solution by designing a new spacer that didn't turn against the lock ring. A five cent solution for a potentially big repair bill.

Another problem showed up in the lubrication system that first winter. Water would get inside the engine from condensation or other sources. In cold weather this moisture would freeze and block the screen in the oil tank which in turn would obstruct oil flow into the feed pump. This either starved the engine of oil or in some cases imploded the oil tank. "There was a baffle plate and screen in the oil tank," said John Nowak. "That thing would freeze up in cold weather. To fix that we'd take the oil cap off and take a chisel and break the screen out of there. Later we took it out and made some oil line changes."

A universal complaint about the 1936 (and 1937) EL model involved the oil return system on the overhead-valve mechanism. We now know the cups were a somewhat make-shift last minute fix. They were semi-open where the top cups were cut away to allow access to the valve stems by the rocker arms and these open slots let oil escape if the return lines became blocked or the oil supply was adjusted too liberally. They also allowed water and dirt to get inside the cups where this contamination would be sucked into the engine. Not a good situation.

A related problem occurred in freezing weather. Water collected inside the cups and would freeze there. Ice is very tenacious stuff and would jam the valve train solid. Next day when the rider gave his bike its morning kick (they rode in cold weather back then) a broken rocker arm, bent pushrod, or snapped head bracket could result.

The return oil lines from the cups were of small diameter and would easily clog. An air nipple was added so the lines could be blown clear with compressed air. The troublesome semi-open cups would be replaced with better covers for the 1938 model year.

As previously mentioned the adjustable oil supply to each rocker arm also proved bothersome. Each had to be individually adjusted just right to provide enough but not too much oil. If set too generously oil could be sucked past the valve guides on the intake stroke and get into the combustion chamber. This would interfere with combustion, foul spark plugs, cause a rough running engine, and create exhaust smoke. Too much oil also caused leakage from the cups and caused those occasional complaints of a messy engine. The factory suggested to set for the "lightest possible...supply without shutting (it) off entirely."

On the first Sixty-ones this adjustment was pretty much trial and error. After each rocker arm supply was set the bike would be test run and readjustments made if necessary—a time consuming and difficult process. Too little and the valve mechanism would squeak. Too much and it would leak. The factory soon developed a better system. After each engine was assembled a man would connect an external oil supply to each head. He would watch the oil flow dripping on each valve stem. With a special T-handle wrench he'd turn the rocker arm adjustment until the supply to the valve stem was right. This was done to each rocker arm. Then he'd stamp the head at that point. This would be the original factory setting and a reference point for future adjustments.

During the first year of production numerous changes were made to the bits and pieces making up the Sixty-one Overhead. Some parts received two or three alterations before a final design was fixed upon suggesting that the Sixty-one was a sort of "pet" around the engineering department that year and the guys there couldn't keep their hands off it until they figured it was just right. As a result a great many parts are unique to 1936, sometimes in very subtle ways. However, the design didn't become "fixed" until 1941. In the minds of many enthusiasts the 1936-1939 Knuckleheads were the best looking motorcycles ever built in Milwaukee.

The 36EL was also fast. It ran a hotter cam than 1937 and later models. The "lightning" or "lightening" cam has been variously interpreted as meaning fast like lightning or lightened by holes drilled in the gear. The cam may have been detuned during the 36EL production year possibly making the earlier (lower numbered) engines faster motorcycles. They were also harder starting and known to spit back through the carburetor. Their frisky reputation was appreciated from the start. John Birch—second owner of 36EL1740—said this, "I had problems with the engine being a little balky until it had warmed up for a couple of minutes. Knuth said the early overhead Sixty-ones were that way. They had high-lift cams that were subsequently modified to be more tractable. Naturally that took some of the steam out of it. I didn't mind the warm-up time after I knew what the problem was. Once it warmed up it would really move. It was quicker than anything else on the road."

Marshfield H-D dealer "Fats" Lauby and wife with Ray Frederick's 36EL2091. Chrome fishtail muffler is enduring classic. Note method of attaching saddlebags to fender. *Courtesy of Ray and Ellen Frederick.*

Winners of uniform contest at Shawano in 1936 was the Wauwatosa Motorcycle Club. Alfred Kuehn's son was a member. Third bike from left is 36EL1284 or 36EL1566. *Courtesy of Ray and Ellen Frederick.*

Shawano 1936 (from left): Norbert Ewald (34VLD5985 in new paint), Edmund Kelly (36EL1307), and "Hal" Deckert (36VLH1060). *Courtesy of Harold Deckert.*

A slightly inebriated William S. Harley at Shawano 1936. There was in fact something to celebrate and Bill Harley was showing it. Formal photos portray founders as a somber crew, but caught on film at Shawano old Bill Harley proved he could still party with the best of them. A beer in one hand, a pretty girl in the other, and a new motorcycle that was the talk of the event. What else could he ask for? *Courtesy of Frank Matheus.*

John Nowak said this about the 36EL cam, "The first thirty-six had a high-speed cam. Later we changed it and scrapped those early cams. I saved six or seven. That cam was an overlap high-speed racing type. They didn't start to perform until you reached a speed of thirty miles an hour. It didn't act right until then, especially with a sidecar. It would blubber or spit. I don't remember which. We changed that cam. Even called some back and replaced them. The later Sixty-one cam didn't have the holes. You couldn't tell much by looking at the lobes. To identify the later ones we made a solid gear. The early one was called 'lightening cam' because of the holes."

Ray Frederick (36EL2091) said this about his Sixty-one, "Very fast. The only problem I had with it was dieseling for fifteen or twenty seconds when I turned off the switch. I thought there was something wrong so I traded for a new thirty-eight model (38EL1027). But I was disappointed. The thirty-eight was a fancy one with a lot of chrome, but the thirty-six was faster. That thing could really roar."

Although he didn't own one, Joe Simandl (30VL11301) recalled the Sixty-one's speed; "Those Seventy-fours and Eighty side-valves seemed a little faster off the line than the Sixty-ones, but the Sixty-ones would get up to eighty and keep right on going. It was a winding type of engine like Shorty (Lindstrom) used to say. Down there in Louisiana they'd go two hundred miles to Texas just for a jaunt. They'd take the Sixty-ones—let them go—'schup'—they're gone. Down there in that wide open country that's where they had the Seventy-fours beat. The Seventy-fours and Eightys would get up there and peak. The Sixty-ones would keep on going."

Another story of a fast Sixty-one was told to the author by William H. Davidson. "There was a dealer named 'Red' Wolverton," Davidson said. "He was a high caliber rider and a hell of a fine person. One year we were at a mile dirt track event. He had a fast Sixty-one with a sidecar. In practice he was out there and went by some guy on an Indian racing Scout which were pretty fast bikes. But he passed him. The guy came

97

Green Bay Motorcycle Club, 1936. Uniforms and formation riding was impressive. *Courtesy of Fred Process.*

into the pits and said, 'I'd better tear this thing down. Would you believe it? Some guy just passed me on a sidecar.'"

If the 1937s were slower, it wasn't by much. John Horstmeier owned 37EL1606. He told of when it was new back when he lived in Aurora, Illinois. "That Sixty-one was a going machine," Horstmeier recalled. "All polished and ported. Guys were always talking about how fast Mercurys were. I remember the first one I saw. I was coming back through Rockford. There was a cemetery there where the kids would race because there were no crossroads. That's where you'd see the new models. I saw one: a jerk in a Merc. I was tooling along and here he comes with his buddy showing him the new Merc. When they went by I put it down in third gear and fired up. I went past him and jerked it back in high and let the clutch in. The wheel came off the ground. When it came down I looked at the expression on his face but he was so far behind he didn't know he had one. He was so bitter! If you like Mercurys you should have been there. You could have bought one for what it was worth."

All the Knuckleheads may have been faster than their aluminum-headed successor: the so-called Panhead engine (1948-1965). According to old factory men the reason could be traced to the 1936-1947 engine's longer valve stems and guides when compared to the 1948 OHV version. The long-stem valves and guides were superior at high revs. Where the shorter Panhead valves would tend to wobble and not find their seats the long Knucklehead valves were more positive. Maybe that's why the Knuckleheads could run with later Panheads and Shovelheads and stay with them. The author recalls one occasion on the freeway south of Milwaukee when he was riding a 1949 FL and had a hard time keeping up with a pal's 1939 EL—and the other guy was packing double!

By the time the bugs were worked out of the 61 OHV the machine was about as bulletproof as a motorcycle could be. It was handsome,

fast, and reliable. There were other fast motorcycles, but anything faster than a stock Sixty-one was probably a specially prepared machine. Anyone with the money could go down to a H-D dealer and buy a hot Sixty-one Overhead right off the showroom floor.

Sixty-ones were taking more than their share of wins in competitions wherever they were entered. But Harley-Davidson was after bigger game with its new model. Even before the Sixty-one was released to the public William H. Davidson had been suggesting to his father and uncles they should make an attempt at a new speed record with it. As a board of director member since 1931 young Bill Davidson had some influence over what was done, but twice he was overruled by his more experienced—and cautious—elders. Finally in early 1937 such an attempt was successfully made on a factory machine piloted by the legendary Joe Petrali.

This story has been told many times and will only be touched upon here. The machine was a special Sixty-one built in the winter of 1936-1937 by Joe Petrali, Hank Syvertsen, Bill Kasten, Ewald "Dutch" Becker, and others in the factory racing department. The engine was modified with higher compression pistons, dual carburetors, magneto ignition, and a special cam. The engine put out sixty-five horsepower at 5700 rpm and was equipped with stream-line cowling. This proved unstable during high-speed running and was removed when the record was set.

Stanley McClintock—personal friend of Petrali—remembered hearing what happened that March day at Daytona Beach, Florida. "They had the whole thing hooked up—tail and all," McClintock said. "Then Joe came down the line and he felt the front end getting light. He wasn't afraid. Not Joe. But he could feel what was happening and it didn't appeal to him. He decided to cut her off otherwise he'd go on his ass. So they took the tail off. Then Joe rode it again and made the speed record. Then they put the tail back on and took the picture."

Johnny and "Bubbles" Spiegelhoff. Milwaukee native Spiegelhoff was a live-wire on the Midwest racing circuit beginning in the mid-1930s. In addition to being something of a rascal he was one hell of a rider. *Courtesy of Gayle Spiegelhoff Renz.*

"Waco" Weigert (left) and Garth Lees, Shawano 1936. Lees rides a Forty-five. Smaller bike was more maneuverable in turns, but Sixty-one had the power to catch up on the straights. *Courtesy of Orville Process.*

The best two-way average speed was 136.183 mph. The highest overall one-way speed was 139.15 mph. These broke the previous American record made by an Indian motorcycle in 1926. Petrali's record stood for eleven years.

The next month Fred "Iron Man" Ham set a new twenty-four hour American and world record at Muroc Dry Lake riding a stock 1937 61 OHV. The first hour he traveled 91.33 miles and then broke every hourly record up to twenty-four hours when he had piled up 1825.2 miles. One interesting note about Ham's record was that at the eight-hundred mile mark the front chain (a new experimental type) seized up and subjected the engine to extreme stress and overheating. No side-valve made could have withstood such punishment, but the Sixty-one did and after the chain was replaced went on to set a new world record. In a fine article written many years ago, Jim Earp described the scene of Ham's twenty-four hour record: "The scene was wild and unearthly. The 5-mile ring of yellow, flickering torches was like a crown in the immense black vault of the desert and the sky. Glowing red flares...lighted the approach to the pits and the crew worked in the harsh white glare of gasoline lanterns. As the rider roared by, light gray ghosts of dust followed along the desert floor through the light of the torches. The cycle flashed its beam powerfully at the pits, moved away dimming the weaker flares, and finally, at the far end of the circle just became just one of the many points of light—but it was always moving."

These are the two best known feats accomplished by the Sixty-one in the first two years of its existence. In the pages of *The Enthusiast* many other exploits were told, yet another early speed contest has gone unrecorded until now. It seems that William H. Davidson couldn't wait for his father and the other founders to show off the Sixty-one's speed, nor was the contest held in any more exotic locale than just outside Milwaukee.

*   *   *

In 1935 twenty year old Harry Sebreny was working at Harley-Davidson. After a year of getting up at four in the morning and standing in line he finally landed a job at H-D helping Joe Traut in the crating department. Later, as the young guy in the paint shop, Harry ran for parts all over the building which was how he got to know every foreman in the shop. He was also a friend of Joe Ryan's son. One day in Ryan's office he saw some photos of a motorcycle lying on the desk.

"I asked him what it was," Sebreny recalled. "He said, 'That's our new model. A Sixty-one overhead-valve.' I didn't know much about motors then except that overhead-valve was a big thing at that time. The

Charles Lehman (left) with his 1936 Big Twin flathead next to a 1934 model. Side-valves were now obsolete but it took several years for this fact to sink in. *Courtesy of Euella Trapp.*

The line-up at the start of the Shawano TT event in 1936. Rider is Steve Kakuk. Motorcycle is 36EL1294. Kukuk loved his Sixty-one. Was told by guys at H-D factory that it was perfect for his weight and size. Bike had been set up at Juneau Avenue for competition minded Kukuk brothers. *Courtesy of Steve Kakuk.*

Bill Knuth (facing camera) enjoys the 1936 Shawano rally. Knuth played key role in organizing event. *Courtesy of Frank Matheus.*

Garth Lees, winner of the 1936 Shawano TT races. Steve Kakuk came in second in last big combined event. *Courtesy of Harold Deckert.*

Wauwatosa Club during uniform contest at Shawano 1936. The Wauwatosa Club claimed to be the first club in the country to be one-hundred percent in uniform. *Courtesy of Ray and Ellen Frederick.*

Heading home. Those saddlebags came in handy to carry a rainsuit in. Guys that were running the new Sport Windshield were smiling when the rains came. Bike is 1935 Big Twin. *Courtesy of Harold Deckert.*

Lime Kiln Hill at Shawano Rally 1936. Brand new Sixty-ones were flung against hillside. Thirties' Big Twin riders make those of today look like wimps. *Courtesy of Frank Matheus.*

Green Bay Club Honor Roll, 1936. Members looked happy and their uniforms spotless. Bikes are flatheads. Dealer "Jib" Arndt tall guy in back row. *Courtesy of Fred Process.*

Adolph Roemer on 36RLDR2232 at the Peshtigo River bridge near Crivitz, Wisconsin. RLDR model was hot and built for Class C competition thus had headlight and road equipment. It was also popular with guys desiring a speedy Forty-five. *Courtesy of Adolph Roemer.*

motorcycle in the picture was beautiful. I put money down right away and paid it off through the Kilbourn Finance Corporation right in the building at Harley-Davidson. Later I went downstairs and watched the first ones come off the line. That was their first big overhead-valve job. It was supposed to be the best they ever made. But mine was the biggest lemon in the beginning."

Strong words, but Harry Sebreny had good reason for feeling that way. That came later, however, and at first he was in the enviable position to watch his own motorcycle being built. The guys told him when it was going through and he went down to the third floor to see it.

"They all knew me," Sebreny recalled. "They knew it was my bike. They put on every piece of chrome they had and didn't even charge me for it. They picked out a special engine. They tested it and that was supposed to be a good one because I worked there."

A dream come true? Hold on. We're dealing with an early first year Sixty-one here: 36EL1489 to be exact.

"It was finished," Sebreny went on, "but they said, 'No, you can't have it yet. Knuth gets it first. He's got things to do to it.' But I think that was just a stall so Knuth could have it on his showroom floor. They might have polished it or something, but that thing looked finished to me."

Finally Harry got his new machine. At first it ran perfect. But after a while it started acting strange. "We used to go out to Lannon stone quarry or down to the lake," Sebreny said. "We'd chip in a few cents and buy beer and hot dogs. One night my motorcycle started missing and fouling plugs. A new set wouldn't make it to the lakefront and back. The guys told me I had the wrong plugs, but I'd already replaced five sets. One night it was missing terrible so I rode it over to Bill Knuth's shop just as he was locking the door. He looked at it and said, 'Bring it back tomorrow.' But I was mad. I said, 'No, right now.' He wanted to put new spark plugs in it, but a new set was just put in. I said, 'Blankity

103

Blank—this machine is the best one you ever had but it won't go twenty miles without fouling plugs.' So Knuth took mine in to fix and gave me a police VL to use. He even put gas in it. The other guys laughed. Here was the prettiest motorcycle built that made fifty others look like junk and it wouldn't run. They razzed Knuth. They said, 'That's supposed to be your King of Motorcycles and it won't run.' They really gave it to him. They weren't saying overhead-valve was no good. They knew something was wrong. Everybody like the way it looked. They fell in love with it. They all wanted to ride it, but I wouldn't let them."

Knuth had 36EL1489 for a long time, or so it seemed to Harry Sebreny. It was sent to the factory for readjustment. Finally Harry got it back.

"It ran like a charm," Sebreny recalled. "As soon as you gave it gas it took off. They fixed it all right. It ran perfect."

The bike was hot. Sebreny's engine had been picked out on the dynamometer as above average. With its problems behind it 36EL1489 now led the pack.

"That Sixty-one was by far faster than Seventy-four and Eighty inch flatheads," he said. "I took off the muffler and put on a straight brass pipe. It echoed like a cannon going off. Once I let a speed cop ride it. He came back and said he never rode anything like it. He told the police department about it and they were interested."

Happy with his bike's performance Harry Sebreny gave his motorcycle a name: "Soupy Sixty-one." He had a front mudflap made with the name outlined in chrome studs. There were plenty of 36ELs parked in the factory garage that first year—36EL1307, 36EL1400, 36EL1519, 36EL1531, 36ES1748, and 36EL2000 among others. But when William H. Davidson wanted a fast one he looked up Harry Sebreny and Soupy Sixty-one.

"The factory knew how fast it was," Harry said. "They tested it when they fixed it. One day Bill Davidson—the younger one— came up to me. He said there was some dealer from California picking up thirteen motorcycles. They had been asking about the Sixty-one and didn't believe it was that fast. They had a car with them. A hot rod. They brought it along to race. Bill Davidson told them, 'I'll bet we got a Sixty-one here that will beat that thing. But I can't promise anything until I talk to the guy who owns it.' They didn't believe anything could beat that hot rod. So they all came up to where I was working and Bill Davidson asked me if I'd race them. I didn't want to. But I was awful proud of that damned thing and when he said, 'Go ahead, Harry' I agreed. We went out right then during working hours. That hot rod guy never saw anything like it."

At that time Highway 100 outside Milwaukee had recently been built. It was finished but not yet open to traffic. It ran through several miles of farmland with no crossroads and it was there the impromptu race was staged.

"They put a car at the end where we were supposed to turn around," Sebreny said. "They put one in the middle, and Bill Davidson and the rest were grouped at the finish. They thought they were going to run away with it. They bet strong on their car. Real strong. All cash. It was three miles out and three miles back. Six miles total. I rode that thing flat out and that Sixty-one went like a dream. It just floated. When you opened it up it was like riding a cloud. They lost their money. I was back before the guy in the hot rod was half and three-quarter of the way. They were surprised. They wanted to buy it right there. They offered me more than I paid for it. After the race Bill Davidson put his arm around me. That was the only time he asked me to race. But later I heard they talked about it to other guys that came from California who asked about it. They pointed me out while I was working and the garage man said Bill Davidson showed my machine to visitors. That hot rod had been beating everything in California, but it couldn't beat Soupy Sixty-one."

36EL1950 stripped for Class C action. Bike shows signs of hard use, inevitable when used for hillclimbing. *Courtesy of Mrs. Harold Helms.*

36EL serves as logo for ad describing 1936 Wausau motorcycle rodeo. Overhead-valve model was instantly identified with speed and power. Nothing much could match it. *Courtesy of Mel and Emma Krueger.*

The event isn't known and while a little blurry, this photo gives excellent feel of Mel Krueger's blazing progress on this Sixty-one. Bike appears to be 1936 model. *Courtesy of Mel and Emma Krueger.*

Balloon busting contest at the 1936 Wausau motorcycle rodeo. Factory encouraged dealers to stage numerous events for riders and spectators. *Courtesy of Ray and Ellen Frederick.*

Here Mel Krueger goes through the board wall on Sixty-one at the 1936 Wausau Motorcycle Rodeo. Modern collectors weep at the sight of priceless antiques being thrown around in this manner. *Courtesy of Mel and Emma Krueger.*

New style sidecar shows up at the 1936 Badger Derby. Bikes, however, are all side-valves. *The Enthusiast.*

Eldy Wheeler; Bernie Ernst, and Syl Fischer working on 1934 flathead. Bike in foreground is 1936 model. *Courtesy of Bernard Ernst.*

Harry and Audrey Sebreny on 36EL1489: "Soupy Sixty-one." Bike was another fast engine picked out at the factory for one of their own. *Courtesy of Harry and Audrey Sebreny.*

CHAPTER FIVE:
Symphony in Steel

The steed carried me as far as my heart desired—the
axle blazing in the socket—for it was urged
round by well-turned wheels at each end.
Parmenides of Elea, 450 B.C.

"Indian Joe" Campbell on way to Florida with 37ULH4190. Eighty flathead with recirculating oil system was H-D's last development of the side-valve Big Twin. In spite of author's bad-mouthing these were very nice bikes if not pushed hard. *Courtesy of Joe Campbell.*

Another quiz bike. Gas tank paint suggests 1936 but frame and rear oil line says 1937 and is correct. Bike is actually 37EL1704. Factory paint followed 1936 style on instructions of purchaser. *Courtesy of Frank Matheus.*

The late 1930s was a time of change for Harley-Davidson. The worst of the Great Depression had passed, Roosevelt's National Industrial Recovery Act and various public works programs put money out into the field, and business started picking up around the country. With cash in their pockets people started buying motorcycles again. At Harley-Davidson more guys were called back and new ones hired, yet there were storm clouds on the international horizon. One sign of this was that the U.S. Army was showing renewed interest in motorcycles.

But things were looking up and that's what mattered. After a slight set-back and layoff in 1937 business continued to improve. Production continued to rise. In its first few years the 61 OHV was built in the following numbers: 1936, 1,704; 1937, 2,250; 1938, 2,478; 1939, 2,909. By today's standards these were small numbers, but there was an advantage to such limited production. Quality was foremost. Each machine

was meticulously crafted to the highest standards of the time and perhaps that's why so many machines of this era survive today.

Riders were highly pleased with the new motorcycles coming out of Milwaukee. If many were still shy about the OHV model the side-valves now looked just as good. Harley-Davidson was still not placing all its bets on the Sixty-one, and plenty steered clear of the 61 OHV. There were even cases of guys going back and forth between overhead and side-valve. Such indecision is hard to understand in a day when the overhead-valve engine reigns supreme. Back then it was a real decision to make—was a guy willing to trade the familiar simplicity of his side-valve for the new-fangled and complicated overhead? Not all were.

Joe "Indian Joe" Campbell received that name one day when he parked an Indian in the H-D company garage. In 1936 he bought a brand new 61 OHV (36EL1400), but sold it shortly afterwards and bought a new Eighty flathead (37ULH4190). Joe said shortly before he died, "She (his wife) didn't like the clicking noise in that first model. So I turned the thing in for a side-valve Eighty. I rode that for a time then went back to a Knucklehead (40EL1584). That's out in the garage. In that respect I had a woman's mind. Never know when you have enough. I liked both."

"Hal" Deckert (39EL3290 and 41EL1678) had several side-valves before switching to the OHV Big Twin. He said, "I wasn't that interested when the Sixty-one first came out. I bought a new Eighty side-valve that year. Maybe I was worried the Sixty-one might not be so good. Yeah? With the Eighty I knew what I was getting. That's why. Most of the guys that rode side-valves said it (61 OHV) would never last. I really have the feeling they thought that way. Guys that had Sixty-ones were crazy for them, but other guys shied away. If it leaked oil—I don't remember that—but that would be a good reason. But here you are working on a side-valve for five or ten years then suddenly you got a different engine to work on. More complicated. So the side-valve guy says we like what we've got and that's it."

That's how it was. In one sense the 61 OHV took the country by storm and yet in another it didn't. While there was a small but growing number of fanatical believers in the OHV there were a lot of others who took a wait-and-see attitude. Some were sceptical, others couldn't make up their minds. It was a little hard to believe a smaller engine could be faster than a bigger one. In Wisconsin there were actually fewer 37ELs sold than 36ELs! But this trend reversed itself in 1938 and never turned around again. That year Milwaukee law enforcement agencies began buying 61 OHV models. Just a few in 1938, then a whole slug in 1939. After that the lid blew off the pot. In 1941 Milwaukee cops got a big fleet of new 74 OHV (FL) models.

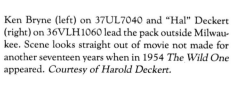

Ken Bryne (left) on 37UL7040 and "Hal" Deckert (right) on 36VLH1060 lead the pack outside Milwaukee. Scene looks straight out of movie not made for another seventeen years when in 1954 *The Wild One* appeared. *Courtesy of Harold Deckert.*

Harley-Davidson service school graduates in 1937. Factory in background. "Professor" Orin Lamb in back row forth from right. Man kneeling on far right is service department boss Joe Ryan. *Courtesy of Mel and Emma Krueger.*

One thing the 61 OHV brought with it was a new standard for high-speed, long-distance reliability. For the first time riders had an engine they could honestly depend upon no matter how many miles they went or at what speed. For OHV riders at least the day of melting pistons was over. Now a guy—or gal—could strap on a pup tent and sleeping bag, throw raingear, extra clothes, and a canteen in the saddlebags, maybe bolt on a new solo "Sport" windshield to keep off the bugs and rain. Then a wave goodbye and hit the open highway.

Then as now the motorcycle offered an exciting and economical means of travel. For better or worse riders were one with the elements and shared whatever storm or sunshine came along. On the nearly indestructable Sixty-one Overhead the rider became a primal force of nature. For here was a mount, as Connie Schlemmer remarked, "That never seemed to get tired."

With the Sixty-one Overhead one could follow the road to the ocean's edge, to the mountain's rocky peak, or, with throttle cracked wide, roar down the highway at midnight. With the 61 OHV anyone who could raise the money ($380 in 1936; $435 in 1939) had a mount with guts enough to go a thousand miles in a day provided the rider did his part. Joe Petrali and Fred Ham's exploits nailed that down once and for all. In 1937 when describing the new models Hap said, "Wire from a roadside fence was a life saver when motorcycling was young. But not now'days with these ultra-modern, up-to-the-second Harley-Davidson motorcycles."

With this new standard of reliability riders took to the highway like never before. Since the early thirties Harley-Davidson had encouraged more touring through better accessories and an open invitation to visit the factory. In 1933 a special "Visitors' Room" had been set up at Juneau Avenue. While visitors waited to take the factory tour they could check out the latest accessories, examine new models, page through motorcycle magazines, or look at photos. Many accepted the invitation and came. Some arrived to pick up new motorcycles to save transportation costs. Others, in the course of their travels, found themselves in Wisconsin. Milwaukee and Harley-Davidson became a mecca for thousands of motorcycle nomads.

In the language of the Chippewa Indians, Wisconsin means "land-of-gathering-waters." The place is best known for beer, bratwurst, cheese, and motorcycles. But Wisconsin is a wonderful land for riding. William G. Davidson—son of William H. Davidson and grandson of founder William A. Davidson—described it this way, "I've been all over the world, and this state (Wisconsin) is one of the best places to ride. You come in from the west over the Mississippi early in the morning, with the steam rising from the river, and see the lush hills and a red barn here and there and you think, 'My God, I'm in heaven.'"

Maybe that's one reason the motorcycle took hold here so early—and stuck. Blue skies, back roads, range upon range of hills stretch on without end. Blond ripe fields and sleepy valleys, lazy clouds drifting across a summer sky. In the north lay primal forest of pine and spruce, wild rivers and blue lakes where the cry of the loon and howl of the wolf is heard. All this calls to the biker's nomad heart with those magical words: Just go!

You know him, have seen and heard him—that dusty traveler reading a map alongside the road. Hunched over the handlebars at some deserted crossroads exhausted and sore. Sulking under a bridge in the driving rain. You've heard the sound of a big V-twin at midnight rolling like distant drums across the land. He—or she—has become immortal

Man and motorcycle: Dallas Little and 37EL2873. White paint jobs had strong following and suggests 1936 and 1937 ELs were not the oil slingers of common myth. *Courtesy of Dallas Little.*

Out along the mighty Mississippi. Hilly terrain and dreamy river landscape has made this a favorite ride for midwestern motorcyclists for ninety-plus years. *Courtesy of Adolph Roemer.*

now, as mythic and enduring in the human pysche as the gods and goddesses of old.

So pack your sleeping bag and fishing pole. Find a companion or go it solo, but go. Hit the trail. Lose yourself. Seek out the sharp tang of the piney woods and the morning mist at the water's edge. Take the road that follows old moccasin trails. Find the spirit of the continent—the *Mizzi Zibi*, the "big river" of the original people of this land. Go up along the shores of those great unsalted seas: Lakes Michigan and Superior. Explore roots of mountains so old they were worn down before the dinosaurs roamed. Find that haunted land where harvest spirits blaze in high autumnal glory. Chase the golden sun into her lair in a hopeless race towards the evening land. Find some misty hilltop far from home and watch the full moon rise over the handlebars like a silent silver goblin, as a distant train hoots a warning stirring something deep and primal in the soul that cries again: Just go!

And if in the course of your travels you come so far—or near—be sure to turn your mount towards the city that once called itself the German Athens. Partake of its famous refreshment and seek out the greatest motorcycle factory on earth.

What was possible in the 1930s is no longer possible today. Then the doors to Juneau Avenue were open. Now Harley-Davidson is spread around in several different facilities in at least three states. The sound of great presses no longer shake Juneau Avenue. Test riders no longer come up the ramps and out of the building heading west. Always west. Milwaukee—*holy* Milwaukee—is no longer the city of yore.

But in the thirties everything was intact. "Ma" Gunderson was just down the street at 3233 Juneau Avenue. For $1.25 you got a place to stay and hearty homecooked meals. She called them "Ma's boys" and wasn't above making small loans to get them home. In twenty years she only got stuck twice.

They came for all reasons. And in spite of their smaller numbers riders of the thirties were as enthusiastic as those from any time or place. They even went to visit the factory on their honeymoon. One couple who did so was Margaret "Mugs" Pritchard and her husband Walter. Back in 1932 Mugs was a sixteen year old girl rider in Appleton with an all-white Forty-five. She soon attracted the eye of Walter

On the road with two 1937 Big Twins. Bike in front is big flathead. Without seeing engine the identity of bike in rear is difficult to ascertain. After 1937 all Big Twins shared a common chassis. *Courtesy of Joe Campbell.*

111

Ken and Elaine Bryne plow through the Milwaukee River on 37UL7040. Bryne was a Milwaukee motorcycle cop after 1941 when the big 74 OHV became the dominant machine on the force. Photo again shows how big men used big motorcycles. *Courtesy of Ken Bryne.*

Visiting the factory. Beaver Dam dealer Jim Trapp picking up well-equipped and well-chromed 37EL2816 outside Harley-Davidson's front door. Bike on right is "Hap" Jameson's personal mount: 36EL1531. Experienced riders like Hap went full out for the Solo Sport Shield. When coupled with windshield and saddlebags 1930s-1940s bikes were practical roadburners with none of the obese excess of later "garbage wagons." *Courtesy of Euella Trapp.*

Pritchard (39E2343). Not long afterwards they ran away to Waukegan, Illinois, and were secretly married. On the way home they went to Milwaukee—and Harley-Davidson—for their honeymoon.

"That's where I told my mother we were going," Margaret recalled. "Why should I lie? We got married in our motorcycle outfits. For our wedding dinner we shared a candy bar. Then we went to the Harley-Davidson factory. It was fantastic. I never dreamed I'd see all those machines and what it took to build them. A nice man came down and we introduced ourselves. When he heard we had just gotten married he treated us like privileged characters. That was our honeymoon."

You could park right out front 3700 West Juneau Avenue all day and not worry about your bike. Inside at the switchboard, Stella Forge would direct you to the Visitors' Room where you could rest after the long ride. If you were lucky there was a brand new Sixty-one Overhead (or flathead model if you preferred) waiting outside at the end of the tour. Whatever model was chosen, those late thirties H-Ds rank as the classiest motorcycles of all time.

The Visitors' Room was a simulation of a Harley-Davidson dealership. On the walls were banners, ads, and photographs. Beneath a large glass showcase all the latest accessories were on display. One whole wall was devoted to a lifesize exhibit of three Sixty-one Overheads ridden by mannequins dressed in the latest snappy outfits. A painted mural of rolling countryside served as a backdrop and a rustic birch log fence in the foreground lent authenticity to the illusion. But the motorcycles were real enough. From the Visitors' Room to the office of Kilbourn Finance Corporation was just a short walk down the hall. More than a few came with no intention of buying a new motorcycle but left with papers in hand.

Pretty soon Hap would show up. He'd crack a joke or two then flirt with the girls. Then he'd lead the way into the heart of the vast Juneau Avenue factory. From then on it was nuts and bolts. How raw steel was transformed into a precision motorcycle. The sound of presses and machinery could be heard up ahead. The smell of hot metal. Fresh paint. Leather. Glittering new machines were coming off the assembly line.

Unlike some manufacturing processes the building of Harley-Davidson motorcycles was a thoroughly honest affair. Outside the engineering and experimental departments the company had nothing to hide. Working conditions were good. No old timer I ever spoke to complained about that. The plant was well maintained. The men were paid a decent wage although absurdly low by today's standards, but then so were prices of new motorcycles.

Margaret "Mugs" and Walter Pritchard. This pair visited Harley-Davidson as newlyweds. When tour guide found out they had just been married he treated them like "privileged characters." *Courtesy of Margaret Pritchard.*

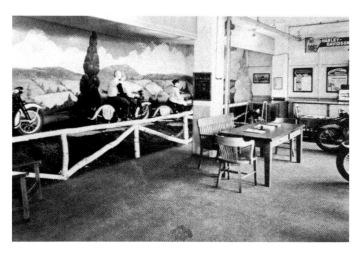

The Harley-Davidson visitors room. Located just inside the front door it was set up to resemble a motorcycle dealership. While visitors awaited the tour they could inspect new models, accessories, and read cycle magazines. Kilbourn Finance Corp. was a short walk down the hall. After one look at the display on left many took that trip. Who could blame them? *The Enthusiast.*

Each machine was built to rigid standards. Nothing was slipshod or phony, there was nothing cheap or ugly hidden behind covers or body parts. These motorcycles were built of the finest materials to the highest standards by the best labor force anywhere. It was old world craftsmanship in a new world setting. While manufacturing capabilities were not as precise as today and belt-driven machinery was still used in the factory, quality was extremely high. The men took pride in their work. The result was a product with a *Made in Milwaukee* mystique famous around the world.

Every motorcycle built had humble origins. Each one began in the vast supply of raw materials purchased by the Harley-Davidson Motor Company. Sheet steel, bar stock, magnet wire, brass, copper—whatever they needed—came from dozens of suppliers. Steel came from iron ore mined on Lake Superior and smelted in the Chicago mills of Republic Steel, LaSalle Steel, Inland Steel, U.S. Steel—maybe twenty steel suppliers depending on what grade was needed. Raw steel came by rail and stockpiled according to grade and size in a low structure behind the south building. Magnet wire for generators came from Phelps-Dodge. Forgings came from Interstate Drop Forge, Walker Forge, and Modern Drop Forge. Castings for cylinders and heads came from Badger Malleable and Liberty Foundry. Aluminum castings came from Eck Foundries in Manitowoc. There were many other suppliers.

Left:
Fred Sherman on his brand new 37EL1704. Another view of this 1937 model with 1936 style paint on gas tanks. Note tire pump attached to frame downtube and small running light on underside of saddle. *Courtesy of Frank Matheus.*

Another 1937 Big Twin flathead. Cool Wisconsin weather was conducive to warm clothing and windshields. Photo taken at Appleton. *Courtesy of Bernard Ernst.*

Milwaukee Motorcycle Club members inspecting a troublesome VL. A 1937 Seventy-four model at left. Guys look concerned. Gals look bored. *Courtesy of Harold Deckert.*

The elegance of the 1930s as expressed in three identically painted machines. Big Twin flathead of 1937 vintage at left stands beside 1936 and 1937 61 OHVs. Even at rest Sixty-ones exude feeling of speed and power. Engines were works of art and stood out a mile away. *Courtesy of Frank Matheus.*

The tour began in the big south building. This was built with profits from the early boom days and finished in 1920. The top floor housed Department 54 where sidecars were built. The entire fifth and part of the forth floor was devoted to Deparment 41: parts and accessories. In the basement was more steel storage and on the west end the racing and experimental departments.

On the floors between it was all machine shop. The steady growl of automatics came from Department 22. Nearly 130 of these machines consumed bar stock and spit out thousands of rough motorcycle parts. Several machines were set up just to turn out roller bearings. By the late 1930s H-D was making millions of rolling bearings each year. The company was famous for its high quality bearings and these were a key part of H-D reliability. Other automatics made a multitude of other parts: washers, pins, screws, shafts, hubs, and gear blanks were produced there. From the automatics nearly eighty tons of waste cuttings per month were hauled off. Ray Griesemer, who worked in the automatic department said, "Harley-Davidson made everything. Nothing was farmed out. It was suprising the stuff they made. The little machines turned out the small parts. The big ones turned out hubs, brake shells—everything. It was noisy and hot work."

Not far away, huge hundred ton presses were turning sheet metal into gas tanks sections and fenders. Smaller presses stamped out instru-

ment panel shrouds, sprockets, tool boxes, footboards, air cleaners, and other parts.

Upstairs in the gear department blanks were put through shapers and gear hobbers. Gears were finished to within "half a tenth" (half of one ten-thousandth of an inch) of concentricity and one-thousandths of an inch of the actual pitch diameter. H-D went to great lengths to reduce gear noise.

Huge Bullard Multi-Matics did the majority of machining on larger parts such as flywheels, connecting rods, rear sprockets and other items. These machines could work on five pieces simultaneously, automatically advancing each part to the next work station. In the lathe and drill press area—Department 3—parts were turned to size and holes drilled in the proper places. In the milling department flat surfaces were buzzed off as if the steel were soft like butter. In the grinding department fine bearing surfaces were put on shafts and hubs. In the plating department chrome and cadmium was applied.

A critical but little known process sometimes preceding, or following, the machining of parts was heat-treatment. While invisible to the eye this vital step gave parts added strength, wear resistance, or flexibility. In the earliest days H-D recognized the importance of proper heat-treating and was one more reason their machines stood up better on primitive roads than other makes long forgotten.

Some twenty furnaces took care of heat-treating duties. Some parts were given different treatments on various portions of their surface. Even big parts, like complete frames, were heat-treated. Paul Maronde spent many years doing that work. He recalled it, "There would be twelve frames to a car. We'd put them in for an hour at 850 degrees. That was hot work. Old Bill Davidson used to come up. He'd say, 'Paul, I really appreciate the way you're doing this work.'"

Proper heat-treatment, annealing, tempering, along with close tolerances, went a long way towards making Harley-Davidson motorcycles durable and strong.

Inspection standards also kept problems to a minimum. Bad parts were marked in red and scrapped. In the inspection department there was a blind woman named Gertrude Weber who worked by touch alone checking surfaces for proper smoothness. Go and no-go gauges were made in the tool room along with countless jigs and fixtures. Tolerances were held to specifications through the use of "Johannson Blocks"—calibrated in millionths of an inch—the equivalent of 1/2000th the thickness of a human hair. Maybe that's why my own dealer back in the 1970s—"Bud" Pater—used to say he'd rather have a good used H-D part than a new reproduction part any day.

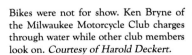

Bikes were not for show. Ken Bryne of the Milwaukee Motorcycle Club charges through water while other club members look on. *Courtesy of Harold Deckert.*

John Horstmeier with 37EL1606 in Chicago at 30,500 miles. At time of photo bike had been painted polychromatic blue. *Courtesy of John Horstmeier.*

Ears ringing from the din of manufacture, the tour goers would pass back outside and cross the street again. On the way they saw the oil house where lubricants were stored and peeked inside the factory service school where Orin Lamb, John Powers, and later John Nowak taught dealers and mechanics how to maintain and fix motorcycles. Some students, however, wanted to learn more than just the basics. John Horstmeier recalled how his friend and business partner Art Seeley obtained some speed secrets right from under Orin Lamb's nose.

"The teacher (Orin Lamb) could tell Seeley very little about engine repair that he didn't already know," Horstmeier recalled. "What Seeley really wanted was information about performance and racing engines. The teacher made it very clear that it was only a repair and a maintenance school for motorcycles. But the teacher had a big book

A new 1937 Seventy-four flathead in Wisconsin Rapids. Owner Russell Johnson with 37UL1284. *Courtesy of Ray Wheir.*

with everything about engines in it. In the morning he'd get the students started on their lesson for the day. Then he'd retreat to the mens room for a while. Seeley spent that time going through the 'big book' and copying down figures and everything he needed to know."

Next the tour entered the big north building again, the first large brick and concrete structure built in the Juneau Avenue complex. It was begun in 1910 and constructed in stages. For a time it stood in two separate sections with a sawmill in between. There's a legend of a hidden room in the basement of the westernmost section. The story first surfaced in the 1920s when "Squibb" Henrich heard it from Edwin "Sherbie" Becker. According to Becker—who worked there with several relatives when the building was constructed—some early belt-drive motorcycles were sealed up at that time. It's unknown whether this legend is fact or myth. A weak attempt to find out in early 1993 proved inconclusive.

The tour then took the west elevator up to the fifth floor, where everything was given over to brazing and welding. Fenders, chain guards, tool boxes, handlebars, leg shields, battery boxes, oil and gas tanks were all fabricated there.

In Department 17 the welding of gas and oil tanks was done. First the filler necks were welded on. Then the tank back and side was tack-welded together. Next the seams were finish welded and the mounting brackets added. During these operations the gas tank was held in a frame-like fixture to guarantee a proper fit. Ralph Behrs worked in the welding department for thirty years. He said, "It was all acetylene welding on gas and oil tanks. The parts came already stamped out and we welded them around the edge. In eight hours a guy made maybe thirty tanks. There was a tester who checked for leaks. He'd seal them up and put them in water. If they leaked he'd mark them. Then we'd weld the leak and he checked again. There weren't many leaks in mine. Too many and the guy responsible would catch it."

Frames and forks were assembled on the floor below. In Department 23 the frames were built. H-D frames were known for their great

One of H-D's best ads of the classic period. Too bad the 61 OHV didn't get similar treatment a year earlier. Improvements of new UL line over older VL model were numerous. UL was basically an EL model with an up-dated side-valve engine. *The Enthusiast.*

strength. They began existence as pieces of seamless tubing and forged fittings and ended up as a finished frame. Joe Seidl came to America from Bavaria in 1924 and worked in the frame department from the late twenties on. When first hired H-D sent Seidl to work in a part of the Pabst Brewery building they were then leasing. Later at Juneau Avenue he became foreman of the frame department.

"My uncle came to visit us in Germany," Seidl recalled. "He asked me if I would like to go to America. I said, 'Why not?' I couldn't speak a word of English and went right away to night school. My foreman was Frank Molitor. He could speak three languages. He said, 'Joe, if you listen to me you're going to be somebody.' That man was right. I had charge of that whole department 23A and 23B."

Frame building was an art. Sections of tubing were cut to length and bent into various shapes. The ends of each section were knurled where they pressed into the forged frame fittings at the neck head, side-car lugs, or axle guides. These joints were then brazed. Every frame had to be perfect so that engine and transmission aligned properly and the motorcycle would track correctly. Without a good frame for a foundation all other precision work would come to nothing.

"Frames were my specialty," Seidl said. "You made the frame joint by joint. Way back we pinned the joints together with nails. We drilled a hole then put a nail through there to hold the pieces together and then we'd chop the nail off. Later we spot welded them to hold them until they were brazed. Each frame was pre-heated. You had pots there with the brass and flux. You had a spoon. You'd feed them just like it was a bottle or something. You could only do that if it was hot enough inside the forging and tubing. When it cooled off it was solid. Just like one piece. I would assemble them and send them to the brazers. There were five or six guys doing that. I could build fifty frames a day. Later they were put in the oven. They came out flexible just like a spring."

"Indian Joe" Campbell was a welder in the frame department. He agreed, "Those frames, you couldn't bust them. They were really strong. I made hundreds of frames. Joe Seidl was my foreman. I'd work there again. Just keep on going."

Joe Seidl had similar feelings, "I loved working for that company. Forty-two years was a short time. That was my first job and my last job. I had thirty or forty innovations on those frames."

The new tubular forks as first used on the 36EL and subsequently on all Big Twin and post-1940 Forty-five models underwent a grueling

Wisconsin State Rally at Shawano 1937. Riders watch from hilltop as TT races begin down below. *Courtesy of LaVern Radke.*

Joseph Borgen was hired in 1925. He worked in riveting for thirty-six years. He must have hammered millions of rivets over that time. He told me what it was like, "At first our rivet machines were belt-drive. They changed to electric motors in the late thirties. The riveting machine had a shaft with a cam that worked a heavy wooden arm with a plunger. There were different rivet hammers for different jobs. You stepped on a pedal and the hammer went down: 'B-r-r-r-r-p.' We stuck wads of cotton in our ears because of the noise. Putting the sprocket and splash ring on the brake drums we used a squeeze machine. At first each rivet was done one at a time. We did one side then turned it over so it wouldn't get too wobbily. Later we got a machine that pressed all the rivets at once. With the single rivet method some sprockets would be off. They'd wobble a little bit. We had to spin them to see if they were straight. If not we had to straighten them. They had to be perfect. They never came loose. If you sawed through the rivets and brake drum you'd see the metal was like one solid piece."

Department 33 was the paint shop. It was located on the sixth (top) floor. John Behrs was foreman. That space was shared with Department 49, where parts were cleaned and prepared for painting. Over ten-thousand gallons of paint, thinner, and varnish were used each year in the late 1930s.

Painting of fenders and gas tanks followed this procedure: first parts were thoroughly cleaned. Then the prime coat was applied and baked for one hour at 325 degrees. Then parts were hand sanded. Next came the color coat, put on in two layers. Parts were baked again, then followed by a final wet sanding and the varnish coat. Gas tanks followed a similar procedure. On tanks, the stripes were painted by hand then the tank transfers applied. Finally came the vanish coat. With this laborious process it's little wonder that H-D paint was famous for durability.

Wilfred Dotter at 1937 Shawano. Known as the "Tomahawk Thunderbolt" for his hillclimbing skills first with a 36EL and then a 37EL. Here Dotter is shown on 37EL2209 ready to take on Lime Kiln Hill. Note white painted forks and dirty knee. *Courtesy of Ray and Ellen Frederick.*

birthing process. Instead of a solid I-beam forging as on the VL the new style fork began existence as plain tubular stock. This was cut to length and fed into a swaging machine utilizing a tapered die. Five times the top end was squeezed until it reached the correct size. The bottom went through a similar procedure and then the individual fork parts were assembled, brazed, and heat-treated.

In 1988 Harley-Davidson stunned the world by bringing the spring fork ("Springer") back. The only hitch was that nobody knew how to build it anymore. H-D engineers had to go looking for somebody who remembered and they found him in John Nowak. "I said go into the archives," Nowak said, "and get the process sheets from chopping the piece off, to doing this, that, for every operation there's a process sheet. They said, 'The archives don't have that stuff anymore. AMF ditched all that.' So they sat here for two days and I told them how we put that thing together. How the tapered tube was put through a swage. A big cylinder with heavy bars that would clop it like this. The more you pushed it in the smaller it got. And the curve. That was formed as a separate piece. It was heated red-hot then a man would take it from the oven with the end glowing and stick it in the press to put in the curve. Then it was assembled. A guy would ladle brass into the joints until it wouldn't take any more."

Part of the fourth floor was taken up by Department 2: small assembly. Here brakes, wheel hubs, foot boards, ride controls, handlebars, and other items were assembled. Attached to this was Department 66 where riveting was done. In the 1930s many parts were riveted that today are welded or of one-piece contruction. Some riveted parts were saddle pans and bars, seat posts, side bars, brake plates, brake drums, footboards, clutch hubs, and many others. They also installed studs and did bushing and reaming work there.

In 1937 the Forty-five model also received a Sixty-one type upgrade. Recirculating oil and tear drop tanks led the change. Curiously, however, I-beam fork was retained until 1940. Proud owner is Ben Wild. Bike is 37WLD1600. *Courtesy of Dallas Little.*

Dallas Little with 37EL2873 at the 1937 Shawano Rally. Little was member of the Beaver Dam Club. Matching oil tank was unique to 1937 model year. *Courtesy of Dallas Little.*

Albert Hech started at H-D in 1927. For forty-four years he worked in the paint shop and even painted some of "Evel" Knievel's motorcycles. He filled in some details.

"All the parts went through the washers first," Hech said. "First came an acid bath. Then they went through clear water and blown off. Then came the prime coat. Most small parts were dipped. Two men worked the dip tank day and night. The parts were put on rods and dipped by hand. The forks were dipped too. Then they were sent to the oven on iron trucks.

"After they put the prime coat on fenders and tanks it had to be sanded. If there were nicks they puttied them up. It had to be perfect. Sanding was all done by hand. They had big benches with seven or eight guys sanding.

"When I started spraying in 1935 they had all kinds of colors. Real fancy stuff. Fenders and tanks came by on an overhead conveyor. You sprayed the part when it went through the booth. We had water

booths. There was waterfall on the sides of the booth so the paint spray wouldn't come back so much. That change was made before the war. Maybe 1936-1937.

"For frames they had a special table. Take it off the truck and put it upside down where the seat post goes in. You turned it as you sprayed until the frame was done. Then you'd pick it up by the neck, hang it on an iron truck, and shove it into the oven. Gas fired ovens. Big enough for a truck of ten frames.

"When they dropped the green for the different colors it worked this way. They would spray the same color for two or three days. Maybe a week. Then the next day maybe half a day. There was a ten gallon tank next to each booth. That would last pretty much all day. The color would change when they needed to. When a special job came you sprayed it with the quart cup. Maybe do that three, four times a day. They'd want it fast. They had a regular shop on the sixth floor where they mixed special colors. Maybe a sample of the color would be sent in. The guy

A 61 OHV goes into the fence. Event was hillclimb at Shawano 1937. Identity of rider not known. *Courtesy of Harry and Audrey Sebreny.*

119

Uniform contest winners at Shawano 1937. The Madison Motorcycle Club. *Courtesy of Ray and Ellen Frederick.*

Outside the TT races, Shawano rally 1937. *Courtesy of Ray and Ellen Frederick.*

would mix it up. He took care of all the paint. He cleaned out the big tanks and filled them up again. That paint had to be mixed just right.

"In those days the parts were hand striped. John Jung did that. For the three-wheeler boxes they had an artist who painted them by hand. He was an old guy already—I can't think of his name—but he used a brush like an artist would. When he had a lot of them he'd chalk an outline, but if it was just one job he'd do it all by hand. He was good. The early men took pride in their work. You couldn't find a better place. Even if I did start at a quarter an hour."

The third floor was a hot-bed of activity. Here engines, transmissions, and final motorcycles were assembled. Engine assembly was Department 8 on the east end of the floor. Max Jansen was foreman. First flywheels, shafts, bearings, and connecting rods were built up and trued into complete assemblies, then installed in crankcases. Timing gears and generator were then fitted. These bottom end assemblies would then go to one of several men who installed pistons, cylinders, heads, manifold, and other parts. Upon completion each engine received its serial number which was stamped on a raised boss on the left crankcase. Engines were then sent to the storage room in the center of the floor or to final motorcycle assembly on the west end.

Frank "Stinky Davis" Matheus worked for a time in engine assembly during the late 1930s. He remembers how it was: "I'd put the en-

gines together so fast I'd have my quota for the day by noon. The older guys didn't like that. There were only so many parts for so many engines each day. If I went over my quota I'd be taking parts away from some guy down the line doing the same thing I was doing. That caused quite a squabble. The older guys would say, 'He's so damned fast. He ain't making them right. He's taking my living away from me. He's making engines I'm supposed to make.' The extras I made went into the 'bank.' I had thirty or forty engines to my credit. That was extra. You'd keep track of those and they'd pay you."

Department 14 was transmission assembly. It was in the southeast corner on the third floor. The foreman there was Elmer Dahlquist. Upon completion transmissions were tested six at a time. Any needing adjustments went to the repair bench. This was "Squibb" Henrich's job in later years. Squibb, now well up in his nineties, recalls his time with H-D, "Those were the great years of my life. I have no regrets. It was a good time there. I met a lot of nice people and it was always a pleasure. The only trouble with age is that all your old buddies are gone."

Finally we come to Department 18: motorcycle assembly. This was located at the west end of the third floor. Ed Stelzner was foreman. There were two assembly lines, but unless they were busy only one was used. About fifteen men worked on the line. Above them hung rows of freshly painted fenders and gas tanks. At the far end of the room wheels

"Al" Witte in sidecar at Shawano. Note the large travel trunk attached to rear. *Courtesy of Harry and Audrey Sebreny.*

were laced. John Buchta, who started in 1928 and worked on the assembly line in the thirties tells what it was like. "When I was first on the line I put motors into frames," Buchta said. "I had a hell of a time. You had a chain and hook to swing them in there. I'd sweat like hell. I wanted to go too fast. Eventually I got it. When I finished I'd lay my tools on the next motorcycle and wait for the bell to ring.

"Later I put on the exhaust pipes, muffler, and footboards. In those days we used hand tools. Put it on tight. That was our orders. You'd have to be a powerful guy to strip anything. You knew. You'd hear that little 'click' and you'd stop. Motors were easier than exhaust pipes. They had to fit just right. If pipes leaked you caught hell. You wouldn't know how good it was until the testers got it and the boss heard, 'Hey, this guy ain't doing his job right.' Because they wrote down whatever they found wrong. It was immediately reported to the assembly foreman and he'd raise hell with you. Before the union came in I seen a good many guys get a kick in the ass. I seen one guy take a poke at the foreman— that was Stelzner—he was a big guy but this guy was bigger."

The assembly procedure went like this: first a bare frame was set on a wheeled truck. This was attached to a track-like belt in the floor. When the bell rang the trucks were moved ahead. Each man then in-

stalled his parts. They were added in the following sequence: first the rear stand and pre-assembled fork, fender, and front wheel went on. Next came transmission and engine. Then the inner chain guard, oil tank, rear fender, and rear wheel. Chains were then installed and adjusted. Handlebars went on next. Then the instrument panel, footboards, horn, headlight, wiring, muffler, brake cable, gas tanks, and oil lines. Last came an inspection, greasing, and then a guy would enter the motor and order number into the log book. Assembly was a tricky job. Everything had to be done right.

One interesting but poorly understood detail about final assembly in those days was the way serial numbers related to the sequence of motorcycles coming off the line. As stated previously some engines were built ahead of time according to orders on hand and projected sales. Engines received their serial number upon completion but before they were put into motorcycles. A card followed every engine and included its serial and line bore number (the line bore number was stamped to identify matching crankcase halves). The card also gave a history of the engine and any repairs or adjustments made. These cards were retained by the factory under Joe Geiger's supervision. They served a purpose long after the motorcycle was shipped out. Not only did they provide

Madison Club women's auxiliary, Shawano 1937. *Courtesy of Ray and Ellen Frederick.*

Two Sixty-one Overheads and a flathead duke it out in the sand during TT races, Shawano 1937. *Courtesy of Ray and Ellen Frederick.*

mechanical information about each engine, but if a motorcycle was stolen and the serial number ground off, the company could identify it by the line bore number.

Engine numbers started at 1000. In those days engines were built in batches according to model. As a rule serial numbers were used only once for each engine type which means there could be a 37EL1000, a 37UL1000, and a 37WL1000, but not a 37UL1000 and a 37ULH1000. That's why you'll find serial numbers far higher than the quantity of that model built in any given year. For example there was a 41FL4836 when only 2,452 FLs were made in 1941. The lower numbers were a mixture of E, EL, F, and FL models. However, there appear to be authentic serial numbers that fall outside this rule. The reason for such discrepancies are unknown to the author.

To complicate the serial number question was Harley-Davidson's practice of not installing engines into frames consecutively by serial

A well-dressed Green Bay couple. *Courtesy of Ray and Ellen Frederick.*

A big flathead stripped for hillclimbing. Royal Beguhl standing. *Courtesy of Joe Campbell.*

Erv Tursky of Fond du Lac, Wisconsin. One guy described Tursky as "hell and sold on Indians." This pugnacious attitude was essential for an Indian dealer in Harley-Davidson's home state. Stories are told of Erv and his H-D dealer brother Ray trading punches while going side-by-side down the race track. *Courtesy of Euella Trapp.* (1938)

number during final assembly. This runs against one's intuition and was a subject that took some time to untangle. But with the help of several old timers from the factory the following is a fairly accurate account of how engine numbers relate to the final assembly process.

A certain number of engines of all models were constructed ahead of time and before assembly of motorcycles began. This represented at most a few days production. As stated earlier they were given serial numbers when the engine was assembled. This initial run of engines was placed in the engine store room until needed.

The final assembly of motorcycles was done in batches according to how many orders were on hand. Batches of less than ten machines of a single model were seldom run. As motorcycles were assembled engines for them were taken out of the store room in racks of ten. As assembly of complete motorcycles progressed additional motors were built as needed. These either went directly to the assembly line or were put into the store room if surplus. When engines were taken out of storage it was by engine type and not by any particular sequence of engine serial number.

This means that just because you possess a motorcycle with a certain engine number—say 37EL1033—this does not mean yours was the thirty-fourth motorcycle of the EL model type assembled in 1937. In general serial numbers of engines going into finished bikes did progress from lower to higher as the production year went on, but no strict sequence of engine serial numbers was followed on the final assembly line except by what rack of motors happened to be brought over. As John Buchta explained it, "Let's put it this way...they'd rack up whatever model (engines) over here. The other model there. The guy gets orders from the assembly department—the final assembly, 'I need a load a motors.' So, do you think he followed numerical order? No he didn't. Because he wasn't told to do it."

When a rack of engines got to the assembly line no account was taken of engine number there either. "You'd get ten on one truck," Buchta continued. "Five on the bottom, five on the top. Engines went into frames whatever way the guy grabbed them off and threw them in there. If he grabbed the end one—okay—if he grabbed the middle one that was okay too. Just as long as it was the right model motor."

A question naturally arises. How far off sequence could engine numbers be when assembled into motorcycles? According to John Nowak usually not more than one day's production or about sixty engines because normally not many more were stockpiled ahead of time. Sometimes engines would go into frames in or near sequence when the assembly line was busy and hungry for engines. Andrew Bushman, who worked on the assembly line and logged serial numbers into the book, said, "Many times they didn't have enough parts to build engines ahead of time. They'd machine parts and they'd still be hot when the engines were assembled. Sometimes the foreman had a hard time getting enough engines for one day's production. He would study the orders and say for that day's production he needed twenty Sixty-one motors and ten Forty-fives. That's what he'd request for engines. The engine department would try to meet those standards because that would keep the production line moving smoothly."

Occasionally, however, engine numbers might be considerably out of sequence. Sometimes engines in the storeroom would languish in a corner while fresh engines with higher numbers went into frames first. Later the lower numbered engines would get their turn and go into

Beaver Dam Motorcycle Club with Safety Award, 1938. Award was given for going a year with no accidents. Mayor of city front row, second from left. *Courtesy of Euella Trapp.*

Two American icons. Harley-Davidson and Coca-Cola. Bikes are 1938 Forty-fives. *Courtesy of Margaret Pritchard.*

finished motorcycles. Another way for engines to get way out of sequence would be if they were set aside for repairs or adjustments before being mounted in a frame. Andrew Bushman said, "Periodically you'd find one that was way off. The reason for that being the engine was worked on or repaired. The number stayed with the engine, but if it had to be retracted or set aside to be fixed it might sit on the rack for a week or ten days. You had to watch each individual number when logging them in the book because they were always mixed up. Eventually the engine cards balanced out, but they didn't come off the line that way."

The conclusion to be drawn is that a certain engine number is only a general guide to when a particular motorcycle was assembled. They were not built into complete motorcycles in a strict 1000-1001-1002-1003 sequence, but rather in batches with a general rise in serial numbers from low to high, with occasional single or groups of numbers slightly, moderately, or way off numerical sequence.

When motorcycles were finished they were taken downstairs via the west elevator to the test room in Department 35 where Leo Connors was boss. Motorcycles were given final adjustments then started up and stand tested. If everything checked out okay they were given a short road test and readjusted if necessary. Most were then sent to the crating department where Joe Traut and his helpers prepared them for shipment out of Milwaukee by truck, train, or boat. Others were set aside for dealers or new owners to pick up.

Occasionally motorcycles would exhibit problems that the testers couldn't fix by themselves. These were sent up to the second floor to the repair shop: Department 21. Walter Leopold was foreman and George Schulteti assistant foreman. "Hal" Deckert worked in the repair shop in the 1930s. He remembers what most problems consisted of. "Noisy gears mostly," he said. "Sometimes they'd rattle like hell. You'd

try different ones and hope they didn't rattle as much. That's where I learned to use a hammer. When a cover didn't go back on I said, 'Hey George, I can't get this gear cover on.' He came over and said, 'What do you mean you can't get it on?' Bang! 'Anything else?'"

Mistakes were rare but occasionally made. John Nowak also worked in the repair shop in the late thirties. He recalled one example, "On one machine the generator wasn't charging. I took the generator off and the gear was missing. I found out from the card who built that motor and went up there and told him. He came down. He couldn't believe he forgot to put the gear in. He was really concerned about it. This guy was hurting because he made a mistake. That's the kind of people they had working there. Before the war nobody ever took an engine out of a frame. It was unheard of. If there was anything wrong they caught the part in inspection. We changed gears left and right—with the engine in the frame—but I never pushed a motorcycle aside to change an engine or transmission. They were all good because the men working on them were mechanics. They knew every part and everything that went wrong."

Part of this high quality originated in the well-organized planning and communication between top men. Once a week they'd meet over a beer and sandwiches to discuss problems that cropped up since the last meeting. This group included Bill Harley or L.A. Doerner, old Bill Davidson (later George Nortman), Rudy Moberg, Joe Ryan, and Ed Kieckbusch. They'd eat, have a few drinks, talk shop, and kick around ideas, discuss problems and plan out their correction. The problem was usually solved the next day. The system was informal, simple, and very effective.

With the factory tour behind them visitors were taken to the historical exhibit. There they inspected an example of each year Harley-Davidson motorcycle from 1903 on up. From machines whose bicycle roots were still very much in evidence to the ultimate road burner: the

Amherst hillclimb, May 1938. *Courtesy of Ray Wheir.*

Alice Kobs Roemer inspecting gate of Waupun State Prison. Bike is 38EL3325. *Courtesy of Adolph Roemer.*

Ray Tursky at the 1938 Madison races. H-D had another ideal dealer in Ray Tursky. He was also quite a rider. His best win was the famed Jack Pine Enduro in 1934 on a 74 ci VLD. At that time—the twelfth running—Tursky was only the second non-Michigan rider to take the Cow Bell trophy home. The first being William H. Davidson in 1930. Ray's brother Erv came in third in the Class B solo division riding an Indian. That only added fuel to the fire of their famous feud whether or not it was real or feigned. *Courtesy of Euella Trapp.*

Lake Mills run checkpoint. No posing. These guys rode and you can see it here. *Courtesy of Euella Trapp.*

Finish line. Beaver Dam TT race, June 1938. Is that Hap out there with the flag? *Courtesy of Euella Trapp.*

Sixty-one Overhead. Outside behind the guard house the last thing they'd see was the original "woodshed" factory of 1903. One could only gaze in wonder at the great advance of just three decades as the immense brick factory towered over the humble, weather-beaten shack where it all began.

*   *   *

Yet the old order was changing at Harley-Davidson. In early 1937 the factory became a union shop. On April 21 co-founder William A. Davidson died following an illness. He was sixty-seven years old. His duties were assumed by George Nortman, who had followed him from the railroad shops many years earlier.

Of the four founders it was Old Bill the men in the shop knew best. Every man who worked under him had a story to tell. Being vice-president and works manager hadn't taken the common touch from Old Bill. Maybe that came from his own humble origins swinging a hammer in the railroad shops. In spite of his high position at Harley-Davidson his name was listed among ordinary factory employees.

You'd think the boss would take some knocks from the working men, but not in William A. Davidson's case. No one told of him ever raising his voice or getting angry. Stories of Old Bill are endless and always positive—stories of the many turkeys he gave away at Thanksgiving, the Christmas baskets, or the tons of coal he had delivered free of charge. But his generosity went beyond this. In the early days a man working in the cylinder department was hard up. His wife and children were living in a windowless shack. When Old Bill heard about this he supplied the materials and the foreman in the cylinder department, Edward Gamm, and his men pitched in and helped built the family a better house by winter.

One long-time employee recalled William A. Davidson, "Old Bill Davidson helped me. I lost a little girl when she was eight months old. I had no money. No insurance. I went and told him. He knew me even though I was just a worker. He asked, 'How much do you need? And you only pay me back when you think you can afford it.' That's the kind of man he was. He had a heart of gold. I can't say enough good about him."

Another employee recalled, "When Old Bill died I heard they went through his desk and found he had given away thousands of dollars. Not to any one person, but if they had a kid that was sick or trouble with payments or something. In that regard it was like a family."

And yet another, "Old Bill would loan the men money. He put it down on a scrap of paper he carried around in his pocket. When they paid back part of it he'd say, 'Aww, forget the rest.' If you meant to pay if off and were honest he might cut it lower."

One of Old Bill's nephews remembered him like this, "He called me 'Little Artie' and my sister 'Little Maudie.' He had a sneaky sense of humor, but was a very generous guy. One time as a youngster I asked

Nor was water an obstacle. Here a Kenosha rider crosses a stream. H-D circuit breaker was actually waterproof. Bike would stall if water reached spark plugs however. Getting close in this example. *Courtesy of Frank Ulicki.*

Dorothy Mollon Ernst sitting on a 1938 Forty-five model. *Courtesy of Bernard Ernst.*

him something dumb like, 'Are you rich?' He stuck his hand into a pocket and a dollar fell out. He said, 'Artie, if you can't get any more in, that's enough.' He was perfectly content. A kindly guy."

Old Bill's son, William H. Davidson, remembered him this way, "My father was a sportsman. He was a hunter and a fisherman, but in a low key sort of way. His hunting was mostly birds. Duck hunting up at Puckaway. He shot a few rabbits. His real interest was fishing. He was good at it. We had a place at Pine Lake for a number of years. He'd go out in the evening and stay until well after dark. After everybody had left the lake you'd hear his little outboard putt-putting back to the dock."

During the years William A. Davidson was production boss at Harley-Davidson he played a key role in helping to make the best motorcycles possible. He lived just long enough to see the successful introduction and initial refinement of the best and most successful machine his company ever built.

Ray and Florence Wheir on trip to Washington state in 1938. Ray Wheir got started with motorcycles by sneaking his sister's Forty-five out of the garage and riding it. *Courtesy of Ray Wheir.*

With the passing of William A. Davidson the remaining founders realized the old order was passing over to the next generation. It was during this time that Walter Davidson began grooming old Bill's son, William H. Davidson, to succeed him as company president several years before his own passing in early 1942. Again here was foresight shown by practical men to ensure an orderly transition. Walter Davidson made his intentions known to other top members of company management. It might seem logical for Arthur Davidson or William S. Harley as original founders to stand next in line if they survived Walter. Yet they knew the wisdom of turning the affairs of the company over to the most capable of the next generation.

From left: 1928 F-head, a 1937 side-valve Big Twin, a 1938 side-valve Big Twin, and a 1936 VL. Photo taken at West Bend airport where Indian Joe was taking flying lessons. *Courtesy of Joe Campbell.*

William H. Davidson spoke about this planned line of succession within the company when he told me, "Why, I will never know, Walter Davidson said simply, 'You're going to be my successor.' That was long before I became president and long before he became ill. That was known to everyone on the board of directors and the top level of the organization including Bill Harley, Sr., who was still living, and Arthur Davidson, who was in fact my boss at the time. So I went over those fellows. Maybe Walter thought that anyone who had the guts to win the Jack Pine should be given a chance."

*   *   *

Between 1937 and 1939 the Sixty-one Overhead model received constant small changes and improvements. As mentioned earlier, in 1937 frames were strengthened. Also the shift lever was made flat with a stepped shifter gate to replace the less conventional 1936 plunger type. The 100 mph speedometer was updated with the 120 mph face—probably for psychological reasons. In 1937 the oil tank was painted to match the color of fenders and tanks, which looked nice but was difficult to keep clean. Black oil tanks were standard in later years.

In 1938 the ammeter and oil gauges were dropped. These were appealing to the eye but road vibration soon killed them and they were replaced by warning lights. Higher handlebars were also fitted. But the big new news for 1938 was full enclosure for the entire rocker arm and valve spring assembly. Return oil lines from the valve spring enclosures were of larger inside diameter. Oil was also routed through additional passages to the upper ends of the pushrods for more positive lubrication. These changes eliminated most of the faults in the original OHV design. The 1936 and 1937 models could be retro-fitted with the full rocker arm enclosures and most were. As "Honest John" Nowak put it, "At first we just had those cups. Later we put on that fancy cover. It had some fancy dips in it. Fancy screws. It was a silly thing to have it partly open in the first place with the rocker arms flapping around."

In 1939 the factory eliminated the adjustable oil supply feature to the rocker arms and replaced it with a fixed supply. The laborious fiddling around to get the adjustments correct was a thing of the past. Outside of occasional and easy tappet adjustment, the OHV mechanism was now largely maintenance free. That same year a new screen was developed for the breather valve to prevent debris from jamming it. Better valve springs were also fitted.

Adolph Roemer on 38EL3325. Bike was purchased "used" from Bill Knuth. To celebrate the arrival of aviator "Wrong Way" Corrigan in Milwaukee Knuth had the celebrity's name painted in gold letters on headlight shell. Corrigan rode the Sixty-one from the airport to downtown. At one point he opened the throttle wide and sped away from the motorcade. Corrigan bike was later owned by Milwaukee motorcycle cop and club member Ken Bryne. *Courtesy of Adolph Roemer.*

Wisconsin State Rally for 1938 was held at popular tourist area of Lake Delton while Shawano was given a well-deserved rest. Note similarity of pilot's wings on sign to Harley wings. Several of the riders mentioned in this book were also pilots. *Courtesy of Ray and Ellen Frederick.*

The 1939 model received a new instrument panel shroud. Today this later style is commonly called the "cat's eye" or "voodoo mask" to differentiate it from the earlier "skull" or "death's head" style. In 1939 the new "beehive" tail light also made its appearance. This year saw a snappy two-tone paint job on the gas tanks. One unusual change in 1939 was altering the transmission so that neutral was between second and third gear instead of the traditional position between first and second gear. This change was advertised as being easier shifting, but was unpopular even with the experimental department let alone the public. It was dropped the next year.

One small but important modification to the sprocket shaft bearing was made in 1939. The man responsible wasn't Bill Harley, his engineers, or the guys in experimental. It was Uke, the Kenosha H-D dealer. Sixty-ones leaving his shop got gotten the reputation for being especially fast and reliable. In 1938 Uke was summoned to the factory in Milwaukee. Walter Davidson asked Uke, "You're selling OHVs like hotcakes. Why are your's so fast?" There was a bunch of company engineers standing around. They had blueprints of the Sixty-one engine spread out. Uke elbowed them aside and walked over to the drawing of the left crankcase. Pointing to the outer bearing race he said imperiously, "You forgot to drill the oil hole." It was another moment of glory for Uke and red faces among the engineers. Uke never received the credit until now, but the oil hole was there in 1939 and later engines.

The 1936-1939 models all used the classic "flying ball" decal on the gas tanks. As fitted with eighteen inch rims and tires these year machines exhibit a lean grace and beauty somewhat lacking in later Knuckleheads.

During these same years there were countless motorcycle events around Milwaukee. There were runs and rallies with food and beer always rounding out the affair courtesy of Bill Knuth. Sometimes the club met in the basement of Wally Waeck's music shop. Of course there were always a couple guys who wouldn't go home until the beer keg was empty.

On one Turkey Run Johnnie Powers and Johnny Spiegelhoff took home the gobbler with their sidecar rig. "Hal" Deckert came in second riding solo. Walter Davidson, Jr. and Joe Petrali were going great guns in a new green 61 OHV sidecar rig until they took a wrong turn. "Sidecar" Werderitsch got mired in a mud hole along the route. The Kenosha Club was pursuing a new activity: ice racing. Now hearty northern motorcyclists had reason not to put their machines away for the winter. In 1937 the Badger Club put on five sanctioned events: a Spring Run, a Field Meet, a TT Race, the Junior Jack Pine, and a Goose Run.

Badger Club members were winning everything in sight around Milwaukee. Griff Kathcart and Wilbert Seidens won top honors in the Tri-Club Trophy Contest. Only George Feith of the Milwaukee Club placed by taking third. After that it was Badger Clubers all the way:

At the starting line. Rivals Ray and Erv Tursky line up at the Lake Delton Wisconsin State Rally hillclimb in 1938. Neither won hillclimb event, but Ray Tursky won the final TT race. Notice "Fat Boy" style front fender on Ray's 1938 Sixty-one. Photo portrays H-D's Sixty-one wonder weapon pitted against Indian's flathead. Handwriting was on the wall for once dominant Wigwam. *Courtesy of Ray and Ellen Frederick.*

Three Kakuk brothers. Three Sixty-one Overheads. From left: Joe, Steve, and Louis Kakuk. *Courtesy of Mary Kakuk.*

Slinger hillclimb in 1938. Note "bobbed" Sixty-ones. Such stripped competition mounts inspired the "bobber" and "chopper" craze of later decades. Contrary to popular notion origin of "custom" occurred before the Second World War. *Courtesy of Joe Campbell.*

Harry Peters, Fred Sadowske, Bob Stuth, and Gus Stenmark. The high scorer was H-D test rider Griff Kathcart. This former Texan also won the Badger Derby, the Wisconson Championship TT, the Northwoods Derby, and the Illinois State TT Championship. In a single year Kathcart made a total of twenty wins.

In 1937 the second Wisconsin State Rally was held at Shawano. Attendance was 2,500, bigger and better than the previous year. And rowdier. Hap greeted the revelers with the following caution, "Respect your sport. Respect your fellow riders. Respect the name of your club. Respect the citizens and laws of Shawano. Then we'll all get along wonderfully and have plenty of fun. You can cooperate or you can spoil it for yourself and others." A list of don'ts—mostly disregarded—then followed.

One noticeable change was the number of clubs in full uniform. There was also a new activity class: motorcycle drill teams. This gave the rally a distinct para-military style. Ray Tursky's Madison Club, dressed in gold and green uniforms, rode onto the field and put their iron steeds through a series of crisscrosses, figure eights, and circular formations. The Wauwatosa Club topped this. Their maneuvers were run with the flood lights turned off. The headlights on their motorcycles had red and amber colored lens, lending a fantastic quality as they rode in figure-eight formation. Erv Tursky's Fond du Lac Indian Club took second place in the drill team event—although news of it didn't make *The Enthusiast.* The Racine Club took first place as best dressed.

The emphasis on uniforms in the late thirties gave a new look to the motorcycle club scene. Gone was the flat top golfing hat that was universal headgear in the twenties. Its replacement was a soft military-style cap with a short stiff visor. Riders cultivated a characteristic "fifty flight crush" for a casual look unlike stiff police and military hats. In the 1930s H-D came out with its own version in both cloth and leather form thereby creating what later generations know as "the Harley hat."

The full uniformed clubs gave the visual impression of motorcycle troops. This was probably a reaction to what was happening in Europe and the Far East and the increasing militarism of the late thirties. Few riders, however, saw anything ominous in these military-like outfits, they were too busy having fun.

William Muehlenbeck of Saginaw, Michigan, won the 1937 Jack Pine and took home the Cow Bell on an H-D Forty-five. A Sixty-one Overhead was right behind him. "Dot" Robinson of Detroit with Glen

38EL3325 wearing winter windshield. With leg shields and sidecar such machines were comfortable riding even in harsh Wisconsin winters. *Courtesy of Adolph Roemer.*

Another trick photo. Bike is 34VD6448 but is sporting a 1938 style paint job. Yet another case of upgrading one's machine with current paint and decals. *Courtesy of Andrew Bushman.*

Pine and took home the Cow Bell on an H-D Forty-five. A Sixty-one Overhead was right behind him. "Dot" Robinson of Detroit with Glen Cole in the sidecar piloted her 61 OHV rig to second place in the sidecar division. Milwaukee was represented by Wilbert Seidens riding 36EL1404. But the upset winner in the solo class was Erv Tursky of Fond du Lac riding an Indian Scout. In an event dominated by Harley-Davidson motorcycles Erv Tursky stood out like a sore thumb.

Steve Kakuk recalled Erv Tursky, "He was hell and sold on Indians. The rivalry between him and his brother (Ray) was real. He was rough competition. Erv was an authoritive sort of guy. When he was right that was it." Other guys told tales of Ray and Erv Tursky trading punches or kicking as they rode side-by-side during races. Like Kakuk, some said this rivalry was real while others said it was for show. But when one brother was a die-hard Indian man in Harley-Davidson country, the potential for sparks was certainly there. Real or not, you didn't want to get caught between them.

Sixty-ones were showing up in ever greater numbers. In the Riverside, California, Cactus Derby seven of the first eight places went to overhead-valve ELs. Sixty-ones also took the first two places in the Ohio State Enduro. At the 100 Mile National held during the Northern Californa Gypsy Tour and Rally in 1938 ten of twelve finishers were riding EL models. At the Class C Hillclimb Championship at Carbon Cliff in western Illinois in 1939, all six first place finishers went to Harley-Davidson with Sixty-one Overheads predominating. There were countless other events where Sixty-ones took top honors during the late 1930s.

The year 1938 saw the Wisconsin State Rally shifted from Shawano to Lake Delton. After hosting hundreds of motorcyclists for two years running, Shawano deserved a rest and now it was Lake Delton's turn. This tourist mecca near Wisconsin Dells and Devil's Lake was located one-hundred and twenty miles northwest of Milwaukee. It was another great affair of the 1930s. "Hap" Jameson was master of ceremonies. H-D's pretty switchboard operator Stella Forge was there wearing a white riding outfit and caught on film sitting on an new all-white 1938 Sixty-one. At Mirror Lake Hill there were one-hundred and forty attempts to scale the sand and jackpine covered mound. Henry Reiman of Port Edwards won the 80 Novice and 80 Amateur events on 36EL2632. Johnnie Powers made two "rocket-like" runs to win the 45 Expert and 80 Expert events. George Hain of Sheboygan won 45 Amateur. Vernon Krause of Beloit was the only non-H-D winner. Of eleven TT races ten went to Harley-Davidsons. "Roaring" Ray Tursky and Merv Molgaard won three and four events respectively. Tursky was riding a new 61 OHV.

In 1938 the uniformed drill teams were a bigger feature than ever. The Madison Club once again led the way with a team sixteen members strong, resplendent in yellow silk shirts and green breeches, riding matching yellow and green motorcycles. Their leader carried the Madison

131

Chitty outside the Harley-Davidson Company with his new 1938 61 OHV. *Courtesy of John Horstmeier.*

Kenneth Gredler on 38EL3286. Author met Gredler when the latter was terminally ill and almost in coma. But when asked which was faster Gredler replied without hesitation: "Sixty-one." Bike was ridden to New York World's Fair in 1939. It was later sold to Bob Peters who took it to California. It may be there yet. *Courtesy of Kenneth Gredler.*

Adolph Roemer at Holy Hill outside Milwaukee. The Kettle Moraine's rolling countryside and scattered woodlots provide wonderful riding. Autumn colors are spectacular. Author spent many happy hours exploring this region. *Courtesy of Adolph Roemer.*

Wausau Harley-Davidson dealer Mel Krueger with a 1938 61 OHV. Note dealer plate. This was Krueger's personal mount. *Courtesy of Mel and Emma Krueger.*

Alice Kobs Roemer on 38EL3325 near Riverview Road. Her father was Max Kobs, who followed Bill Davidson and George Nortman from the rail shops to the Harley-Davidson Motor Co. He named one of his sons Walter William Arthur Kobs to honor the founders. Max Kobs owned and registered for road use one of twenty-seven V-twins H-D built in 1909. He was killed on a motorcycle in 1922. *Courtesy of Adolph Roemer.*

Club colors. They dazzled the crowd with spinning circles and intertwining figure eights. Across the field the Madison Club Womens' Auxiliary stood at attention and saluted the riders. Precise control and discipline was apparent in every maneuver.

The Racine Club wore uniforms in H-D's own orange and black colors. They circled the field then split into separate columns. Onlookers were dazzled by the overhead spotlights glittering off their chrome rim strips. The small but ambitious New London team sported gray shirts and tan breeches. They went through their formations with military precision and wound up forming the letters "NL" with headlights flashing as the overhead lights were dimmed.

But the Wauwatosa Club upstaged them all. On all-white motorcycles each rider was dressed in white uniforms and white helmets. First they made an intertwining figure eight. Then they shifted into a fast spinning circle. Next they split into two smaller but even faster spinning circles. They finished with a flying V-formation down the length of the field, coming to an abrupt stop in front of the announcer's stand. That must have given old Hap a thrill. Such enthusiasm—just what Harley-Davidson loved so much to see!

The Badger Club's Goose Run in the autumn of 1938 was one to remember. It was a fifty-seven mile long course over sand dunes and beach along Milwaukee's northern lakefront. Then it led over ploughed fields, dirt roads, and through a two block long swamp. Bob Stuth riding 37EL1468 took first prize—a goose—with the runners-up receiving a duck, a chicken, and a pigeon.

The Appleton Club invited riders to take part in their Class C hillclimb at Mosquito Hill. Since the hill had never been successfully topped, a special cash prize was offered to the first person to scale it. The nearby Beaver Dam Club put on their Turkey Run through a hundred and fourteen miles of swamps, marshland, and woods. Gus Stenmark took first place. Wilbert Seidens and Bill Nadler second and third. Some riders got stuck in the mud up to their knees, and eight were stuck in one spot alone.

The Madison Club tried to outdo this by running their New Year's Reliability Run through and over the following obstacles: a stone quarry, old farm roads, swamp, frozen bogs, open creeks, fire lanes, more swamp, and a railroad right-of-way. Donald Arendsee was responsible for laying out the course. Dealer Ray Tursky won it.

The 1938 Jack Pine was noteworthy as the first time a 61 OHV was ridden to victory by Ted Konecy of Saginaw, Michigan. Five hundred and ten miles of sand, swamp, logging roads, river crossings, and

Francis Fredericksen of Racine on 37EL2489. Place is Waukesha hillclimb, July 1938. *Courtesy of Kenneth Gredler.*

Late thirties Forty-five at Waukesha hillclimb, July 1938. Pros didn't approve of riders who dragged their feet. *Courtesy of Kenneth Gredler.*

Indian rider going up—and possibly over backwards. Waukesha hillclimb, July 1938. *Courtesy of Kenneth Gredler.*

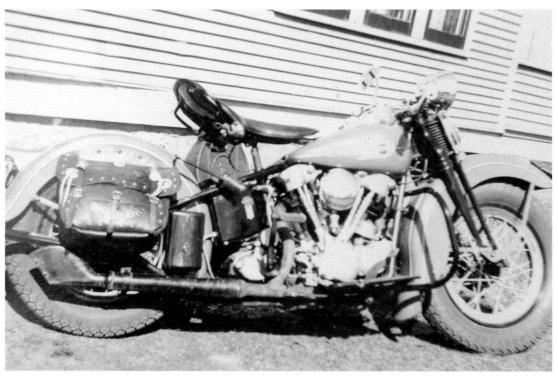

Original owner of 38EL1027 was Ray Frederick. He recalled it being not quite the speedster of his previous 36EL. *Courtesy of Ray and Ellen Frederick.*

Green Bay Motorcycle Club displaying awards, 1938. Dealer "Jib" Arndt, rear row, forth from right. *Courtesy of Fred Process.*

They even dressed up the kids. Child is said to be Earl and "Dot" Robinson's little girl. *Courtesy of Mel and Emma Krueger.*

mudholes over northern Michigan's roughest terrain couldn't stop Konecy's Sixty-one. The Class A solo and Class A Sidecar events were also won by Sixty-ones. Milwaukee was represented by Wilbert Seidens, "Sidecar" Werderitsch, and Bill Nadler.

In the October issue of *The Enthusiast* Hap gave a good description of the conditions riders encountered during that year's Jack Pine, "...they came to a long stretch of dry, hummocky swamp. Actually it seemed almost impossible to cross, even to experiencd Jack Pine eyes. Yet, somehow, the next check, Pioneer, was reached. Arms were numb and sore by this time; yet no one whimpered. As they neared McBain they encountered a black, mucky stretch of swamp. It was tough to drop out here but several just couldn't navigate any farther...Before the devilish Jack Pine country let the riders out of its grasp, there was a washed-out uphill gully to traverse. This monstrosity of nature was four feet deep and so narrow at the bottom that sidecar outfits rode with one wheel in the bottom and the other up the side at a precarious

The Kenosha Motorcycle Club, 1939. Dealer Frank "Uke" Ulicki on left. Given the okay by Arthur Davidson in 1930, Uke is the oldest dealer still running his shop on a daily business. Uke says he'll stay that way until they carry him out. *Courtesy of Frank Ulicki.*

angle...After hearing what the finishers had to say, this year's course would have been ideal for testing army tanks."

Army tanks? Where did that come from? Perhaps a mere slip of the tongue—or did Hap have something else on his mind? What's interesting in these late thirties enduros were the combat-like conditions under which they were run. The spartan meals under canvas had a military flavor. The special Jack Pine fenders with their cut-away side panels bear great resemblance to those on later WLA army Forty-fives. By this date the military was snooping around Juneau Avenue and showing renewed interest in combat motorcycles. One wonders how innocent Harley-Davidson's interest in these endurance runs actually was.

One interesting contest of 1939 began with a notice in the June issue of *The Enthusiast*. The newly organized Jackpine Gypsies Motorcycle Club of Sturgis, South Dakota, announced some dirt track races for August 12 and 13. They added this final challenge, "Here's hoping that some of those boys who think they are good on the dirt track will come up and take a shot at our $750 worth of prize money."

That was big money in 1939. You could buy a brand new 61 OHV and still have three hundred bucks left over. No wonder it caught the attention of a young hot shot with racing ambitions named Johnny Spiegelhoff. It was at Sturgis he got his first chance at fame.

Every 1930s rider from Milwaukee and environs knows of Johnny Spiegelhoff. He was a flamboyant racer with a style all his own and his personality matched. As Andrew Bushman recalled him, "Spiegelhoff was a rascal. We drank together and went to the clubhouse. He was a dynamic rider. At the start he was a big Harley racer."

That will come as a surprise to Indian fans who know Johnny Spiegelhoff best for his win at the Langhorne 100 and a spectacular victory at the Daytona 200, both in 1947. These wins are noteable in that they came during Indian's twilight years when the field had turned against that once proud make. What Indian fans might not know is that

Early Sixty-one Overhead at the Fond du Lac TT race, July 1939. Sharp turns and loose dirt turned such contests into "tricky trials." *Courtesy of Adolph Roemer.*

Mary Trapp (right) and friend at 1939 rally. Three bikes in foreground (left to right) are 39EL2625; 37ULH4741; and 37WLDR1098. This last belonged to "Hal" Deckert's other brother-in-law Fred Sadowske. He also worked at Harley-Davidson for a time and was successful racing before being injured in 1939. *Courtesy of Euella Trapp.*

before the Second World War Spiegelhoff was a hard-core Harley-Davidson man. By the late thirties he was making quite a name for himself on Midwest dirt tracks. In 1938 Spiegelhoff took both the Wisconsin and Minnesota dirt track championships. He was also a mechanic for Bill Knuth and for a time worked at Harley-Davidson in the inspection department and on final motorcycle assembly.

"Hal" Deckert was married to Spiegelhoff's wife's sister, making them as he said, "More or less brother-in-laws." For a while Deckert served as pit crew for Spiegelhoff and that's how Deckert knows what happened at Sturgis in 1939.

"John D. thought he couldn't miss going up into that area," Deckert said, "but it got to be very interesting. We had a racing machine and were practicing on the Sturgis track. Then a local rider named Al Nelson came roaring out from town on his Indian. He didn't have a muffler and we could hear him coming. He got on the track and made a couple circles. I said to my brother-in-law, 'Boy, that looks like trouble.'

"Well, came the races and poor Spiegelhoff never had a chance. Nelson whipped the pants off him. That evening the two dealers—Indian and Harley-Davidson—decided tomorrow would be the payoff. When we went out Sunday morning Spiegelhoff gets over there by Nelson and says, 'Look, I know you can beat me, but why not put on a show for the people? Let me get ahead of you once and vice versa.' Nelson agreed. But once John got ahead of him he never let go. Nelson was new to the dirt and it was real dusty. John said the only way he knew he was still on the track was to watch the posts go by. But he whipped Nelson. That made the Indian riders crazy. The next year they made Sturgis into a rally."

In 1940 the Jackpine Gypsies obtained an AMA sanction for a Gypsy Tour of the Black Hills to compliment their races, and it was the official beginning of the great annual rally held to this day at Sturgis. In the beginning, however, it was just some local races on a dusty, half-mile track, at least until some Milwaukee boys showed up and created a stir.

Shortly afterwards Spiegelhoff switched loyalties from Harley-Davidson to Indian. It was a radical move to make. Brand loyalty was more polarized than ever; if you rode an Indian with a bunch of Harley riders chances are you brought up the rear. So why did a Milwaukee boy with factory connections like Spiegelhoff jump ship? From time to time this question comes up. Spiegelhoff's freedom loving and rebellious personality alone might explain it, but those who knew him shed addi-

Elaine Byrne on a 1939 61 OHV. This machine is another with an all white paint scheme. Spotlights were increasingly popular but six volt generator wasn't quite up to the job. Outside charging was needed when machine was used frequently after dark. *Courtesy of Ken Bryne.*

Bernie Gessler at the Cedarburg races, May 1939. Gessler was a test rider at the factory for a short while. One day on an experimental machine he stopped at Ralphie Heger's West Side Cycle—something strictly forbidden. By chance a second generation Davidson happened by, saw the factory machine parked outside, and gave Gessler hell. *Courtesy of Virginia Gessler.*

Below:
Caption on original, "Alice holding the Sixty-one—Yep, she can handle it—she did ride it!" *Courtesy of Adolph Roemer.*

Pretty girls and motorcycles always go together. Ann Hendricks of Milwaukee. *Courtesy of Dallas Little.*

Kenosha TT races, 1939. Notice bike on right is off the ground. *Courtesy of Adolph Roemer.*

Starting line at the Racine races, 1939. *Courtesy of Virginia Gessler.*

Beaver Dam dealer James Trapp wife and child in sidecar outside H-D factory. Rig is 39EL4039. Several old photos show neighborhood kids hanging around H-D's front entrance. *Courtesy of Euella Trapp.*

tional light. While not privy to Spiegelhoff's exact reasons "Hal" Deckert knew the immediate cause.

"He gave up Harley-Davidson after Sturgis," Deckert recalled. "When he came back the guy who built the engines for Nelson—the Indian dealer out there—got him to go over to Indian. Spiegelhoff wasn't working for Harley-Davdison then."

Andrew Bushman recalled a little more, "Spiegelhoff was disappointed with the way the (Harley-Davidson) racing department handled him. He wanted certain alterations done on the motor and it wasn't meeting their expectations and they wouldn't help him so he helped himself. He got disgusted with the Harleys and got an Indian. He was out to win and that was his alternative. Believe me he had a knack of doing it too. Spiegelhoff beat a lot of Harleys. But then I lost touch with Spiegelhoff because Indian people and Harley-Davidson people didn't get along together theoretically."

During Indian's last years Spiegelhoff was their Milwaukee dealer. He had a small shop on North Avenue but that didn't last either. Spiegelhoff never could settle down for long. He ended up packing his worldly goods on a Servi-Car and moving down to Mazatlan, Mexico. He died there sometime in the 1960s and so ended the colorful career of John D. Spiegelhoff.

*   *   *

The biggest news of 1939 was not available on an order blank or on the dealer's floor, at least not yet. Riding high on their success with the Sixty-one Overhead model, Harley-Davidson had two new OHV models up their sleeve. By 1939 these were in the prototype stage and ready for extensive road testing.

Two years earlier Bill Harley and his engineers began working on a smaller companion for the 61 OHV. With performance and piston reliability in the Sixty-one vastly improved over the side-valve engine a 45 OHV seemed a logical additon to the line-up. This 45 OHV project, however, was not a new machine from the ground up like the Sixty-one had been. New overhead-valve cylinders and heads were grafted on the standard Forty-five bottom end. Valve enclosure was complete and the pushrod side of the heads bore no resemblance to the Sixty-one. The cylinders, however, were in essence miniature Knucklehead barrels. The standard Forty-five piston had a cute little dome on it. The bottom end was built around WR (racing) components with ball bearings for the timing gears and cams. The gear cover looked identical on the outside to that on the standard Forty-five side-valve engine, but inside it contained a maze of oil passages. The oil line to the heads came off the oil pump. With experience gained from the Sixty-one H-D engineers had

Ray Tursky hitting another rider at the Madison races sometime in the late thirties. Is it brother Erv? Not likely. The other bike is a Harley. *Courtesy of Royal Beguhl.*

Original caption: "Alice trying sidesaddle." *Courtesy of Adolph Roemer.*

Beaver Dam TT races, June 1939. Two Sixty-ones duke it out. *Courtesy of Adolph Roemer.*

come up with an improved second generation overhead-valve engine. It was designed to be a motor that would not leak, but was built as a perfectly sealed unit. Other than the engine the motorcycle utilized standard Forty-five side-valve parts. In this way the factory could test the 45 OHV without going to the great expense of designing a totally new machine.

The other new OHV in 1939 was a bored and stroked Big Twin displacing seventy-four cubic inches. On the outside you couldn't see any difference from the Sixty-one, but this was the future 74 OHV model.

By early 1939 both prototypes were ready. Like other times in Harley-Davidson factory history officials turned the experimental machines over to test riders who packed some tools, spare parts, and promised to go easy on the expense account. Then they pointed their machines in the direction of distant lands. This time two machines and two riders would go. The destination was Texas—by way of Florida.

The riders on this trip were Art Kauper and Art Earlenbaugh. They were gone six weeks, during which time they put five thousand miles on the prototype 45 OHV and 74 OHV machines. As mentioned earlier Earlenbaugh died in 1941. Kauper went on to take charge of the entire H-D experimental department but in the late 1930s he was a test rider. This would be the longest trip he ever made in that position. What makes it interesting is that it was taken on a machine H-D enthusiasts know little about, for while the 74 OHV went on to achieve immortality the 45 OHV died prematurely, just like Art Earlenbaugh. In recent years Art Kauper spoke at length about the 1939 trip. Because the 45 OHV had no subsequent career this solitary description of its road performance over fifty years ago has special value.

"We left Milwaukee in February of 1939," Kauper began. "It was the longest trip I ever made as a test rider. We were gone six weeks. We came close to riding five thousand miles during that time. We were testing new models. One was a model we never came out with. It was a type of Forty-five. An overhead-valve Forty-five. The other machine was an experimental Seventy-four (OHV). On the outside it looked pretty much like our existing Sixty-one.

"There was just one Forty-five Overhead on the trip. It was built of parts not all intended for use on the production model. A mock-up in the sense that it wasn't made on production tools. It was one of a kind. They did have others, but only one went on the trip.

"Along with me was a fellow by the name of Art Earlenbaugh. He died many years ago. We rode both machines, but I mostly rode the Forty-five. We were told, 'Just test it.' We left in wintertime. Both machines had winter windshields and sidecars. There was snow and ice. A

Another tricky one. A 1929 Forty-five wearing a 1936 style paint job. Rider is Bernie Gessler. Place is Shawano State Rally, June 1939. *Courtesy of Virginia Gessler.*

Getting ready to go. Milwaukee Motorcycle Club members outside clubhouse before leaving for 1939 Shawano rally. From left is a 1939 Forty-five, a 1939 Big Twin side-valve, and a 1938 61 OHV. *Courtesy of Harold Deckert.*

Beaver Dam club looking good at the 1939 Shawano Rally. Bike is 1939 61 OHV. Clean late thirties lines evident on this fine machine. Paint job on 1939 model carried frame line up through gas tanks. Nice. *Courtesy of Euella Trapp.*

On the road: 1939. Bike on left is 37EL1987 with thirty-six style gas tank paint. Bike on right is a 1934 Forty-five wearing 1939 paint. Owner of Sixty-one was Joe Zedoff of Milwaukee, who recalled his bike this way, "That bike didn't accelerate, it exploded." *Courtesy of Joe Zedoff.*

storm like you wouldn't believe. It was cold when we left Milwaukee. Very cold. But it wasn't snowing yet. By the time we got to Racine County down old Highway 41 there was snow coming down and it was blowing hard. When we got to Kenosha County there was an awful lot of snow. Of course we had the third wheel, but it was getting to be pretty tough going. When we got to Illinois the police were stopping people from going farther. Earlenbaugh and I talked. What are we going to do? We could go back. That would be the sensible thing. But our foreman at that time (Ed Kieckbusch) was the kind of guy who would tell you how once he got stuck in the desert and built a wheel up that collapsed in order to go farther. That's the kind of guy he was. So we didn't want to go back and spend the rest of our lives listening to how *he* could have gotten through there.

"Well, we couldn't go through on Highway 41 so we rode across a farmer's field where the wind had blown the snow off. Then we took side roads until we got to the outskirts of Chicago. Here there were streetcars running so we got into the streetcar tracks where the snow was piled to the side and followed them to a hotel. We were glad of that.

"Next day they cautioned everyone to stay off the road. But we decided we better go anyway. They had cleared the streetcar tracks so it was like a canyon with snow walls on both sides. We started up and headed out behind a streetcar which was really slow picking up passengers. Then the Big Twin (74 OHV) got a flat tire. There we were in this snow canyon with no place to go. Finally we found a filling station that was shoveling out. We asked to go in there. At first the guy didn't want to let us. Then he gave us a corner and we repaired it and got back on the machines. We had that kind of snow until we got to Danville then it began to let up. We just couldn't stand the thought of going back and not getting through."

From there Kauper and Earlenbaugh rode south to Pensacola, Florida. Then they followed the Gulf of Mexico to Texas. The factory wanted the machines tested in Texas, but they wanted road miles too. The side trip to Florida seemed a good way to get some mileage in. Besides, after surviving that Chicago blizzard the two Milwaukee boys were anxious to get south as soon as possible. In Texas they made their headquarters at San Antonio. From that city to the Mexican border was about a hundred fifty miles. They rode it every day.

"When we got to San Antonio we took off the windshields and

Tired of looking at Harleys? Try this OHV Crocker. Machine was built in small numbers in California by former Indian man Albert Crocker before the Second World War. Machine shown was registered in Wisconsin to Edward Rushka and is number 3961107—probably the seventh machine built in 1939 of sixty-one cubic inch displacement. Crockers were fast, possibly faster than H-D's 61 OHV, but made in numbers so small they made no inroads. *Courtesy of Royal Beguhl.*

sidecars," Kauper continued. "We stored the sidecars at a garage that we could use for whatever service we might have to do. We changed sprockets for solo riding. Then we did some high-speed testing. We did some off-the-road testing too, but not to any great extent. Nothing unusual. Mostly it was an endurance test to see how things went. Some fast riding. Some rough riding."

And the performance of the 45 OHV?

"Good," Kauper said, "Exceptionally good. It was a very good

Jim Trapp mired in the mud. Assistance provided by Clarence Thiede. Bike is 1939 Sixty-one Overhead. When they called these endurance runs they weren't kidding. *Courtesy of Euella Trapp.*

Slinger hillclimb July 1939. Bike is a Super X. Rider unknown. *Courtesy of Adolph Roemer.*

Mary Trapp sitting on 37ULH4528. Bikes built that year were heavily pin-striped on both fenders. *Courtesy of Dallas Little.*

Participants in the November 1939 Beaver Dam Turkey Run. Hitching post in lower left-hand corner was a remnant of a fast vanishing age. *Courtesy of Euella Trapp.*

Late thirties endurance runs were no picnic. Here Al Campshure on 39WLDR2021 (left) and Roland Bent with a 1936 Indian urge their bikes through a river crossing. *Courtesy of Orville Process.*

Cool couple on their Sixty-one, 1939 model. *Courtesy of Euella Trapp.*

Original caption: "Alice riding it backwards after a few beers, Betty and Warren's Tavern, Germantown, Wisconsin, 1939." At one time Milwaukee's Schlitz brewery was world's largest. Now defunct except for the name used by a Detroit brewer for its cheap label. *Courtesy of Adolph Roemer.*

motorcycle. Very fast. Fast and very responsive. It was pretty close to the Big Twin (74 OHV) we had along with us. There was another nice thing about it. With the sidecar and windshield it was still very responsive. The regular Forty-five wasn't so good with a sidecar. But that Forty-five Overhead pulled a sidecar exceptionally well. It was a very good motorcycle. When we got back I wrote a positive report. I was disappointed that it didn't go into production."

But if the 45 OHV was so good why was it dropped before it was ever produced?

"The transmission," Kauper said. "That might not have been adequate for what power that engine could produce. But all that was determined during the inspection made after we got back. Decisions were made on the top level. The decisions that the company made were never discussed with the people in the testing department. Those were management decisions and that's the way it went."

In order to build a motorcycle able to withstand the power output of the 45 OHV an entirely new transmission needed to be developed. Several factors weighed against going that route. One was the increased costs of building a 45 OHV and the slight profit margin involved. Another was a new improved piston Harley-Davidson had developed for the big side-valve models.

One reason for developing a 45 OHV was the plan to drop the flatheads because of continuing piston trouble. Side-valve piston skirts would sometimes get so hot that the alloy would fail or seize in the cylinder bore. Over the years all sorts of slots and braces had been incorporated into pistons to stop the heat flow or hold the piston together. Finally in 1937-1938 Harley-Davidson developed an improved piston that worked fairly well. This was patented in 1939 under Bill Harley's

This looks serious. Knuckles on Ken Straub's 39E1334 nearly submerge as he hits a hole following in the wake of Roger Harper's Sixty-one. Bill Harley's right hand man when 61 OHV was designed was an ex-U-boat engineer. But it's doubtful he had this in mind. Why not try it with your Evolution? *Courtesy of Orville Process.*

Some things never go out of style. Three pretty girls on a motorcycle. Sidecar is a Goulding. Cycle is 39E2343. *Courtesy of Margaret Pritchard.*

A well-dressed 39EL with some of the Beaver Dam gang. *Courtesy of Euella Trapp.*

name, but old factory men say that Ed Kieckbusch was instrumental in the improved piston's development.

This piston had a steel web or strut that was anchored along the entire inner length of the opposing piston-skirt thrust faces. Because the steel strut had a lower co-efficient of expansion than the aluminum piston body, it kept the piston-skirts from over-expanding and sticking in the bore. The practical result was increased piston reliability in the Big Twin side-valves. This somewhat altered plans to replace the side-valve line with overheads and gave the flatheads a few more years of life. It also helped kill off the 45 OHV. "Hap" Jameson, long an advocate of lighter weight sporting models, was furious when the 45 OHV was dropped, but then Hap might have been privy to other reasons too.

Since 1937 the U.S. Army had been working with Harley-Davidson on improved military motorcycles. The army wasn't interested in a speedy, high-performance bike. For them the utilitarian Forty-five flathead was ideal and as time went on the army was looking like H-D's biggest potential customer. This time the riders weren't consulted.

Yet the 45 OHV did not totally die. It probably influenced the redesigned rocker arm assembly on the 1948 Big Twin OHV engine—the Panhead. During the early 1950s when Harley-Davidson was developing an overhead-valve successor to the K-model the 45 OHV was taken out of storage and dusted off for another look. When the brilliant all-aluminum KL engine proved too troublesome the heads from the old 45 OHV were lifted and grafted to the K-model. It was an easy job because the pushrods already lined up. The head was restyled but left in its orginal iron form, thus in a way the old 45 OHV lives on in a model that exists to the present day: the "Sportster."

The above tale shows the luck of the draw for both humans and motorcycles. Two test riders named Art, two OHV motorcycles. One man and one motorcycle went on to long and productive careers with the Harley-Davidson Motor Company—both Art Kauper and the 74 OHV retired together in 1978. But the other Art—Art Earlenbaugh—died in 1941. By chance that was the same year the 45 OHV would have been introduced to the public. Coincidence? Most likely. Such are the whims of fate and the toss of the dice!

Herbert Raabe raises dust on 38EL3069 during the July 1939 Fond du Lac TT races. Raabe was a well-known Milwaukee rider. He also owned an early 1936 Sixty-one: 36EL1507. In 1940 he upgraded again with 40EL1762. A new Sixty-one every two years. *Courtesy of Adolph Roemer.*

James Trapp on a Turkey Run. Bikes took some hard knocks as evidenced by bashed-in headlight. This was the main reason why fenders and headlights were removed. It wasn't a fashion statement. *Courtesy of Euella Trapp.*

Texas has produced many talented racers. One was Tommy Hayes. Here he's shown at the State Fair Park racetrack near Milwaukee in 1939. Hayes was killed along with another rider at the Oakland 200 Mile race in California in August 1941. Remembering Hayes, one guy from Harley-Davidson said, "Hayes was clipping off firsts and seconds all the time. He was hot. Those guys used to live right in the factory watching their motors being rebuilt." *Courtesy of Ken Bryne.*

Unknown rider showing good form at the Slinger hillclimb, July 1939. *Courtesy of Adolph Roemer.*

On hands and knees checking out his Sixty-one. Bumper on bike in front is first hint of coming "garbage wagon" trend. *Courtesy of Margaret Pritchard.*

Madison TT races. Sharp curves and uneven terrain marked this type of race. Cycles are stripped of front fenders, headlights, rear fender ends, and mufflers in usual manner. More inspiration for "bobber" and "chopper" craze. *Courtesy of Euella Trapp.*

Johnny Spiegelhoff near the end of his racing career as a Harley-Davidson rider. Spiegelhoff worked both for Bill Knuth and the Harley-Davidson factory where he was an inspector and worked on final assembly. Here Spiegelhoff is shown on a late thirties Forty-five racer, possibly the same bike he rode at Sturgis in 1939. By 1940 he had switched over to Indian. *Courtesy of Ken Bryne.*

Indian rider crashes wall at Sturgis in 1939. Dirt track races were initiated in 1938. Big $750 prize money the next year tempted Johnny Spiegelhoff and his brother-in-law "Hal" Deckert up from Milwaukee. Spiegelhoff's tricking the Indian rider may have helped change the course of history. *Courtesy of Harold Deckert.*

Sheboygan hillclimb, July 1939. *Courtesy of Adolph Roemer.*

Forty-five overhead-valve engine shows distinct style all its own. Heads and cylinders may have been designed by skilled hands of Charlie Featherly in H-D's engineering department. In the early 1950s it was taken out of storage and dusted off when the Sportster was being developed. It may also have influenced the Panhead. *Courtesy of Carman Brown.*

Opposite page, top:
45 OHV in the snow. Setting is appropriate as test prototype model was caught in a Chicago blizzard on way south in February 1939. Machine is essentially a factory Forty-five except for cylinders and heads. Bike was reported to be a snappy mount. *Courtesy of Carman Brown.*

Opposite page, bottom:
According to factory test rider 45 OHV was a sweet machine and a positive report was written. Factory didn't pursue concept for a variety of reasons. Dropping it made "Hap" Jameson furious. It's easy to see why. This sole surviving example is a beauty. *Courtesy of Carman Brown.*

CHAPTER SIX:
74 OHV and Rumors of War

Just go!
William S. Harley

By 1940 the country was drifting towards war, yet most motorcyclists had little interest in events in Europe and Asia. That was ironic because if war came their generation would do the fighting. But war wasn't on their minds, having fun was—and what do riders enjoy most but their motorcycles!

In Milwaukee a dozen motorcycle clubs were in existence. Nationwide the AMA could boast seven hundred clubs under its auspices. Bill Knuth sponsored his third club: the Sky Chief Motorcycle Club. Their headquarters were an abandoned house members had acquired and renovated. Not much is known about them as the club's existence was cut short by Pearl Harbor.

Endurance runs were as much fun—and tough—as ever. Griff Kathcart or Gus Stenmark usually took first place at the events held around Milwaukee. These guys thought nothing of flinging 45s and Big Twins over river crossings, bumping over plowed fields, slogging through swamps, and crashing through thickets. The Beaver Dam Club was noted for its tough runs laid out by dealer James Trapp. The Rock Valley Club (Lake Mills) fielded several good riders; member Bill Nadler took the State Novice TT Championship in 1940 at Madison.

That same year Beloit hosted the Class C Hillclimb Championship. As usual Harley-Davidson reigned supreme in its Midwest stronghold, taking five of six first place wins. Uke was caught on film roaring up Big Hill on 40EL1428. Hank Reiman won the 80 Expert Event. The Waukesha Club entertained the crowd—ten-thousand strong—with a fine display of stunt riding. Pete Ulicki, the third and youngest brother in that H-D loving family, did well in the 45 Amateur Event riding 37WLD3291. Pete worked at the factory and would help assemble the first prototype XA experimental army model.

Elkhart Lake was the scene of the 1940 Wisconsin State Rally. By now just about everyone attending was in full uniform. Eddie Underburg and Frank Werderitsch were mobbed at the registration table. Ken Beschta of the Badger Club was top motorcycle game winner and Miss Beatrice Bare of Lake Mills was top woman rider. Again motorcycle drill contests were prominent, as were American flags. Madison took first and Waukesha—with a drum and bugle corps—took second place. Ray Tursky won the big final TT event.

The new 1940 models saw several changes, including a new gas shut-off and instant reserve valve located in the left gas tank. Instead of fumbling under the tanks for a petcock riders now simply unscrewed a handy knob for the main supply and yanked it up for reserve.

The 1940 models no longer sported the classic gas tank decals of former years. In their place were chromed nameplates and in 1941 two metal trim strips were added. The 1940 models also received new footboards of curved design replacing the older rectangular style that went back to 1914. The timing gear cover was given a ribbed design. The 1940 pattern cover was unique to that year only.

A new teardrop shaped toolbox also appeared in 1940 but the biggest change that year was the introduction of 5:00 X 16 inch wheels and low pressure tires. These soon became standard and were popular for their easy riding qualities. Handling suffered, however, as did the Sixty-

Ready to go. Pete Ulicki with a 37WLDR before the TT race. *Courtesy of Peter Ulicki.*

one's former sleek good looks. Although the bigger tires were advertised as being safer they actually created handling difficulties. At highway speed the bigger tire was prone to wobble, at low speed the big wheel and tire gave the motorcycle a heavy feel. The big tires tended to develop square edges as they wore down, which made cornering less precise than the older 4:00 X 18 inch tire.

In 1941 the frame neck angle was increased for greater fork trail and better stability at speed. For earlier frames running the five inch wheel and tire the factory had a quick fix. John Nowak recalled, "We'd tell the dealer to 'bump' it. Take a sledge hammer to the top rail give it a whack. That would bring it up closer to thirty degrees. That was a field correction to make it handle better."

Beloit hillclimb. *Courtesy of Adolph Roemer.*

The author has a pet peeve here. In 1974 he was riding 50FL1578 along the Wisconsin River south of Tomahawk on County Trunk E. The bike had stock sixteens front and rear. Coming out of an S-curve at about 30 mph those tires led to trouble. They were worn a little squarish and there was some sand on the road and as a result the machine wasn't leaned over as much as it should have been. The bike got over on the shoulder slightly which would have been okay except for an old iron bridge suddenly blocking the trail. Luckily a wooden post and sign reduced the impact somewhat. After a moment of unreality as bridge, motorcycle, and author merged, the author found himself lying peacefully on road. But the Big Twin had vanished. Above the song of birds, however, came a curious bubbling sound—looking over the embankment author saw his motorcycle beneath six feet of water!

During impact the author's helmet (mandatory in those days) went flying and ended up floating down the river where it caused wild speculation among fishermen downstream who saw wreck occur. "He's dead! He's dead!" a little girl screamed. Author blandly asked, "Who?" By luck a farmer happened to come past with a front end loader. A heavy rope was obtained and attached to the motorcycle frame. Mr. Farmer then proceeded to lift the FL out. The wheels were turning as they climbed the concrete embankment. It looked like a big brown carp coming out of the water. A bystander hollered, "Catch anything, Charlie?" The author still owes that county for post and sign. Back home the author's dealer "Bud" Pater said, "If you want that thing to handle like a sport bike dump that fat doughnut up front for an eighteen." True words of wisdom!

Back in the thirties it wasn't always fun and games either, then as now riders got themselves in trouble. Some bikes obtained the reputation of being jinxed or unlucky and stories got around—true or not. Ed Kubicki told the tale of 38EL2529. "I bought that thing from a Chevy garage in Stevens Point," Kubicki said. "It was like new, but it was a hoodoo. I had problems. I ran into a wall with it. Another guy was killed. That was a fast buggy. I never really opened it up, but once had it up to ninety. There were washouts in the road. Ice underneath. I gave it a little too much—zip—and then went into a wall. I got banged up pretty bad and sold the bike. The guy who bought it was going to Wausau to join the motorcycle club. He never made it. He ran into a car and was killed. It was a bucking bronco that one. Maybe it was too fast. Nobody had any luck with it."

Usually it was the rider and not the motorcycle. Anyone who rides two wheels knows how easy it is to get into trouble. Heck, it happened to Ray Frederick one Sunday on 36EL2091 on his way to church. "It was on Christmas," Frederick recalled. "I was dressed up real nice. There

Henry Hartlaub with a 1940 Big Twin flathead. That year saw the first 5:00 X 16 wheels and tires. *Courtesy of Andrew Bushman.*

Fun and games 1930s style. Milwaukee Motorcycle Club frolics in the Milwaukee River. This same photo ran with author's article about test rider "Hal" Deckert. Author's caption was changed by editor who called these guys and gals H-D test riders. Not true. Modern minds have difficulty believing ordinary riders and not test riders had the courage to pull such stunts. *Courtesy of Harold Deckert.*

Jim Trapp (left) and Clarence Thiede. Bike is 40EL1138 stripped for Class C action. Curved footboards first appeared in 1940. Seen here on Thiede's bike. *Courtesy of Euella Trapp.*

was no snow, but some kind of fog that made a glaze or ice you couldn't see. I hit it right in front of the church where people were going in. The bike began to slide sideways in front of the crowd. I received some very stern looks. They all thought I did it on purpose."

A similar case of unexpected trouble that looked like a planned stunt happened during a 1940 trip made to the West Coast. John Horstmeier was riding 37EL1606 and his friend Roger Ames was on a new Forty-five. In North Dakota they saw a sign on the highway warning of a "dip" up ahead.

"In Illinois you could hit a dip at seventy," Horstmeier remarked. "Up there the road was gone. The front wheel went over and when the rear wheel hit it flipped me right up in the air. I was actually doing a handstand on the handlebars. There was a VFW meeting in Grand Forks and the cars were all coming at us so I had to keep the motorcycle going straight. I had it with one hand and almost missed it with the other when I came down. Somehow I managed to get back on the seat. My knee was hooked over it and my collar bone dented the headlight."

One can only speculate what the occupants in those automobiles thought when they saw a motorcycle coming at them with the rider doing a handstand—it probably wasn't pleasant.

Some flathead riders spread stories that Sixty-ones were more dangerous than other motorcycles, but as the Sixty-one's reputation grew, guys switching over from the side-valve saw the transparency of those claims. John Benner, owner of 38EL2627, told that story, "They said that Sixty-ones were killers. But I think a lot of guys were jealous. The Sixty-ones were beating them. The one I had, a guy named Schleuter took it for a ride and flopped it. Then the guys told me, 'Don't take that bike. It's a killer.' But I wanted that Sixty-one bad. It was a better running bike than my 31VL. Faster. You could run it sixty-five, seventy-five miles an hour all day and it didn't bother it one bit."

The big news for 1941 was the 74 OHV Big Twin. While the Sixty-one had a reputation for being smooth running and plenty fast, riders always preferred more power and speed and Harley-Davidson was will-

ing to give it to them. Here was Harley-Davidson's ultimate king of the highway. Bore and stroke was increased to 3-7/16 inches by 3-31/32 inches yielding 73.66 cubic inches (1207 cc). Larger flywheels were fitted. At 5,000 rpm output was forty-eight horsepower. The machine was good for an honest one hundred miles per hour. The 74 OHV would go through several incarnations while remaining Harley-Davidson's top-of-the-line model until 1978 when it was superseded by·the 80 OHV.

In 1941 a totally new clutch was introduced. This clutch—supreme in ruggedness—did away with the old splined clutch hub and discs for a simple, heavy-duty design. The older style had the tendency to stick and drag but the new clutch incorporated hardened steel pins upon which the fiction discs rode and was smooth and dependable. The friction area was increased sixty-five percent over the former style. Harley-Davidson clutches had always been good, but this one was near perfection. They were quite justified calling it a "Super Clutch." It was designed to handle the additional horsepower of the 74 OHV twin although in reality hefty enough for a small car. This clutch was so good that H-D kept it intact for forty-three years.

The continuing improvement in the national economy and the increasing popularity of the OHV Big Twins can be seen in a rise in production numbers—the figure rose from 2,909 Sixty-ones built in 1939 to 4,069 in 1940. Production of overheads in 1941 increased to 5,149; more than half—2,608—were 74 OHVs.

A few beers and it's time to go wading. George Fronson (left) and Joe Zedoff at the Elkhart Lake State Rally, 1940. *Courtesy of Joe Zedoff.*

Milwaukee Motorcycle Club members at Elkhart Lake, 1940. New Sixty-one at left. *Courtesy of Henry Seebooth.*

Beaver Dam Turkey Run, 1940. *Courtesy of Euella Trapp.*

Gaining the road during a Lake Mills Run. Endurance runs and reliability trials covered both wild country and roads. Bike appears to be a 1936 flathead. *Courtesy of Euella Trapp.*

"I was excited about a Seventy-four Overhead," Horstmeier recalled. "They had been talking about one for a couple years. We rode up for the races and got there early. We had something to eat then I said, 'Let's go over to the factory and see if there aren't some new models around.' The place was locked up, but there were some sidecar outfits parked out front. I started rapping at the door. There was a hall and the switch-board operator was inside to the right. Just down the hall was a big arch into the Visitors' Room. Right in that arch was the new 1941 model. It had that crossbar on the gas tanks. Different from the 1940 model.

"Anyway, while I was rapping at the door Walter Davidson (Jr) came over. I could see his elbow. I rapped louder and he looked around and said, 'Beat it!' Then I kicked at the door. He came over and opened it. He said, 'What's the idea coming around here kicking on peoples' doors?' I told him we wanted to come in. He said, 'Wait outside. It ain't raining.' I said there was new models inside and that we wanted to see them. He told us, 'You're welcome after the race but not now.'"

That was no good for Horstmeier. He had to go back to Illinois and get up in the morning and go to work. Besides, he was too enthusiastic to be put off that easy.

"I told Walter that, but it didn't help," Horstmeier continued. "Now this guy I was with—his girlfriend—she was so cute. She was looking real pretty that day and she vamped old Walter. He looked at her. Then he looked again. Finally he stepped back and I dashed inside and under

Fog and mud lend atmosphere to this 1940 Turkey Run. Note cut-back front fender on bike. *Courtesy of Euella Trapp.*

One of the first riders to get a crack at the new 74 OHV was John Horstmeier. He was up from Aurora, Illinois, in Milwaukee to attend motorcycle races held during State Fair week. It was H-D tradition to introduce the new models after the races. Riders were then invited over to the factory to see them. Already owner of 37EL1606, Horstmeier was in the market that year for a new motorcycle—the eagerly awaited 74 OHV. Here's the story of how he tricked Paul Barger, the Aurora Harley-Davidson dealer, into selling him his 74 OHV demonstrator.

Elkhart Lake Rally 1940. Overhead twins predominate: a 1940, a 1939, and a 1938. *Courtesy of Henry Seebooth.*

that arch. There was the Seventy-four. I said, 'Oh Walter. I've got to have one.' I told him exactly what I wanted but he said, 'Wait a minute. We don't know if guys want motors that big. We're going to make just one (74 OHV) per dealer for the rest of the year.' I said, 'Oh Walter, don't tell Paul that.' Then he said, 'You're the one I shouldn't have told.'

"We ran back over to the race track where Paul was taking movies of the time trials. I told him I was thinking of buying a new motorcycle. He guessed right away. He said, 'You've been over to the factory and they're building a Seventy-four Overhead.' I said, 'Oh no, I think I've got a short in the wire and need a new motor.' He said, 'I don't believe it. That's a lie. I know you better than that. You plan weeks and months and years ahead. How come you're talking to me now? Come over to the shop Monday.' I said, 'No, I'm afraid I'll change my mind.' He said, 'Everything you say is a lie. I don't believe a word of it.' Then he turned away.

"Dealers didn't normally sell motorcycles on race day, but they had an order blank in their pocket. So when they knocked the time trials off at noon we went up to the grandstand. I reached into Paul's pocket and took out the order blank. Then I crossed out 61 OHV—there was no Seventy-four Overhead listed—and wrote down 74 OHV. Then I pinned a ten dollar bill to it and put it back into his pocket. Paul said, 'I'm

making a mistake. I can't imagine what it is, but I'm doing something stupid. I can feel it.'

"After the race we went back to Illinois and Paul went over to the factory and found out it was only going to be one Seventy-four Overhead per dealer. Next morning the phone was ringing off the hook. Paul said, 'I've got bad news.' I said, 'What? Did you fall off your bike on the way home?' He said, 'No, I didn't fall off. Harley-Davidson is going to make a Seventy-four Overhead.' I said, 'That's good news!' He said, 'That's not the bad part.' I told him, 'There can't be a bad part.' He said, 'Yeah there is. They're only going to made one per dealer.' I said, 'But all I need is one.' He said, 'That's my demonstrator!' I said, 'Forget that demonstrator. That's mine.' He said, 'That's the first time I got cheated out of my demonstrator. Bill Thede, Harry Molenaar, Kemper, that guy in Joliet—they'll all have one and I won't.' I told him, 'I'll come over to your shop every night with it.' He asked, 'Will you let anyone ride it?' I said, 'No, but I'll let them watch me.'"

Horstmeier rode his 74 OHV all right. In 1940 he rode it to California when he moved there permanently. After polishing and cleaning up the ports Horstmeier took 41FL1199 to Muroc Dry Lake and ran 114 mph with it. That was during the last speed trial held before the government took Muroc over for Edwards Air Force Base. After stroking it to 80 cubic inches Horstmeier ran 117.07 mph with it at Rosamond.

Royal Beguhl tries out the first Triumph motorcycle in the hands of a private owner in Harley-Davidson's home state. It was owned by Herbert Borer of Milwaukee and is a 1940 Speed Twin: 40T1C029940. Before the Second World War foreign bikes were almost unknown in Milwaukee. A couple of others trickled in about the same time: including another Triumph, an Ariel, and a German DKW. After the war this trickle became a flood and foreshadowed the Japanese invasion of more recent years. *Courtesy of Royal Beguhl.*

Another Sixty-one taking swimming lessons. In this case a 1940 model. Old timers report such antics did little harm to machines although a transmission oil change and greasing of hubs and controls would be in order. Water in engine was not usually a problem as engine heat would soon burn it out. *Courtesy of Ken Bryne.*

Another first. Shortly before the Second World War this 61 OHV with travel trailer passed through Appleton. It appears to be home-made. Rider unknown. *Courtesy of Bernard Ernst.*

These weren't record times but good standing. In California, Horstmeier was partner with Art Seeley in the Horstmeier and Seeley Engineering Company. They made custom single and dual carburetor manifolds and heavy-duty clutch pressure plates for H-D Big Twins. The manifolds were used on many record-setting Knuckleheads at dry lake speed contests in the late 1940s and early 1950s.

Speaking of manifolds, Horstmeier's 41FL came under factory scrutiny under somewhat humorous circumstances. It's also a lesson in how conscientious the factory was over model changes—in this case the new oil pump introduced in 1941.

Shortly after taking delivery of 41FL1199, Horstmeier noticed the bike had developed a sort of "squeak or wheeze." Because that particular machine was one of the first Seventy-four Overheads built, the factory kept tabs on it every time dealer Paul Barger visited the factory.

Horstmeier mentioned the unexplained noise to Barger who in turn casually mentioned it to Walter Kleimenhagen at the factory. At once Kleimenhagen demanded to see that oil pump. Ever the good dealer, Barger asked Horstmeier to bring his bike in. Then he removed the oil pump and took it the eighty miles to Milwaukee. The factory went over that pump with a fine tooth comb and proclaimed it perfect.

Back in Aurora, Paul Barger was beside himself trying to figure out what was causing that noise. After putting the oil pump back on while Horstmeier and a couple of other riders watched, the truth came out. One guy was named Rudock. Horstmeier recalled what happened.

"When Paul was finished," Horstmeier said, "he sat on a box next to my Seventy-four just thinking. No one said anything. Then Rudock said, 'It might be a leaking manifold nut.' Paul said, 'Why that was the *first* thing I checked.' But he started acting strange. Looking over his

State Fair Park races, West Allis, July 1940. *Courtesy of Adolph Roemer.*

Stuck in the mud at Horicon Marsh and working up a sweat. Check out the snappy twin fox tails attached to Buddy Seat. *Courtesy of Adolph Roemer.*

shoulder until Rudock said goodbye and left. As soon as Paul heard Rudock's engine start, he looked out the window to be sure he was leaving. He grabbed a manifold wrench. Sure enough. They were a little loose."

*   *   *

In spite of the war in Europe and the Far East, the motorcycle scene around Milwaukee retained much of its old flair in that last year of peace. There were still plenty of activities and new motorcycles around. The Milwaukee Motorcycle Club ran a full schedule of events in 1941 including new dirt track races at the Cedarburg Fairgrounds on Memorial Day. At the Badger Club "perfessor" "Hap" Jameson was conducting his regular courses at Knuth's Kollege. The graduation quiz was rollicking fun with gut splitting questions and answers. Kollege president was Bill Knuth. Minister of "Propergander" was Frank Werderitsch. Master of ceremonies was "Mordiburp Snurd." The Badger Club now had forty-three members—its peak.

A disconcerting note had appeared on the scene. Some club members were departing for army camps in the south for what were vaguely described as "defense measures." The first peacetime draft in U.S. history was instituted in 1940 and its effects were now being felt. A farewell party was held for departing club members in early 1941. Many more would follow.

But club life went on. The Oshkosh Club—sponsored by dealer Joe Robl—finished building a new clubhouse. Kenosha was doing what it liked best during the winter months—ice racing. The new West Allis Club had just sixteen members but made up for their small size by putting on a Class A hillclimb at Slinger in early 1941. In August the Racine Club sponsored the Wisconsin Hillclimb Championship. Henry Reiman made the fastest time and took home the biggest trophy. Up in Green Bay they were building a new clubhouse on the edge of town under dealer "Jib" Arndt's supervision.

The Wisconsin State Rally took place in June at Sturgeon Bay. This was Door County, an eighty mile long limestone escarpment jutting out into Lake Michigan. This lovely realm was covered with cedars, cherry trees, and apple orchards and it was ringed by quaint fishing

Milwaukee Motorcycle Club picnicking along the Milwaukee River before the war. Idyllic scenes such as this showed the good times and camaraderie of the organized club scene. War on horizon ended this chapter in U.S. motorcycle history. *Courtesy of Harold Deckert.*

Another teaser. A VL with 1940 gas tank badges. *Courtesy of Ray Wheir.*

John Horstmeier and Roger Ames on a 1940 trip to the West Coast. Here shown along the rugged Klamath River in Oregon. Trip was high adventure. *Courtesy of John Horstmeier.*

Another pretty girl on a motorcycle. Rosemary White Mislin on what appears to be a 1940 model. *Courtesy of Ray Wheir.*

villages and lovely vistas of Lake Michigan. Door County contained some of the best riding in the region, but in spite of this favorite destination attendance was down from previous years. Many were already in the military. With the pick-up in the economy others had less free time than formerly, but those who came made merry while the good people of Sturgeon Bay smiled tolerantly at the noisy motorcycle celebration.

With so many gone the drill team competition was canceled. Madison won the club uniform contest. There was a tour of beautiful Door Peninsula. Bernie Gessler, Johnny Spiegelhoff, and Bob Stuth took the prizes in the dirt track races. When the motorcyclists went home on Sunday many wondered when they would meet again. Some never would.

For the seventeenth year in a row a Harley-Davidson motorcycle won the Jack Pine that autumn. It was an unusually rough course, only twenty of seventy-five entries finished. Sixteen of these were H-Ds. An interesting development was the presence of foreign motorcycles in a

contest traditionally waged between H-D, Indian, and an occasional Super X. But this new competition didn't stop Don Loucks on a 61 OHV with military style cut-away fenders from winning.

Many riders knew they'd soon be leaving for unknown destinations on military careers so some decided on one last fling. One who did so was Lester Burmeister of Marshfield, Wisconsin. In the spring of 1941 he bought a brand new 74 OHV from "Fats" Lauby. He ran it about a year before leaving for the military.

Burmeister had previously owned a Forty-five, but liked the looks of the big overhead Seventy-four better. Lauby made the arrangements in Milwaukee including an overnight stay at "Ma" Gunderson's. It was early in the year when Burmeister picked his machine up, a bit too early as things turned out. He found himself riding home in a spring blizzard. As he put it, "A baptism in snow for its maiden trip."

Milwaukee Motorcycle Club members with a VL. Note higher than stock handlebars. *Courtesy of Harold Deckert.*

Milwaukee Motorcycle Club members show their stuff. Bikes include (from left) a 1940 Sixty-one and three Big Twin side-valves. New 5:00 X 16 wheel and tire on Sixty-one shows up clearly in this photo. Chrome rims were available in 1940 for the first time. Cost: five dollars extra. *Courtesy of Ken Bryne.*

Alice Kobs Roemer looking over the Mississippi River valley at Palisades State Park in Illinois, August 1940. *Courtesy of Adolph Roemer.*

"Indian Joe" with 40EL1584. After having 36EL1400 for a year this H-D welder switched to a 37ULH. But in 1940 he went back to the overhead model. He kept it until the day he died. But Joe liked the side-valve enough that he kept a spare Eighty in his garage in case he felt nostalgic for the flathead. *Courtesy of Joe Campbell.*

Horstmeier and Ames at the summit of the Washington Cascades near Mt. Ranier, 1940. *Courtesy of John Horstmeier.*

Paul Barger, the H-D dealer at Aurora, Illinois. Here he's shown with a 1940 61 OHV, his personal mount. Unique 1940-only timing gear cover can be seen in this photo. John Horstmeier tricked Barger out of his 1941 74 OHV demonstrator. At first only one FL model was allocated per dealer. *Courtesy of John Horstmeier.*

Burmeister remembered 41FL3853 well, "That was a fine machine. I especially liked the hand shift with the gate and long gear shift lever. You knew just what gear you were in instead of tippy-toeing around poking at it like they do today hoping they're in the right gear."

Burmeister was a serious rider. He belonged to the local motorcycle club but did most of his riding alone. He had a reason. "They were like a flock of birds," he said. "They would all get on their machines at the same time and ride like mad to the next bar. That didn't appeal to me. I wasn't interested in going just a few blocks."

Today Lester Burmeister is in his mid-eighties. He's a neat, dapper, soft-spoken man. It's a little hard picturing him on a big Seventy-four Overhead blasting across the continent, but that's what he did on the eve of the Second World War on his new 74 OHV. It was a trip a man would recall for a lifetime. Nowadays any number of Jap bikes or fast cars can blow a Harley-Davidson Big Twin off the road, but in 1941 the Seventy-four Overhead was pure dynamite.

"One hundred miles-per-hour (by speedometer) was my cruising speed," Burmeister recalled. "That was on the flatlands of Oklahoma where you can see the curvature of the earth quite plainly. Eighty-five became monotonous under those conditions. The Seventy-four was very stable and comfortable at eighty-five to one hundred miles-per-hour. That bike had everything: windshield, leg-guards, spotlights, leather saddlebags with fringes, Delco-Remy seashell airhorns. I ran into a rainstorm at sixty and didn't even get wet. The windshield took the wind and rain right over me. The back fender got wet but I didn't."

Burmeister was headed to Los Angeles on old Route 66. In Oklahoma he had the opportunity to test the speed of his new mount. It was a pastime of local Indians who'd come into oil money to cruise up and down the highway in fast cars looking for somebody to race and in Burmeister's big new Seventy-four Overhead a couple guys met their match. As Burmeister recalled it, "They were cruising along at a very reasonable speed in the proper lane. It was a big Chrysler touring car and they were itching for me to pass. When I came alongside they wound that big car up. But I left them behind me as if they were standing still. I could see them in the rear view mirror. They were all giggles when I pulled away. I don't imagine that happened to them very often."

After visiting his California friends, Burmeister decided to take the northern route home. It was April and snow still blocked some mountain passes but he didn't know that until reaching Grand Junction, Colorado.

"The road was closed and so marked," Burmeister said. "I inquired and they told me to find a place to stay for about six weeks when the road would be plowed out. But I had to get back to the induction center in Milwaukee. So I went through anyway. There was no turning back."

The motorcycle has always encouraged a daredevil attitude, from the day Pennington jumped rivers in his dreams, to when guys like Floyd Clymer raced up and down Colorado mountain peaks for the hell of it. At last there was a motorcycle strong and dependable enough to truly inspire such confidence and it did so that day for Lester Burmeister. The highway hadn't been open since the previous autumn. He had no idea what he'd encounter. Deep snow might be up there. There was the danger of avalanches, falling rocks, and tunnels drifted shut. But

Original caption, "Alice resting." Tower Rock, August 1940. *Courtesy of Adolph Roemer.* (1941)

15336

Below:"
The stream-line 1941 dash first appeared on 1939 models. Here shown on a 1941 Forty-five, it is often called "cat's eye" or "voodoo mask" dash. Fuel valve can be seen just ahead of gas cap. On Forty-five right cap is for oil. Big Twins carried gas in both tanks with oil in separate tank beneath the saddle. *Author's Collection.*

Above:
All rise and hail the king! The son of Sixty-one arrives in 1941. No other motorcycle in history has been more influential. Machine is landmark first year 74 OHV. Machine was basically unchanged for the remainder of Knucklehead production run. Its successor, the Panhead, was essentially the Knucklehead model with restyled aluminum heads in 1948 and hydraulic forks in 1949. *Author's Collection.*

Nicely styled welded tanks first appeared on 36EL. Similar tanks are still current today. 1940 and later tank badges lack appeal of earlier decals. Another hint of "garbage wagon" excess to come. *Author's Collection.*

Rear end of machine is dominated by fat sixteen inch tire. Up front this same unit caused handling problems and helped create the "chopper" craze of later years. *Author's Collection.*

Burmeister pushed ahead up the "Million Dollar Highway" where the road was cut into near vertical cliffs. It was a hundred miles or better to the other side.

"There was deep snow," Burmeister recalled, "but it wasn't frozen into solid ice. That was underneath. I could plow through the snow up to the axles. Beneath that was ice hard enough to ride on. Some of the tunnels were nearly drifted shut. I had to sight pretty well to run through the small opening in the center."

Near Silverton the curves got steeper and the road was banked for four-wheel, not two-wheel vehicles. He was so high up in the mountains that rivers down below looked like silver threads.

"There was a thunderstorm down in the valley," Burmeister said. "You could see the lightning flash below and the thunder sounded like crumpling paper. I didn't get into that storm until I reached Durango on the Animas River. The storm had loosened up the road and I mired down. I pulled the wrinkles out of my boots so the mud wouldn't go over the tops. Then I pushed the machine about six inches at a time. With accessories it weighed about six hundred pounds. I'd rest and then push again until it was out of the mud. The motor wasn't running. I didn't want mud to get inside and ruin everything.

"There was no avalanche, but I was conscious of that possibility. At fourteen-thousand feet—so marked in those solid granite mountains— the deep drone of that big Harley engine was like the beat of Indian drums. The vibrations went all the way back into the rock. But the good luck angel was looking after me."

She must have been. After getting past snow-drifted passes and avalanche danger Burmeister and 41FL3853 encountered another inhabitant of the Colorado mountains.

"Wolves," Burmeister recalled. "Wolves in the San Juan National Forest. It was a place named Wolf Creek Pass. I know why it was so called. A pack of wolves came off the steep slopes and followed me a couple bike lengths away. I couldn't accelerate very fast under those conditions so the only thing to get rid of them was to retard the spark and open the throttle. The backfires were like cannons going off. That knocked the wits out of them and they went rolling down in the snow. That was the last I saw of them."

Andrew Bushman on a 1941 model. Bike is a Sixty-one but nothing visible on outside of motor differentiates it from the 74 OHV except serial number. *Courtesy of Andrew Bushman.*

While Lester Burmeister was struggling across the Colorado mountains other guys were already in active service. Sometimes their motorcycles were pressed into duty as well. Among them was Ray Wheir and 36EL1981. They were with the Wisconsin Rapids National Guard unit of the 32nd Division. The division had gone south to conduct military maneuvers. Four motorcycles accompanied the convoy.

"That was the slowest and fastest trip I ever made," Wheir said. "Our job was to block main intersections and guide the convoy through. Our commanding officer had a 1940 Pontiac. He'd lead the way every morning at about seventy miles an hour until we came to an intersection. Then he'd stop and say, 'You stay here and after the convoy goes by catch up with me.' Then he'd take off. The convoy was doing about thirty-five. By the time they passed through it was almost impossible to catch him. But we tried. That's how Don Henry was killed (39EL1368). Down in Tennessee there was a station wagon hauling booze. The guys driving were drunker than lords. They pulled out and hit him. He was killed instantly."

Even before Pearl Harbor the country was in a war-time mentality, as evident at the Harley-Davidson factory where Lieutenant J.J. Roth was the military liaison man overseeing army mechanics being trained in motorcycle maintenance and repair. At home people were catching war hysteria—some were already scanning Wisconsin skies for enemy aircraft. The Milwaukee County Defense Council formed the Civilian Motorcycle Dispatch Corps to carry messages over the battlefield should it come to the Dairy State. One meeting was held at the Milwaukee County Courthouse to teach the riders the use of hand signals to coordinate movement over the battlefield. According to Dispatch Corps member Adolph Roemer, one of the guys came charging up to the group and then slammed on his brakes for effect. "But it didn't work like in the movies," Roemer recalled. "He wound up sliding on his backside before the whole group."

Thirty-one motorcyclists took part in the first test exercise over a course that included the Menomonee River valley. Ironically this was where Harley-Davidson would soon be testing some of their military motorcycles. Now civilian riders participated in this new kind of endurance run. But it was no longer for fun: if the predictions some were

1940 Forty-five at the Beaver Dam TT races, September 1941. Rider unknown. *Courtesy of Euella Trapp.*

Motorcycle parking at a 1941 event. *Courtesy of Peter Ulicki.*

By 1941 most clubs were in full uniform. The Wausau Club pictured had different color schemes for men and women. Contrast is striking. Looks good. *Courtesy of Mel and Emma Krueger.*

Mary Trapp (left) and Mertes Feely at the Rhinelander beer truck. Waupun TT races, September 1941. *Courtesy of Euella Trapp.*

The good husband. Jim Trapp turns over winnings to his wife Euella. Beaver Dam races, 1941. Note trailered bike in rear. In the beginning Class C events mandated that bikes be ridden to events, but trailers soon crept into picture. *Courtesy of Euella Trapp.*

167

Bill Nadler at a Beaver Dam Turkey Run. Nadler later became the Aurora, Illinois, H-D dealer. His father, Walter Nadler, was H-D dealer at Lake Mills from the teens to the late 1940s. *Courtesy of Euella Trapp.*

Erv Tursky on his beloved Indian leads the pack during an Elkhorn TT race, June 1941. *Courtesy of Euella Trapp.*

Walter Davidson, Jr. just outside H-D's front door with John Horstmeier's early production 74 OHV: 41FL1199. Photo taken at time of bike's fifth birthday. Note the sidecar rigs, probably ridden by office men, including then president William H. Davidson. *Courtesy of John Horstmeier.*

A 1937 61 OHV going in and a 1941 74 OHV coming out of Barger's dealership. Sixty-one had 42,367 miles on it. Red headlight lens on 41FL1199 is for police model and apparently a production error. *Courtesy of John Horstmeier.*

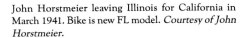

John Horstmeier leaving Illinois for California in March 1941. Bike is new FL model. *Courtesy of John Horstmeier.*

mouthing came true the dispatch riders might soon be dodging bomb craters around Harley-Davidson and the Gettelman and Miller Breweries!

On the first exercise run Clayton Kasten—son of Milwaukee pioneer Excelsior dealer Emil Kasten—made it the entire distance without a spill or any assistance. Another rider was Adolph Roemer on 38EL3325. That particular Sixty-one had a little bit of history behind it.

After pilot Douglas Corrigan conned everyone into thinking he was flying from New York to California but flew to Ireland instead, he earned the nickname "Wrong Way" Corrigan. When he visited Milwaukee, Bill Knuth had a brand new 61 OHV waiting for him at the airport. On the headlight shell was painted the words "Wrong Way" Corrigan. When he got on it and twisted the throttle it nearly got away from him. Adolph Roemer bought it off Knuth's showroom floor with only thirty-some miles on it. Now Roemer and 38EL3325 were running military-like maneuvers for the defense of Milwaukee County.

"The most difficult part of the run," Roemer said, "was alongside a small creek on the left and an embarkment on the right. The path was narrow and if one didn't pay strict attention to the clearance on his right there was the danger of the crash-guard or footboard digging into the embankment and throwing the cycle and rider. That happened to one guy. His cycle wound up in the creek but the rider was fortunate to remain on the footpath high and dry. My incident happened where the path made a ninety degree right turn. Not wishing to go 'ass over appetite' as some of the hillclimb racers did on occasion I didn't give the engine full power and stalled half way up."

A few nights later forty-nine motorcyclists went on a blackout exercise over city streets and open countryside. Outside the city limits no lights were permitted.

"The city was under a test blackout," Roemer continued. "All the cycle headlights were blackout painted with just a small slit in the center. Each rider was given a test message to deliver. My destination was less than a mile but located in the maze of the old Schlitz railroad mar-

169

shalling yards. I had to stop and read the city map by the light of the blackout headlight to get my bearings and successfully deliver the message."

On Memorial Day the group formed part of a parade through downtown Milwaukee in shirtsleeve weather. One by one, however, the members were inducted into the military. Two women—Josephine Kopca and Clara Holstein—signed up as motorcycle dispatch corps riders, but it's not known whether they participated in maneuvers.

The Goose and Turkey Runs, Junior Jack Pines, Midnight Mystery Trials, Badger Derbys, hillclimbs, and countless other activities had not been frivolous play after all. In a strange way motorcyclists had been training for this day ever since the club scene was resurrected in the 1920s. Everything from a Sunday Gypsy Tour to nearby Tichigan Lake to the meanest reliability run of all—Michigan's Jack Pine Enduro—had been conditioning riders in one aspect or another of what could be translated into military service. Strict discipline. Group maneuvers. The emphasis on uniforms. Constant rough riding under field conditions. Mechanical knowledge of motorcycles and the general skill in handling dangerous machinery. All these were skills easily incorporated into military life with little or no modification.

Coincidence? Perhaps. But don't forget. Harley-Davidson got its deepest breath in the Flanders mud of 1918. The founders were experienced and intelligent men. Maybe they had seen another war on the horizon long before most others. If so, they were determined the mili-

Milwaukee Motorcycle Club president Ken Bryne (right) presents Carl Griesbacher with a trophy. Griesbacher was a consistent winner at various endurance runs in the sidecar class. *Courtesy of Ken Bryne.*

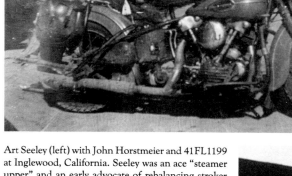

Art Seeley (left) with John Horstmeier and 41FL1199 at Inglewood, California. Seeley was an ace "steamer upper" and an early advocate of rebalancing stroker engines. This machine was later stroked to eighty inches. *Courtesy of John Horstmeier.*

Cedarburg half-mile flat track, 1941. The crowd is big. The bikes are loud and fast. *Courtesy of Adolph Roemer.*

tary motorcycle would play a key role. At the beginning of the war in Europe Germany's success with motorcycle reconnaissance and combat troops seemed to bear this prediction out.

But that's another story.

Perhaps the most evocative description of the beginning of the Second World War came from a man who served in a special liason position between Juneau Avenue and the U.S. Army throughout that conflict.

"We started making army motorcycles in 1937," he told me. "We had a mockup of what they wanted. There was one guy from the army. He had a fancy new pair of leather shoes. He was going to show *us* how to start the motorcycle. He put his foot on the crank and his shoe split wide open. He was quite provoked at that.

"We were preparing for that war at the factory five years before it began. Just like Pearl Harbor. We knew why it was getting bombed. We wanted to get into that war. That was between Churchill and Roosevelt. That bothers me though. Killing. Bombing cities. Blowing everything to hell. And then we're human. That whole damned war was planned."

A few weeks before Pearl Harbor a small notice appeared in *The Enthusiast*. It quietly notified riders that the government had requested that H-D discontinue its factory tours as they stated simply, "for the duration of the present emergency."

Unidentified rider at the Cedarburg races, 1941. *Courtesy of Euella Trapp.*

Bill Nadler (left) and another Forty-five rider, Janesville races, 1941. *Courtesy of Euella Trapp.*

Appleton races, June 1941. Center bike is 1940 Sixty-one Overhead. *Courtesy of Euella Trapp.*

Laying it down. Waupun TT races, September 1941. *Courtesy of Euella Trapp.*

The first three 74 OHVs in Aurora, Illinois. *Courtesy of John Horstmeier.*

Getting a little assistance during a Beaver Dam Turkey Run, November 1941. Bike is 1939 Sixty-one.
Courtesy of Euella Trapp.

Ray Tursky (left) at Janesville races 1941. *Courtesy of Euella Trapp.*

Pete Ulicki, the third Ulicki brother in that Harley-Davidson oriented family. Pete worked at the factory, helped assemble the prototype XA model, and pursued a racing career before and after the war. *Courtesy of Peter Ulicki.*

Jefferson races 1941. *Courtesy of Euella Trapp.*

Motorcycle parking at the Cedarburg races, 1941. Note Indians in foreground. That make is hard to spot in the rest of the crowd. *Courtesy of Ken Bryne.*

Bob Stuth (right) was a winning racer around Milwaukee before the Second World War. TT Forty-five has been stripped of fender, lights, and speedometer. *Courtesy of Euella Trapp.*

Leaving for the Sturgeon Bay State Rally 1941. *Courtesy of Euella Trapp.*

This unfortunate 39EL caught fire during a TT race. What is more interesting, however, is that front and rear fenders on this machine might have been inspiration for current H-D items on "Springer" and "Bad Boy" models. *Courtesy of Adolph Roemer.*

Byron Long on 41E2392. By 1940-1941 actual military uniforms were quickly superseding club uniforms. *Courtesy of Andrew Bushman.*

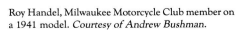

Roy Handel, Milwaukee Motorcycle Club member on a 1941 model. *Courtesy of Andrew Bushman.*

Moving out. Members of the Wisconsin Rapids unit of the 32nd Division heading for maneuvers in Louisiana. Bike with winter windshield and skull and crossbones motif is 36EL1981. Owner Ray Wheir sitting on it. *Courtesy of Ray Wheir.*

Adolph Roemer and 38EL3325 were members of Milwaukee County Motorcycle Dispatch Corps on the eve of Second World War. Their job was to carry messages should the battle come to "Beer City." Roemer's motorcycle riding career ended in eastern France when a mortar blast took off his left leg. *Courtesy of Adolph Roemer.*

Parks in Louisiana with his 1940EL. Bike is unusual in that it has the 1941 style timing gear cover. Tilted toolbox probably the result of a missing mounting bolt. *Courtesy of Ray Wheir.*

Don Henry and friend. Photo taken at Wisconsin Rapids before leaving for Louisiana. Henry's bike is 39EL1368. *Courtesy of Ray Wheir.*

Don Henry's 61 OHV after the wreck. Henry was killed instantly. In spite of condition 39EL1368 was fixed by a Louisiana dealer and sold to a Michigan man. *Courtesy of Ray Wheir.*

CHAPTER SEVEN:
Legacy of the 1930s

It is all one to me where I begin;
for I shall come back there again in time.
Parmenides of Elea, 450 B.C.

The period between 1930 and 1941 was a time of creativity unmatched in the long history of the Harley-Davidson Motor Company. They rode into the 1930s on the flathead VL and rode out on the 74 OHV. By the standards of the day the Seventy-four Overhead was damned near perfect. Today—more than five decades later—it retains an influence and force unmatched in the annals of motorcycling worldwide.

For the 1930s never ended. The "EL" and "FL" models never died. The 61 OHV was so fundamentally correct, so right, so true, that later Harley-Davidson OHV Big Twins—Sixty-ones, Seventy-Fours, and Eighties—have been mere refinements upon the 1936 version.

Evolution not revolution.

Place an original 36EL next to the newest Evolution Big Twin and the heritage is obvious. Just two generations: the Panhead engine (1948-1965), and the Shovelhead engine (1966-1983), stand between. Successors of the 36EL motor have merely been improvements upon the original form. The basic design remains intact to this day. The Knucklehead was the founders' idea of the ultimate motorcycle engine. Time has proven them correct. As William H. Davidson, H-D president 1942-1971, described it, "In many respects it's the same design they're still using today. You look at a 1936 Sixty-one overhead-valve and except for cosmetic and mechanical improvements it's basically the same motor. I think that's one of the reasons that Harley succeeded."

The legacy of the 1930s goes deep. As time passes and earlier decades become tangible and nostalgic, old becomes new and the beauty of the 1936 Harley-Davidson takes on new life and charm. Witness the return of items first seen on the 1936 61 OHV model: the EL style "Springer" and early style spot lights, rigid frame look-alike in the "Softail" models, the "horseshoe" style oil tank, and smaller early style teardrop gas tanks or "Fat Bobs."

Other parts brought back from that era include the round air cleaner, fringed leather saddlebags, teardrop toolbox, and thirties style horn. Some parts never left production. The 1936 transmission has come down the years in a manner similar to the engine. There have been changes but the basic design endures. Bill Harley's integrated frame mounted instrument panel has been continuous through the years, although the present shroud lacks the charm of earlier styles. The rear, full valance fender—with some modification—has never missed a year of production. The solo seat even pre-dates the thirties and still carries its 1925 part number, which goes to show that some things simply cannot be improved upon.

Many dream of the day when the 36EL is reborn in Harley-Davidson's styling department. The vitals already exist. The only parts missing include the original springer style front fender and 4:00 X 18 inch wheels. Combined with the existing "Springer Softail" this envisioned "Springer Heritage" would have all the taste and visual charm found today in the "Heritage Softail" model which replicates so wonderfully the style of the classic 1950 FL model.

But the 1930s gave us more than hardware. An entirely new cultural pattern arose in the motorcycle scene. The organized club movement first found its modern expression at that time. Paradoxically, however, as the AMA clubs—so strong in the thirties—lost favor after the Second World War, their antithesis or mirror opposite appeared in the outlaw biker movement. But even here the pattern followed the AMA clubs of the thirties. The very terms "outlaw club" and "outlaw motorcyclist" were first coined in the 1930s, long before the appearance of the "biker movie" or post-war motorcycle gangs.

Even in revolt the outlaw biker uniform inversely mimicked that of the organized clubs. Instead of white they favored black. Ironically, today the biker look is just as universal and conformist as any uniformed club of the 1930s. Instead of selling para-military style uniforms Harley-Davidson now markets the outlaw look. But even here the high boots, the leather pants and jackets first gained popularity in the 1930s. Heck, for thirty-eight bucks (1995 prices) you can still go down to your dealer and buy a Harley hat or as Juneau Avenue appropriately calls it, "the Club Hat."

Even that most destructive and perverse reaction against stock motorcycles—the "chopper" or "custom"—found its inspiration in the stripped down track racers, hillclimbers, and TT Knuckleheads of the 1930s. Some of the blame, however, must be laid at Harley-Davidson's own doorstep. When they mounted that big wheel and tire in 1941 they sacrificed looks and sport handling with dire consequences. They also came up with dozens of non-functional accessories. These various bits of superfluous chrome, "beet-cutter" bumpers, and covers upon covers helped create that often despised syndrome: "the garbage wagon."

A backlash was inevitable. It came via southern California and Hollywood then progressed through an LSD-laced fantasy that lingers to the present day. Windshield, saddlebags, Buddy Seat, big fenders, front brake, chain guards, stock wheels, and gas tanks—the result of millions of hours of engineering and experimental testing—were cast aside in a search for some nebulous quality that had little if anything to do with motorcycling. It finally came to the point where these chopped or custom "hogs" were more abstract art than motor vehicle. The irony here being that the climate and road conditions over most of the continent far more resembles the area around Milwaukee, Wisconsin, than it does some southern California Disney Land fantasy. Even the author admits falling sway for a time to this weird mentality in the early 1970s.

By the late 1960s and throughout the following decade many dealers had to accept this fad in order to survive. Most were hard-core thirties riders and hated choppers with a passion even if they didn't show it on the surface. As one dealer told me, "I didn't like the looks of choppers. They didn't handle right. No control. Ape bars. No front brake or fender. They cut the fittings off frames. I hated all that. But what could I do?"

For years H-D resisted this movement. Finally the factory saw the light and in 1971 brought out a brilliant compromise in the Harley-

Davidson "Super Glide." This project, which turned out to be incredibly successful, was seen as a gamble at the time. It was also the first Willie G. designed "factory custom." It should be noted that the Super Glide was the last big project brought out during William H. Davidson's tenure as company president. This father and son team opened an entirely new field for Harley-Davidson upon which much of that company's success is based today.

Yet what is the Super Glide at heart but a motorcycle with a Big Twin OHV engine and sport handling? This is exactly the same design concept of the 36EL and its late thirties successors. Nothing very new after all. So it's all coming full circle. Slowly. Inevitably. Wherever you jump on the wheel it brings you round to the same place.

This is not to suggest that the 1930s Big Twin overheads were superior or better than what H-D is building today. That's simply not true. Ralphie Heger, whose West Side Cycle rebuilt thousands of H-D OHV Big Twins between 1939 and 1976, said that Knucklehead and Panhead engines were typically good for twenty-five to thirty-five thousand miles before an overhaul was needed—far less than the current Evolution motor. Then they'd need everything: valves, pistons, rods, bearings, the whole works. On the other hand transmissions would go right on through. They seldom gave trouble unless the rider let them run dry.

Not to say a well-balanced Knucklehead wasn't a rugged engine. It definitely was. When John Horstmeier sold his 1941 FL it had been stroked to eighty cubic inches and rebalanced by Art Seeley. Ray Miller, the El Centro, California, Harley-Davidson dealer couldn't believe how smooth it ran and spent one afternoon trying to blow it up. Horstmeier recalled that day, "Ray kept it wide open in low gear, back and forth up and down in the desert. I told him, 'You're going to leave me stranded in this forsaken place.' But that thing was unreal. For an hour wide open in low. He was exhausted. I took off for Pasadena and the stroker purred like a kitten."

As to which Big Twin overhead gained the greatest following in later years, Ralphie Heger said this, "Knucklehead. Definitely the Knucklehead. The Knucklehead looked better in the frame. There was something about it. Prestige. The Panhead didn't have that look. Everyone said Knucklehead. Now you can't find one. And if you do it's a museum piece."

Around Milwaukee the 1930s were unique in another respect as well. Those years formed a sort of golden age between local riders and the factory. This is no nostalgic fantasy either. A combination of tough times, hard riding second generation Davidsons and Harleys, a desire to reinvent the motorcycle, and the presence of the founders brought about conditions that will never be seen again. As one Milwaukee Motorcycle Club member who also worked at Harley-Davidson recalled, "(Before the war) Gordy and Wally Davidson, young Bill Harley; they were still with the club members. They rode with the club at different times. Yeah, I remember it best up to 1941 when our whole nucleus was all together. Before the war we could be buddies. But afterwards nothing came together anymore. People were in different frames of mind. They had new intentions. Before the war things were different. Very much so."

The 1936 EL—the original Sixty-one Overhead—was the final expression of the combined genius of Harley-Davidson's four founders. And not just the founders alone, but the awesome talent of that generation who had grown up with the motorcycle and whose experience went back to the origin of the invention. Guys who rode year round and didn't become martyrs doing it. Guys who rode motorcycles, not slogans, stickers, or barstools, guys who would have died laughing at the sight of a chopper or the idea of trailering a big road bike to a motorcycle rally instead of riding it there. Guys whose understanding and grasp of what a motorcycle should be was more profound and deeper than any of us who came later.

Nor was the 61 OHV developed any too soon. Within a year of its introduction one of the founders was dead. Two more followed during the war years. Only Arthur Davidson lived to see the second generation OHV Big Twin of 1948 and in 1950 he was gone too. Thereby ending a chain unbroken back to 1903, yet unbroken to this day.

Bibliography

Bach, Sharon, and Ken Ostermann. *The Legend Begins, Harley-Davidson Motorcycles, 1903-1969*. Milwaukee: Harley-Davidson, Inc., 1993.

Bolfert, Thomas, Buzz Buzzelli, M. Bruce Chubbuck, and Martin Jack Rosenblum. *Harley-Davidson,Inc., Historical Overview, 1903-1993*. Milwaukee: Harley-Davidson, Inc., 1994.

Bolfert, Thomas C. *The Big Book of Harley-Davidson*. Milwaukee: Harley-Davidson, Inc., 1989.

[Davidson, William H., and John Nowak.] *The Story of Harley-Davidson*. Milwaukee: AMF/Harley-Davidson Motor Co., [1970.]

Halla, Chris and Art Gompper. *The Harley-Davidson Story*. Milwaukee: Harley-Davidson, Inc., 1982.

Harley-Davidson Motor Co. *Service Shop Dope. Vol. 3: 1934-1939*. Reprint. Cedar Springs: Antique Cycle Supply, Inc., 1986.

Hatfield, Jerry. *American Racing Motorcycles*. Osceola: Motorbooks International, 1989.

Hatfield, Jerry. *Inside Harley-Davidson*. Osceola: Motorbooks International, 1990.

Hatfield, Jerry. *Indian Motorcycle Photographic History*. Osceola: Motorbooks International, 1993.

Hendry, Maurice D. *Harley-Davidson*. New York: Ballantine Books, 1972.

Holliday, Bob. *Motorcycle Panorama*. New York: Arco Publishing, 1974.

Lyons, Gerry and Lisa. *36EL: Registry of 1936 O.H.V. Harley-Davidson Motorcycles*. Winter Garden, Florida, 1992 to date.

Palmer III, Bruce. *How to Restore Your Harley-Davidson*. Osceola: Motorbooks International, 1994.

Staff of *Motor Cycling*. *The Motor Cycling Manual*. USA Edition. Los Angeles: Floyd Clymer Publications, [1955].

Staff of *Mechanix Illustrated*. *The Motorcycle Book*. Fawcett Book 123. Greenwich: Fawett Publications, Inc., 1951.

Sucher, Harry. *Harley-Davidson: The Milwaukee Marvel*. Newbury Park: Hayes Publishing, 1979.

Sucher, Harry. *The Iron Redskin*. Newbury Park: Hayes Publishing, 1977.

The Enthusiast. Milwaukee: Harley-Davidson Motor Co., 1930-1941.

Tragatsch, Erwin. *The Illustrated Encyclopedia of Motorcycles*. London: Quarto LTD, 1977.

[Uncle Frank (pseud. for Howard E. Jameson)]. *Questions and Answers*. Reprint of 19th revised edition. Cedar Springs: Antique Cycle Supply, Inc., 1984.

Wiesner, Wolfgang. *Harley-Davidson Photographic History*. Osceola: Motorbooks International, 1989.

Index